"Funny, informative. . . . Chock-full of ideas for reducing stress and having fun. A great handbook for lifting anyone's spirits (teens or light-hearted adults), whether or not substance use is an issue."—*KLIATT*

"Written with wisdom and wit, *Wise Highs* is an am[...] to live a better, fuller life. One of the best life-skills bo[...] should be on every teenager's bookshelf."—*School Library Journ[...]*

"*Wise Highs* is jam-packed with useful, fun, and weird ideas, information, random quotes, and so much more. I made a floating sausage with my fingers and found my missing third thumb. You'll have to read *Wise Highs* to know what I'm referring to!" —Petric Kerley, teen reviewer, *Orlando Sentinel*

"Recommended, enlightening, and readable! This humorous and enjoyable book discusses the various ways teens can feel good without the use of alcohol or drugs." —*The Book Report*

"*Wise Highs* is a great choice for when you're feeling stressed out. So go on—find out how to get high the right way."—Sephra Mattocks, teen reviewer, *Miami Herald*

"*How Rude!* author Alex Packer has hit the jackpot again, this time with *Wise Highs*, a book overflowing with effective ways to chill out or feel exhilarated without using drugs or alcohol. Packer's personal approach and steady stream of suggestions give teens plenty of ways to feel good about themselves and life."—*Booklist*

"Book for the Teen Age"—New York Public Library System

"Quick Pick" selection—American Library Association/YALSA

WISE HIGHS

How to THRILL, CHILL, & Get Away from It All
Without Alcohol or Other Drugs

Alex J. Packer, Ph.D.

Edited by Pamela Espeland
Illustrated by Jeff Tolbert

free spirit
PUBLISHING®

Library of Congress Cataloging-in-Publication Data
Packer, Alex J., 1951-
    Wise highs : how to thrill, chill, & get away from it all without alcohol of other drugs / Alex J. Packer ; edited by Pamela Espeland ; illustrated by Jeff Tolbert.
        p. cm.
    ISBN-13: 978-1-57542-198-8
    1. Pleasure. 2. Cheerfulness. 3. Happiness. 4. Conduct of life. I. Espeland, Pamela, 1951- II. Title.
    BJ1481.P33 2006
    646.700835--dc22   2005036746

At the time of this book's publication, all facts and figures cited are the most current available. All telephone numbers, addresses, and Web site URLs are accurate and active; all publications, organizations, Web sites, and other resources exist as described in this book; and all have been verified as of December 2007. The author and Free Spirit Publishing make no warranty or guarantee concerning the information and materials given out by organizations or content found at Web sites, and we are not responsible for any changes that occur after this book's publication. If you find an error or believe that a resource listed here is not as described, please contact Free Spirit Publishing. Parents, teachers, and other adults: We strongly urge you to monitor children's use of the Internet.

Cover design by Marieka Heinlen
Interior design by Percolator

10 9 8 7 6 5 4
Printed in the United States of America

Free Spirit Publishing Inc.
217 Fifth Avenue North, Suite 200
Minneapolis, MN 55401-1299
(612) 338-2068
help4kids@freespirit.com
www.freespirit.com

Free Spirit Publishing is a member of the Green Press Initiative, and we're committed to printing our books on recycled paper containing a minimum of 30% post-consumer waste (PCW). For every ton of books printed on 30% PCW recycled paper, we save 5.1 trees, 2,100 gallons of water, 114 gallons of oil, 18 pounds of air pollution, 1,230 kilowatt hours of energy, and .9 cubic yards of landfill space. At Free Spirit it's our goal to nurture not only young people, but nature too!

Printed on recycled paper
including 30%
post-consumer waste

To the staff and teachers of FCD Educational Services, Inc.,
for their tireless work in schools across the United States and abroad
to empower young people to make healthy, responsible choices
regarding alcohol and other drug use.

Permissions and Credits

The sugar quiz, tips for cutting back on sweets, healthy snack suggestions, fast food guidelines, and breakfast suggestions in Chapter 5 are all excerpted from *The Right Moves* by Tina Schwager and Michele Schuerger (Free Spirit Publishing, 1998), pages 63–64, 65, 99, 100–101, and 111, respectively. Used with permission of the publisher.

"How Much Caffeine?" in Chapter 5 is © 1998 CSPI. Reprinted/Adapted from *Nutrition Action Healthletter* (1875 Connecticut Ave., N.W., Suite 300, Washington, DC 20009-5728).

"A Silent Man" in Chapter 9 was adapted from an article by Lynda Gorov that originally appeared in the *Boston Globe* (March 2, 1988). Used with permission of Lynda Gorov.

"10 Tips for Traveling with Parents" in Chapter 9 is adapted from an article the author wrote for *U.S. News and World Report* (May 25, 1987). © 1987 U.S. News and World Report. Used with permission.

"12 Reasons to Roleplay" in Chapter 9 is from "Why Roleplay?" by Dru Pagliassotti, Ph.D. © 1999 by Dru Pagliassotti, licensed to About.com. Used by permission of About.com, Inc., which can be found on the Web at www.about.com. All rights reserved.

"12 Reasons to Write" in Chapter 10 is from *Write Where You Are* by Caryn Mirriam-Goldberg (Free Spirit Publishing, 1999), pages 7–10. Used with permission of the publisher.

The advice on how to make family meetings work in Chapter 11 is from the author's *How Rude!*™ (Free Spirit Publishing, 1997), pages 116–117. Used with permission of the publisher.

The tips on doing service work as a family in Chapter 11 are adapted from *Children as Volunteers* by Susan J. Ellis, *et al.,* © 1991, Energize, Inc. Used with permission. Energize, Inc. can be found on the Web at www.energizeinc.com.

Acknowledgments

Even though all of these people have been rewarded with the "high of giving" for helping me with this book, I would still like to thank them for their advice, support, and expertise.

Beth Seiser, Director of Curriculum at FCD Educational Services, Inc., for her invaluable help in conceptualizing the book, researching healthy highs, tracking down resources, and reviewing the manuscript;

Ross Herbertson, Executive Director, Slide Ranch, Muir Beach, California; Will Slotnick, Director of Education, FCD Educational Services, Inc.; Rence Soulis, Director of Client Relations, FCD Educational Services, Inc.; and Maurice Soulis for providing suggestions, resources, and encouragement;

The teachers at FCD Educational Services, Inc. for their help in distributing questionnaires;

The hundreds of FCD client schools for their commitment to preventing drug abuse, and for allowing us to conduct surveys with their students;

The thousands of teenagers who participated in our surveys and shared their tips and techniques for healthy ways to get high;

Robin Wood and members of SALSA (Students Advocating Life without Substance Abuse) at the Cambridge School of Weston, Weston, Massachusetts, for their brainstorming and dedication to promoting alternative highs;

Annie Bell, Mikell Belser, Jason Burks, Carter Coe, Rachel Covert, William Hall, Hunter Johnson, Elizabeth McInturff, Kate Melman, Kimberly Shearer Palmer, Nikki Routhier, Ellen Sawyer, Evelyn Sawyer, Sarah Stillman, Hunter Strong, Annie Wengenroth, and Guillermo Zavala for the marvelous ideas, comments, and essays they contributed to this book;

Judy Galbraith, president of Free Spirit Publishing, for her courage and creativity as a publisher, and her patience and encouragement as a friend;

Darsi Dreyer, Betsy Gabler, Marieka Heinlen, Nancy Robinson, Jessica Thoreson, Tim Woessner, and the entire staff of Free Spirit Publishing for their enthusiasm, good cheer, and unswerving professionalism;

And finally, I wish to thank Pamela Espeland for her wisdom and creativity as an editor; for pulling me out of authorial funks; for keeping me within the bounds of good taste (or at least trying to); and for the respect and good humor that make our collaborations so enjoyable.

Contents

Physical and Sensuous Highs

Social, Spiritual, and Creative Highs

Introduction

Why High?

This is a book about getting high—without alcohol or other drugs. Now, some people may object to the very idea of telling teenagers how to get high. To those people, I say "Poo."

Getting high is fun. It's natural and healthy. In fact, the desire to experience ecstatic moments and alternative states of consciousness is in our genes. Andrew Weil, a famous doctor with a very large beard who is an expert on drugs, healthy living, and natural highs, writes in his book *The Natural Mind* that the pursuit of alternative states of consciousness occurs in all cultures, and can be witnessed in children too young to have been influenced by parental or cultural conditioning.

Think about it. Infants know what feels good, and they seek it out—whether it's a bottle or a cuddle. Little kids "get high" by rolling down hills, looking at the world upside down through their legs, going higher and higher on the swing, staring at clouds, banging on drums, and having Daddy toss them in the air. They don't know that they're altering their consciousness; they just do it. And if they do it once, they want to do it again. And again.

The pursuit of delight and sensuous gratification is all part of nature's grand design. Do you think it's an *accident* that behaviors necessary for the survival of the species are pleasurable? Just how

"We like to get together with a few close friends and hang out. Sometimes we listen to old music or the Spice Girls, even though we might not like it, and it really makes us laugh. We get really hyper and laugh a whole lot. When we settle down a bit, we are all exhausted and a lot happier. We think laughing is the key to happiness."

MIKELL BELSER AND
KATE MELMAN, 15

1

long do you think the human race would have lasted if every time someone ate a meal or had sex they said "YICCCHH, BLECCCCH, I HATE THIS!!!!"? We're *supposed* to enjoy life.

The problem with the pursuit of pleasure is that there are many ways to go about it. Some are more lasting, effective, easy, difficult, accessible, simple, complicated, risky, stupid, legal, moral, meaningful, practical, healthy, addictive, and/or costly than others. This is why, since the dawn of time, parents and teenagers have disagreed over the relative safety and propriety of different pleasure-seeking behaviors. Davy Crockett was forever telling his son "No drinking and driving the buckboard!" And Socrates advised his pupils to "Just say no" when offered hemlock.

Which brings us to drugs. Virtually every culture throughout history has used (and abused) psychoactive drugs. Some cultures embrace certain drugs while condemning others. Go anywhere on the planet and you'll find tribes, religions, and/or societies using alcohol, peyote, opium, and other drugs as part of their rituals. Why is drug use so widespread? Because alcohol and other drugs are means to alternative states of consciousness. They are probably the easiest and quickest routes to changing the way you feel. And some people have used them without any *apparent* ill effects (although the long-range consequences of using certain drugs are still unknown).

Some mood-altering drugs, such as anti-depressants and sedatives, can be used safely, legally, and responsibly under the care of a doctor. Alcohol, consumed in moderation by adults as a complement to other social activities (e.g., a dinner, wedding, or Super Bowl party), can be a pleasant way to relax. Alcohol, consumed in excess by teenagers as the main event of a party, can be an unpleasant way to get sick, vomit, lapse into a coma, and even die as a result of alcohol poisoning.

The use of illicit and/or unprescribed drugs can pose serious health and developmental risks. For example, drug use can cause or contribute to:

- legal troubles
- school problems
- relationship problems
- accidents
- injury
- coma
- death
- conflict with parents
- arrested emotional development
- impaired memory function

- blackouts
- brain damage
- decreased problem-solving capabilities
- mental confusion
- learning difficulties
- diminished attention span
- impaired immune function
- decreased sperm counts
- irregular menstrual cycles

- poor judgment
- slowed reflexes
- psychological scarring
- depression
- criminal activity
- jail
- lack of motivation
- cancer
- liver damage
- respiratory diseases
- addiction
- high-risk behavior

- sexual promiscuity
- unintended pregnancies
- sexual dysfunction
- sexually transmitted diseases
- feelings of guilt, paranoia, isolation, and worthlessness
- loss of friends
- barf on the carpet

You may think that I'm giving you the old scare tactic routine. Or that I'm talking about real "hard-core" drugs like heroin or crack cocaine. But every potential consequence listed above can be linked to one or more of the *four drugs most commonly used by teenagers:* nicotine, alcohol, marijuana, and inhalants.

It's true. There's tons of research to back this up. These are the things you know if you have a Ph.D. (pronounced *fidd*) in developmental psychology and run an organization called FCD Educational Services, which provides drug education and prevention programs for schools in the United States and abroad.* In fact, thousands of students tell us every year that the reason they love our programs and really listen to what we say is because we *don't* use scare tactics, preach, or tell them what to do.

One of the things we've learned at FCD from talking with over a million students is that when teenagers take drugs, it's not necessarily because they want to "do drugs." It's because they want to relax or "get away from it all." They want to stop feeling bored, angry, hurt, afraid, inadequate, or stressed out.

A senior at a boarding school confided: "I have a few hours the whole week to myself. I don't have time to do yoga or breathing exercises to unwind. So my friends and I get wasted. It's instant relief, no messing around."

As this student discovered, the main "advantage" of drugs is that they work quickly. But the problem with drugs is that they mess with your mind and body. You introduce what is often a poison into your system (certain chemicals in cigarettes, for example, are so toxic that you'd never be allowed to dump them in a landfill), and your mind and body go into hyperdrive or zombieland. You feel weird, giddy, happy, relaxed, stoned, confused, uninhibited, brave, scared, creative, sexy, paranoid, cosmic, and/or out of control because

"My friends feel that you can't have fun unless you're high. But when I'm not high and they are, they look so incredibly stupid."
UN-HIGH HIGH SCHOOL STUDENT

* Which I have (the *fidd*) and do (run FCD).

Wise Highs

the drug has altered your circuitry and chemistry. The drug is in charge, not you. Over time, more of the drug may be needed to achieve the same result, and you can become dependent on something outside yourself to feel good or deal with life.

Now, don't get me wrong. I'm not saying "Don't get high." I'm saying "Get higher—naturally." Why spend Monday through Friday in stress city, living for a drug-induced weekend blowout, when, with a little effort, you can experience safer and better highs all week long? Why smoke cigarettes if you can smoke an opponent in a race? Why sniff glue if you can sniff a hot apple pie with your name on it? Why shoot heroin if you can shoot rapids? Why inhale propellants if you can inhale spring after a rain? Why pop pills if you can pop bubble wrap? (Yes, people *do* get turned on by this.)

It's true that many non-drug highs require practice, knowledge, patience, or training. But people who seek natural highs report that they get *more* peace, pleasure, excitement, and insight from these kinds of experiences than they ever did from taking drugs. And natural highs don't leave you feeling dull, exhausted, or hung over. The best highs come not from a chemical substance, but from a way of life. The best highs are the ones you create for yourself. And this book will tell you how.

We'll look at all sorts of different highs including rushes, thrill-seeking, X-treme sports, inner journeying, adrenaline highs, sensuous highs, visual highs, interpersonal highs, spiritual highs, deprivation highs, creative highs, intellectual highs, and Rocky Mountain highs. Highs that will calm you down. Highs that will jazz you up. From free to expensive. No-risk to high-risk. Easy to hard. Highs that will take you deep inside yourself. And waaaay outside. Highs that will change you forever.

Along the way, we'll learn what other teens do to feel really, really good without alcohol or other drugs. During 1998–99, FCD surveyed 2,000 students ages 11–18 from all over the United States, and they had plenty to say that will interest you. You'll also read quotes from teens who responded to the survey with their own insights and experiences.

So…wanna get high? Let's begin.

CAUTION!!! Some of the activities described in this book require special equipment, expertise, safety measures, and/or supervision. For example, skydiving is not something you should try on your own. Don't build a bonfire unless you know what you're doing. And deprivation tanks aren't for everyone.

Please use good judgment and common sense. Before diving into (or out of) something that might be the least bit dangerous for you, talk it over with your parents or other adults you trust. If I hear that any of you went bungee jumping without tying the cord to your ankles, believe me, it will be a real downer.

Chapter 1

All Stressed Up and No Place to Go

Serenity Highs

One of the greatest highs you can give yourself in today's rude, noisy, fast-paced world is *serenity.* Contentment. Peacefulness. A feeling of calm amidst the storm; the ability to let deadlines, pressures, and inconsiderate buffoons huff and puff and threaten to blow your house down—while you maintain your balance, perspective, and sense of humor.

Since so many teenagers today are super-anxious and harried, let's begin the journey to altered consciousness with some strategies for dealing with stress. After all, how can you get high if you're a nervous wreck?!?

In fact, everybody gets stressed. And up to a point, stress is good. For example, the stress you feel when you're on deck to bat, or preparing for a test, or about to go on stage, can actually improve your performance. This is because it gets you "psyched."

Stress is also nature's way of alerting you to danger—the so-called "fight or flight" response.

Let's say you're out for a stroll. You round a corner and come face-to-snout with an alligator. If you were to yawn and say "Yo, alligator-dude, them's mighty big choppers you have," you wouldn't be long for this earth. That's why evolution, interested as it is in the survival of the species, has seen to it that you go into major nuclear alert. Your body thinks "FIGHT???? Nahhhh. FLIGHT!!!!"

> "Stress is an ignorant state. It believes that everything is an emergency."
> NATALIE GOLDBERG

You take off as if you were being chased by...an alligator! Your stress response is in high gear: Your body floods with cortisol and epinephrine, hormones that boost your heart rate, blood pressure, and energy levels. Muscles tense, sweating increases, digestion shuts down, your breathing becomes shallow and fast. You race across a highway (looking carefully before you cross) and glance back to see Mr. Alligator getting flattened by an 18-wheeler. The danger is over, and before you can say "Handbags, third floor," your stress hormone levels begin to return to normal.

Sources of Stress

Fleeing an alligator is an extreme example of a stressful situation. But stress comes in many varieties:

Minor everyday hassles
- missing your car pool
- having a surprise quiz in math
- losing your keys
- stepping up to the free-throw line with the whole game riding on whether you make the shot
- having an argument with your brother
- forgetting your lunch
- getting stuck in traffic

Moderate, persistent anxieties
- studying for SATs
- being out of commission for six weeks with a broken leg
- having a summer job with a boss who's always criticizing you
- problems with friends
- breaking up with a boyfriend or girlfriend
- constant conflict with, or criticism from, parents or teachers
- academic problems
- wanting to fit in and be popular
- worrying about your looks or sexuality
- physical and emotional changes during adolescence
- pressure to do well, get into college, please parents

Major transitions and life traumas
- parents arguing or divorcing
- death, serious illness, or injury of a parent, sibling, relative, or close friend

"Stress, in addition to being itself and the result of itself, is also the cause of itself."
DR. HANS SELYE

"If I knew what I was so anxious about, I wouldn't be so anxious."
MIGNON MCLAUGHLIN

6

- constantly being bullied or harassed
- suffering from a chronic illness
- moving to a new school or community
- experiencing war or a natural disaster
- living in an impoverished, abusive, or violent environment

Serenity Highs

You might think that major traumas cause the most damaging stress. And certainly, a terrible tragedy or an abusive environment can affect someone for life. But research suggests that it's the cumulative effect of *daily* hassles that does the most damage.

Think of it this way: A major blow to your life is like a faucet bursting in a bathroom. All of a sudden there's a flood of water (stress) gushing everywhere. It demands your total attention. You can't ignore it. You can't hide from it. So you deal with it. You get help. People rally around. The water gets turned off. The pipe gets fixed. There may be some damage to the walls and floor, but in time it will go away or you can get it repaired.

Smaller, daily hassles are like a dripping faucet. Lots of drops all day, but each one doesn't amount to much. It's annoying; maybe one day you'll fix it, but you can live with it. You can even shut the door and forget about it. But come back after a year of ignoring the drips and you'll find a dark, corrosive stain in your sink that you'll never get out.

Many teens live with a steady drip of stress in their lives. Day in, day out, they get teased, criticized, and nagged. They live with fears, worries, and insecurities. They get jostled on the bus, shoved in the hallways, assaulted by noise. Too much to do, not enough time. Homework. Tests. Papers to write. Rushing. Racing. Gulping meals. Running to class. Trying to meet everyone's demands and expectations. Peer problems. Romance problems. Family problems. School problems. Inconsiderate roommates. Not enough privacy. Not enough money. Not enough confidence.

Even happy events can cause stress. For example, the birth of a brother or sister is a joyful occasion—but a new sibling could mean sleepless nights, preoccupied parents, baby-sitting obligations, sharing a room, and less money to go around. Preparing for a Bar Mitzvah, confirmation, graduation, prom, or Sweet 16 party can overwhelm your "To Do" list. Getting the lead role in a school play may be something you've always dreamed of, but now that you have it, your anxiety level is off the charts.

8 STRESSORS TEENS FACE

1. Wondering if you're normal
2. Worrying about the future
3. Feeling powerless
4. Family problems
5. Money problems
6. Pressure from parents
7. Peer pressure
8. General doubts, anxiety—"teen angst"

Wise Highs

Effects of Stress

Whether the cause of your stress is a troubling emotion (e.g., worry, guilt), a chronic situation (e.g., illness, family conflict), or a once-in-a-lifetime trauma (e.g., an alligator with an attitude), your body responds in the same way. And that response can cause or contribute to a host of physical, psychological, and social problems, such as:

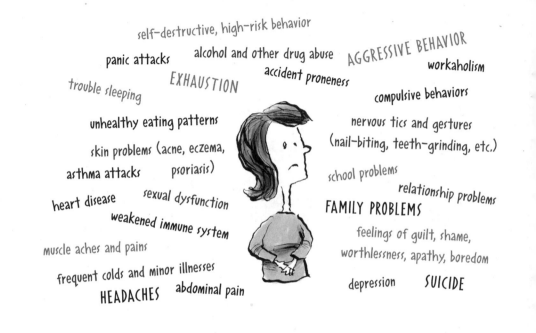

self-destructive, high-risk behavior
panic attacks   alcohol and other drug abuse   AGGRESSIVE BEHAVIOR
EXHAUSTION   accident proneness   workaholism
trouble sleeping   compulsive behaviors
unhealthy eating patterns   nervous tics and gestures
skin problems (acne, eczema,   (nail-biting, teeth-grinding, etc.)
asthma attacks   psoriasis)   school problems
heart disease   sexual dysfunction   relationship problems
weakened immune system   FAMILY PROBLEMS
muscle aches and pains   feelings of guilt, shame,
worthlessness, apathy, boredom
frequent colds and minor illnesses
HEADACHES   abdominal pain   depression   SUICIDE

You may be on stress overload if...

...you have outbursts of uncontrollable anger
...you feel depressed or sad most of the time
...you think about death or killing yourself
...you're drinking or abusing other drugs
...you hate yourself
...you hate everybody
...you avoid your friends
...you have a secret life that troubles you greatly yet nobody
    knows about it
...you feel lonely and misunderstood
...you have a hard time focusing or remembering
...you think a lot about running away
...you're addicted to computer games or the Internet
...you burst into tears for no reason

...you feel that your problems are different from everyone else's

...you believe that if people only knew the real you, they wouldn't like or respect you

...your self-talk is constantly negative, angry, or resentful

...you feel irritable, impatient, restless, hopeless, helpless, angry, depressed, resentful and/or frustrated

Serenity Highs

Please don't read this list and decide that you need to check into the stress ward just because you feel lonely or blue on occasion. Virtually all human beings find a match with some of the items on this list. Things go wrong. Life isn't fair. People hurt your feelings. And you'd be unhealthy if you *didn't* feel angry, resentful, or idiotic from time to time.

So how do you tell if the amount of stress in your life is something to be stressed about? Go back over the list and, for each item, ask yourself:

1. How *often* do I think, feel, or behave this way?
2. How *long* does the thought, feeling, or behavior last?
3. How *strong* or *extreme* is the thought, feeling or behavior?

Frequency, chronicity, and intensity are clues as to where you lie along the stress continuum. In other words, the more frequent, persistent, and/or intense the thought, feeling, or behavior, the more likely it is to harm you physically, mentally, emotionally, or socially.

> ## STRESSED PETS
>
> Pets seem to have it made: they nap and eat all day, and people pick up their poop for them. But they feel stress, too. The causes may be different (Fluffy doesn't worry about flunking that chemistry final), but prolonged stress can cause physical and psychological harm in animals just like it does in people. In fact, stress may be a much more serious problem for them because many stress-inducing situations—travel, allergies, noise—go unnoticed by their human caretakers. Symptoms of a stressed-out pet include illness and/or sudden behavior problems.

That's the bad news. The good news is that there are all sorts of things you can do to a) keep from getting stressed in the first place, and b) minimize the negative effects when stress does strike.

Handling Stress

There are healthy and unhealthy ways to deal with stress. "Type A" people wear stress as a badge of honor. Aggressive and super-competitive, they want the world to know how overscheduled, hurried, pressured, counted upon, responsible for, and answerable to they are. "Type A" people can even get addicted to stress; they get a rush out of doing three things at once and racing from deadline to

Wise Highs

deadline. Not surprisingly, these are the folks who are most likely to end up with high blood pressure and heart disease.

Other people eat, drink, smoke cigarettes, guzzle coffee, pop pills, abuse drugs, seek thrills, watch TV, pound pillows, sleep, get sick, or go shopping to "deal with" stress. These types of distractions, avoidances, and coping mechanisms may have temporary effects that make us forget our problems or feel more relaxed, energetic, or secure. But the effects are short-lived, and invariably these "solutions" turn on us, creating more problems and more stress.

The only healthy way to deal with stress is to eliminate the cause and/or reduce your vulnerability. When you do this, you experience the incredible high that comes from feeling calm, confident, and in control.

*"Being outside—calms me.
Walking—clears my head.
Running—makes me feel better about myself.
Dancing—gives me energy.
Sleeping—relaxes me.
Being in a good conversation—makes me secure."*

CALM, CLEAR, ENERGETIC,
RELAXED HIGH SCHOOL
STUDENT

THE SURVEY SAYS...

We asked teenagers "How do you relieve stress without alcohol or other drugs?" Here are their Top Ten ways:*

1. watch TV or a movie
2. talk to friends
3. play a sport
4. listen to music
5. go shopping/go to the mall
6. sleep
7. cry
8. take a bath/shower
9. exercise/run
10. play video games

And here are some other ways mentioned by teens in our survey:

- take deep breaths
- get a massage
- do transcendental meditation
- bake/cook
- beat up a pillow
- get into my computer
- make a comic book
- make a home video
- make music
- sing
- paint

- write in my diary everything I'm feeling
- write poetry
- read
- pray
- scream
- make a cup of tea
- talk to my parents
- talk to my shrink
- talk about the causes of stress
- laugh with friends

* From a survey of 2,000 students ages 11–18.

- tell extremely stupid and pointless jokes
- play our favorite music and light incense
- have a girls' night out
- do each other's hair
- give each other hugs
- act silly
- play board games
- have a sleepover
- do youth group activities
- play with a pet
- clean
- do homework (to feel the relief)
- fix things
- sit outside/look at the sky
- go to the beach or lake
- listen to the rain
- go for a drive in the country with the windows down, music blaring

One serene teen wrote "If I get completely stressed out, I'll go into my room and turn on some calming music. Then I'll grab some paper and a pen and write. I'll write poems and whatever comes to mind, and this usually helps clear my head. If this doesn't work, I'll go for a walk and watch other people and wonder about their lives. I'll picture what they're having trouble with and remind myself that I'm having the same problems as other people. Or I'll just lie down on my bed and think. Soon my mind starts to wander and I forget about how bad I think my problem is."

Serenity Highs

"When I'm stressed, I read a really good book. (Only four really good ones I know of.)"

STUDENT READER WITH DISCRIMINATING TASTE

How Stress-Resistant Are You? A Quiz

Read each of the following statements and decide if it applies to you:

1 = always   **2** = most of the time   **3** = sometimes
4 = rarely   **5** = never

Circle the number that corresponds to your answer.*

1 2 3 4 5   1. I eat balanced, nutritional meals.

1 2 3 4 5   2. I give and get lots of hugs and affection.

1 2 3 4 5   3. I do something fun at least once a week.

1 2 3 4 5   4. I am able to organize my time and meet deadlines.

1 2 3 4 5   5. I have enough money for my everyday expenses.

1 2 3 4 5   6. I practice deep breathing exercises.

---

* Or, if this isn't your personal copy of *Wise Highs,* be a polite borrower and list your answers on a separate sheet of paper.

Wise Highs

"I am relieved from stress when I play guitar."
STRUMMING STUDENT

1 2 3 4 5   7. I have one or more friends that I really enjoy and trust and can tell my innermost thoughts and feelings.

1 2 3 4 5   8. I can talk about my feelings when I'm upset.

1 2 3 4 5   9. I can discuss almost anything with my parents.

1 2 3 4 5 10. I have at least one parent or other adult who lives with me (or nearby) that I admire and trust.

1 2 3 4 5 11. I get seven to eight hours of sleep most nights.

1 2 3 4 5 12. I avoid smoking cigarettes.

1 2 3 4 5 13. I drink fewer than three caffeinated beverages (sodas, coffee, tea) a day.

1 2 3 4 5 14. I avoid drinking alcohol.

1 2 3 4 5 15. I avoid using illegal or other mind- or mood-altering drugs.

1 2 3 4 5 16. I am in good health.

1 2 3 4 5 17. I exercise or play sports to the point of working up a sweat at least three times a week.

1 2 3 4 5 18. I participate in social activities.

1 2 3 4 5 19. I do something positive for myself every day.

1 2 3 4 5 20. I can ask for help when I need it.

1 2 3 4 5 21. I enjoy most of the things I do.

1 2 3 4 5 22. I find that there are a lot of interesting and exciting things to do in life.

1 2 3 4 5 23. I feel that I can handle most things that come my way.

1 2 3 4 5 24. I like myself, flaws and all.

1 2 3 4 5 25. When I make a mistake, I use the experience to grow and become a better person.

1 2 3 4 5 26. I derive faith and security from my religious and/or spiritual beliefs.

1 2 3 4 5 27. I meditate.

1 2 3 4 5 28. I use visualization and/or relaxation techniques.

1 2 3 4 5 29. I am able to talk myself down from self-defeating attitudes and worries.

1 2 3 4 5 30. I use a repertoire of healthy strategies (e.g., taking a hot bath, talking with a friend or trusted adult, reading, getting exercise) for dealing with stress.

When you're through taking the quiz, total your score.

- If it's 75 or less, you're probably pretty stress-resistant. You use a combination of physical, mental, emotional, and interpersonal strategies to maintain a healthy lifestyle and support network.
- If your score is between 75 and 85, you're getting close to stress overload.
- If your score is over 90, you may be in the red zone of serious stress territory.

Serenity Highs

INCREASE YOUR STRESS RESISTANCE   TRY THIS!

Look at the items on the quiz for which you gave yourself a 3, 4, or 5. Improvement in any of these areas will make you more resistant to stress.

Don't try to work on all of these items at once. That will only add to your stress. Instead, pick one or two to start with. For example, if you rarely eat balanced meals or do anything fun, make a point of having at least *one* healthy meal a day. Schedule at least *one* fun activity into your week. Once these become habits, move on to some of the other factors.

"Sometimes in-line skating helps me feel confident and stress-free."
ROLLING STUDENT

LESSEN THE STRESS IN YOUR LIFE   TRY THIS!

One of the first steps in dealing with stress is understanding the cause(s). You may want to keep a "stress journal" in which you list the daily hassles, ongoing pressures, and disturbing events or relationships that make you anxious. Then decide which ones you want to address.

You'll find that some of the stressors in your life can be eliminated simply by learning to say no, changing your routine, or getting out of certain relationships. Others will require you to master specific skills to make yourself more stress-resistant. Many stress-reduction techniques have the fringe benefit of getting you high—just as many techniques for getting high have the fringe benefit of reducing stress.

Here's a guide to where in this book you'll find strategies that can give you a high while alleviating stress:

"When I'm stressed, it's really hard for me to not get stoned. But sometimes I feel better when I just stay home on a Friday night and watch movies with my mom. She's great to talk to."
HIGH SCHOOL STUDENT WITH MOM AND POPCORN

13

Wise Highs

deep breathing: Chapter 2 • laughing: Chapter 2 • meditation: Chapter 3 • progressive relaxation: Chapter 3 • guided imagery and visualization: Chapter 3 • self-hypnosis: Chapter 3 • exercising: Chapter 4 • eating right: Chapter 5 • avoiding nicotine and caffeine: Chapter 5 • getting enough sleep: Chapter 5 • meditating on a mandala: Chapter 6 • getting (or giving) a massage: Chapter 7 • communing with nature: Chapter 8 • taking a long bath: Chapter 8 • going for a walk: Chapter 8 • taking time for yourself: Chapter 9 • expressing your thoughts and feelings: Chapter 10 • listening to music: Chapter 10 • finding things you enjoy and care about: Chapter 10 • creating connections in your life: Chapter 11 • building and using a support system: Chapter 11 • getting a pet: Chapter 11

8 SELF-DEFEATING STRESS MYTHS

1. If I tell people I'm losing my grip, they'll think less of me.
2. Only weak people get stressed.
3. Nobody will care or understand how I feel.
4. Something must be wrong with me for feeling the way I do.
5. If I were stronger or smarter, I wouldn't feel this way.
6. I should be able to figure out life for myself.
7. If people would just get off my back, everything would be all right.
8. My whole life rests on what I do now.

 BE OPTIMISTIC

The way you look at yourself, your life, and the world around you makes a *big* difference in how much stress you feel. Researchers at the University of Wisconsin studied the biology of optimism—what actually happens to body chemistry when you have an upbeat outlook on life. They found that optimists have higher levels of natural killer-cell activity, so they're more capable of fighting disease. Optimists also have lower levels of the stress hormone cortisol.

What if you're naturally pessimistic? You can do something about it. Make a conscious effort to look on the bright side of life. (Okay, it's a cliché, but give it a try!) Start each day with a smile. Decide to be happy. Understand that when bad things happen, they're not your fault. Tell yourself that defeats and setbacks are temporary.

It's possible to redirect your thinking and change your frame of mind from pessimistic to optimistic. You might be able to do this on your own, or you might need help. (Which doesn't mean you're helpless.) Talk with optimistic friends and adults you trust. Find optimistic role models and choose to be like them.

> "Adopting the right attitude can convert a negative stress into a positive one."
> DR. HANS SELYE

> "I've always believed that you can think positive just as well as you can think negative."
> SUGAR RAY ROBINSON

TRY THIS!

Serenity Highs

If you're feeling stressed or depressed, lonely or sad, hopeless or angry, don't suffer in silence. Call a teen hotline. Talk to somebody you trust: a friend, teacher, coach, or school counselor; a parent, sibling, or other relative; a doctor, priest, rabbi, or therapist. You'll feel better, and you'll have someone on your side who can steer you to sources of help.

FIND OUT MORE

Learned Optimism: How to Change Your Mind and Your Life by Martin E.P. Seligman, Ph.D. (New York: Pocket Books, 1998). Psychologist and researcher Seligman has been studying optimists and pessimists for 25 years. His book teaches specific skills that can help you retrain your thinking habits from pessimistic to optimistic.

The Relaxation & Stress Reduction Workbook by Martha Davis, Ph.D., Elizabeth Robbins Eshelman, M.S.W., and Matthew McKay, Ph.D. (Oakland, CA: New Harbinger Publications, 2000). A comprehensive, well-organized, easy-to-read book on relaxation and stress management strategies. Clear, step-by-step directions show you how to master self-hypnosis, meditation, visualization, breathing, and progressive relaxation techniques. Should be in the library of every teen who wants to feel *really, really* good.

Too Stressed to Think? A Teen Guide to Staying Sane When Life Makes You Crazy by Annie Fox, M.Ed., and Ruth Kirschner (Minneapolis: Free Spirit Publishing, 2005). This book is based on teen stress workshops the authors run and addresses making choices under stress. There's also info on how stress affects your brain and how you can use the mind-body connection to manage your hectic life.

"The sovereign voluntary path to cheerfulness, if our spontaneous cheerfulness be lost, is to sit up cheerfully, to look round cheerfully, and to act and speak as if cheerfulness were already there."
WILLIAM JAMES

Chapter 2

How to Be an Airhead

Breathing Highs

Everybody knows how to breathe, right? You're born, you get whacked on the fanny, you cry, you breathe. What's the big deal? Breathing is so simple most people can do it in their sleep.

I've got news for you, befuddlement breath: Most people *don't* breathe correctly. This is usually for one of two reasons. Either they're sucking in their gut to look thin, or they're stressed out of their gourd—both of which interfere with airflow to the lungs.

Re-learning how to breathe properly is the single most powerful thing you can do to alleviate stress. And without the weight of stress on your shoulders, you'll feel light and high.

Let's take a look at a typical teenager in a typical situation and see how stress affects breathing.

It's 7:20 A.M. You're standing at the corner of Elm and Maple waiting for the school bus. Along comes a 30-foot-high velociraptor. (I know, you thought they'd been extinct for millions of years. Nah. They've just been hiding out in a trailer park in Arizona.) The raptor towers over you, snarling, spitting, and humming a hip-hop tune while sharpening its talons. The phrase "breakfast meat" goes through your mind.

You begin to feel anxious. So, instead of breathing from your diaphragm, you take shallow breaths using your chest muscles. This

> "The process of breathing is one of the great miracles of existence. It not only unleashes the energy of life, but it also provides a healing pathway into the deepest recesses of our being."
> DENNIS LEWIS

16

means that only the top part of your lungs fills with air. Your brain doesn't receive enough oxygen, so it hits the panic button and floods your body with STRESS CHEMICALS!!!! These chemicals make you feel *more* stressed, so you breathe *more* shallowly, your brain gets *less* oxygen, pumps *more* chemicals, you get more tense, less air, more chemicals, more stress, **more stress, more stress,**

Breathing Highs

more stress,

more

more stress

until your friend says, "Hey, dude, you gonna take the bus or stand there all day reading *Jurassic Park?*"

Breathing from Your Diaphragm

The diaphragm is a dome-shaped muscle located between the thoracic and abdominal cavities. When you breathe deeply, your diaphragm contracts, pulling air into the *lower* portion of your lungs. This ensures that your brain gets the oxygen it needs.

Diaphragm breathing, by lowering your heart rate and blood pressure, reduces stress. As your diaphragm moves, it also stimulates important internal organs such as the kidneys, pancreas, stomach, liver, and spleen, which keeps them in tiptop condition.

Babies and children practice diaphragmatic (sometimes called abdominal) breathing naturally. By the time they're teenagers, however, many have forgotten how, which means they expend more effort for less air.

Posture also affects the way you breathe. If you slouch, slump, and sag your shoulders, your diaphragm won't be able to move. This prevents diaphragm breathing. It also puts an extra strain on your heart, since it has to work harder to supply the amount of oxygen your body and brain require.

"Sooner or later, every one of us breathes an atom that has been breathed before by anyone you can think of who has lived before us— Michelangelo or George Washington or Moses."
JACOB BRONOWSKI

"As we free our breath (through diaphragmatic breathing) we relax our emotions and let go our body tensions."
GAY HENDRICKS

17

Wise Highs

Know Your Breathing

You can easily tell whether you're breathing from your chest (bad!) or diaphragm (good!). Lie on your back on the floor. Breathe naturally. If your chest rises, you are breathing with your chest. If your abdomen rises, you are breathing with your diaphragm.* If you want to experience both types of breathing more fully, here's how:

Shallow (chest) breathing

- Lie down. Contract your "stomach" muscles. They will feel hard to the touch.
- As long as your abdominal muscles are tensed, your chest will rise every time you inhale. If you place a hand over your abdomen, you'll see that your diaphragm doesn't move. This means you're breathing through your chest and very little air is getting to the lower portion of your lungs.

Deep (diaphragm) breathing

- Relax your abdominal muscles. Place a hand on your abdomen.
- Take a deep breath. Pull the air all the way down into your "stomach"—not by sucking it in, but by expanding it (as if you're trying to give yourself a pot belly). Your hand should rise about an inch. If this happens, it means you are breathing from your diaphragm.
- Now exhale. Your stomach will drop.
- Repeat the process. Breathe in...abdomen rises. Breathe out... abdomen drops.

If you're used to shallow breathing, deep breathing may feel strange at first. This is because it's the exact opposite of how you've been breathing for years. But deep breathing is well worth mastering, since it's your first line of defense against stress, tension, and fatigue.

Check for Stress

Being stressed out can be such a natural state for some people that they don't even recognize it. So you don't become a mess o' stress, give yourself a tension test. Here's how:

---

* If your legs rise, I don't have a clue what's going on.

Breathing Highs

1. Several times throughout the day, stop what you're doing. Tune into your mind at that very moment. Do you feel angry? Upset? Nervous? Are you rehashing conversations? Holding debates in your head? Carrying on internal tirades? Is your mind plagued by endless, self-badgering tapes of the "should-have," "why-didn't-I?" and "how-could-I-have-been-so-dumb?" variety?

2. Next, give your body an anxiety exam. Is your jaw clenched? Does your neck ache? Are your shoulders stiff? Muscles tense? Are you biting your nails, picking your cuticles, tapping your feet, wringing your hands, drumming your fingers, biting your lip? Do you feel light-headed? Are you taking short, shallow breaths? If you answer yes to any of these questions, you're either watching a *Star Wars* battle scene or heading for the red zone on a stress chart. Time for some deep breathing!

The great thing about deep breathing is that you can do it almost anywhere. Some people find it works best if they lie down. Since this isn't always possible (for instance, when you're taking part in a spelling bee), it's nice to know that deep breathing can also be done sitting or standing. If you aspire to respire with full, deep breaths, the following techniques will show you how.

> *"Breathing is the first place, not the last, one should look when fatigue, disease, or other evidence of disordered energy presents itself."*
> DR. SHELDON HENDLER

CAUTION!!! If any of these exercises make you feel dizzy or light-headed, stop *immediately.*

BREATHE YOUR STRESS AWAY
TRY THIS!

Practice this exercise at least once a day. If you can do it more often, so much the better. You'll see faster results.

1. Sit up straight in a chair without armrests. Place your hands in your lap. Keep your feet flat on the floor. (You can also lie on your back on a carpet, blanket, or pad on the floor.)

2. Breathe in smoothly and deeply through your nose. Allow your abdomen and chest to expand and your shoulders to rise slightly. Visualize the air flowing into your lungs, chest, and abdomen.

3. S-l-o-w-l-y breathe out through your nose. Exhaling should take longer than inhaling.

> *"Improper breathing is a common cause of ill health."*
> ANDREW WEIL, M.D.

19

Wise Highs

4. Continue to breathe this way for at least a minute. Fill your lungs to capacity, but don't hold your breath or strain yourself. You want to find a rhythm that feels easy and natural.

Doing this for a minute will refresh you. If you do it for 10–20 minutes a day, you'll notice even greater benefits.

Variation #1 for Math Wizzes

1. Breathe in through your nose as in the exercise above. As you breathe in, *count slowly from 1 to 4.*

2. As you breathe out, *count slowly from 4 back to 1.*

3. Continue to breathe deeply and count slowly until you feel refreshed.

Variation #2 for Math Wizzes

1. Breathe in through your nose—a nice, deep, abdomen-expanding breath. As you exhale, think to yourself the word *ten.*

2. Breathe in.

3. Breathe out again. Think *nine.*

4. Breathe in.

5. Breathe out again. Think *eight.* (Are we beginning to see a pattern here?)

6. Breathe in.

7. Continue to count down with each exhalation until you get to zero.

You should now feel refreshed and more relaxed. If you don't, repeat the exercise. Show-offs may want to start at 20, or 50, or 100 and count down from there.

The Pause That Refreshes

This modification can be applied to any of the preceding deep breathing techniques. Follow the directions as stated except, as you breathe...

1. Hold your breath for 4 seconds after each inhalation.

2. Wait for 4 seconds after each exhalation before you breathe in again.

Breathing Highs

HIC!

It's hard to achieve serenity if your breathing is disturbed by hiccups. A hiccup (*hiccough,* for our British readers) is an involuntary contraction of the diaphragm, which pulls air sharply into the lungs. When this happens, your vocal cords close suddenly, causing that funny *hic* sound.

Sometimes hiccups are caused by eating or drinking too fast, stomach irritation, or stress, but most often there isn't any apparent cause. Most bouts of hiccups last only a few minutes, but it's possible for them to linger for hours or days. One man, Charles Osborne from Iowa, started hiccuping in 1922 and didn't stop until his death, 68 years later!

As Mr. Osborne discovered, there is no foolproof cure for hiccups, and everyone seems to have their own ideas. Treatments range from homespun remedies (holding your breath, breathing into a paper bag, bending over and drinking from the far side of a glass of water) to medical interventions (drugs and, in at least one documented case, rectal massage). The mere thought of these medical solutions is enough to scare the hiccups out of most people.

> "Our band director makes us breathe deeply and in different ways. You always feel alive and awake after that."
>
> WIDE-AWAKE TUBA
> PLAYING STUDENT

REALLY DEEEEEEEEEEEEEEEP BREATHING

TRY THIS!

When regular deep breathing just won't do, try a bit of X-treme breathing.

1. Sit or stand up straight.

2. Breathe in slowly, deeply, and continuously through your nose while counting to 10 (in your head).

- First, fill the lower portion of your lungs. Your abdomen will expand.
- Second, fill the middle portion of your lungs. Your ribs and chest will expand slightly.
- Third, fill the top portion of your lungs. Allow your chest and shoulders to rise.

Visualize the air as it fills the lower, middle and upper portions of your lungs.

Wise Highs

3. Hold your breath for a count of 10. Keep your muscles relaxed.

4. Breathe out while counting to 10. Visualize the air as it leaves the upper portion of your lungs, then the middle portion, and finally the lowest portion.

Note: If you feel uncomfortable doing this exercise to a count of 10, start with a count of 5 and slowly work your way up.

Tension Prevention

You don't have to wait until you're *in* the stress zone to practice deep breathing. You can use it to *prevent* stress by making deep breathing a part of your daily routine.

Link it to activities you do every day. For example, you could practice deep breathing in your morning shower, again during fourth period history class, and once more while waiting for your car pool home.

It's even better if you can do your deep breathing at those times of the day when you typically feel anxious or lethargic. If you dread a particular class or teacher, take a few moments ahead of time to breathe deeply. If your energy fades after dinner, lie down and do some "power breathing" before you face your homework. And when you're face-to-face with a stressful moment—your teacher hands out a test, you're waiting in the wings to go on stage, you're getting ready to ask someone out on a date—take a few deep, fortifying breaths. You'll feel calm and focused.

BREATH AND TENSION

Tense your muscles as if you're in danger or being threatened. Keep them tightened for a few seconds. Now relax them. When you tensed your muscles, did you hold your breath? Most people do. This is because holding one's breath is a natural response to stress. In fact, people experiencing panic attacks feel as if they can't breathe, as if they're being choked. Everyday stress may not cause you to hold your breath for weeks on end, but it can, without your even knowing it, result in shallow, rapid, inefficient breathing.

SIGH HIGH

We usually sigh when we're feeling relieved, tense, disappointed, world-weary, or blue. A sigh is a respiratory lament. To get rid of sad breath:

1. Sit or stand up. Keep your spine straight.

2. Now *sigh*. Deeply and audibly. Let everything you're feeling escape with the air flowing out of your lungs.

3. Breathe in naturally.

4. Once again, sigh away the contents of your lungs.

5. Take 10–15 "sigh breaths." You'll feel much calmer and better equipped to face the day.

Breathing Highs

BREATHING TIP

The word element *pneumo,* which refers to the lungs or respiration, comes from the Greek word *pneuma,* which means soul or spirit. Breathing is your link to your spiritual self.

As you practice these deep breathing exercises, imagine that you are breathing *in* hope and vitality, breathing *out* hurt and fear. Breathe *in* faith and confidence, breathe *out* insecurity and despair. Breathe *in* boldness and determination, breathe *out* tension and doubt.

You can actually say this silently to yourself. As you inhale, say "Breathe *in* peace." Pause for a few seconds. Then exhale while saying to yourself "Breathe *out* stress." Choose words that most pertain to your wishes and needs (e.g., acceptance/anger, clarity/confusion, etc.).

"Sometimes the most important thing in a whole day is the rest we take between two deep breaths."
ETTY HILLESUM

SWAT BREATHING

TRY THIS!

People often get hurt or into trouble by losing control when thrust unexpectedly into a high-stress situation. If you suddenly find yourself in a heavy-duty conflict or an adrenaline-pumping predicament, it's time to bring rapid-action deep breathing to the rescue.

1. First, say "Stop" in your mind.

2. Take three or four long, deep breaths.

3. Breathe normally.

4. Take a few more long, deep breaths.

"The breath is invisible, yet it affects the visible."
KYLEA TAYLOR

Wise Highs

This exercise not only helps you to breathe rhythmically, but it also gives the old schnozzola a good workout.

1. Take the edge of your right thumb and press it against your right nostril to close the airway. (You can rest your fingers on your forehead.)

2. Inhale through your left nostril while counting to 8. (No snorting please. Hay fever sufferers may want to blow their nose first.)

3. Next, squeeze your right index finger against your left nostril. (This is the famous *peee-yooo-what's-that-smell* gesture.) Hold your breath while you count to 8 again.

4. Continue to press your right index finger against your left nostril while taking your thumb off of your right nostril. Breathe out to a count of 8.

You have just completed the basic maneuver. Now, begin the sequence again, only this time, reverse the rights and lefts. In other words...

NO PICKING!

Clear nasal passages are essential for proper breathing, but there's a right way and a wrong way to remove boog—I mean, obstructions. A University of Wisconsin study found that 91 percent of adults surveyed admitted (anonymously) to picking their nose regularly. But *you* shouldn't. When you pick, whatever bacteria you've touched end up in the warm, moist environment of your nose, where bacteria flourish. Also, picking can cause small cuts and lacerations of nasal tissues and may cause pimples on or in the nose from increased amounts of oils left there by probing fingers. Use a tissue.

5. Left thumb over left nostril; inhale through right nostril; count to 8; left index finger over right nostril *(peee-yooo);* hold breath; count to 8; release left thumb from left nostril; exhale; count to 8. (Whew! Did you actually follow that?!?)

6. Do five reps of the total sequence.

Note: While many breathing exercises can be done "invisibly" in public places, you might want to think twice about doing this one on the subway. From the wrong angle, it will look like you're picking your nose.

BREATHE OUT LOUD **TRY THIS!**

Finally, here's a breathing exercise that lets you make some noise.

Breathing Highs

1. Stand up straight, feet about 6 inches apart. Inhale through your nose while counting to 4 (silently will do for the time being).

2. When your lungs are full, expel the air forcefully and explosively through your mouth while saying OUT LOUD "shoo" or "hoo" or my favorite, "poo." Stretch out the word and the exhalation for as long as you can. As you breathe out (pay attention now, you're going to have to do several things at once), drop your upper body toward the floor, bending your knees.

3. Hang there limp and relaxed for a couple of seconds. (If you feel like an orangutan, that's okay.) Then slowly rise while inhaling to a count of 8. Once you are fully standing, breathe out to a count of 2.

4. Repeat the sequence until you feel alert and relaxed.

Note: Do not do this in a crowded elevator.

REFRESH YOUR BRAIN **TRY THIS!**

1. Stand, sit up straight in a chair, or lie flat.

2. Close your eyes. Empty your lungs.

3. You're going to breathe in while counting slowly to 3. As you count 1, fill the top portion of your lungs. As you count 2, fill the middle lobe. At the count of 3, fill the lower portion of your lungs. Do not break your inhalation into 3 separate stages. Rather, do it as a fluid, continuous process.

4. Once your lungs are full, purse your lips as if to blow out candles, pucker up for a kiss, or blow out through a straw. (Choose the image you like the best.) Now exhale slowly but *forcefully* to the count of 6. Empty your lungs from the top down. Take twice as long to exhale as you did to inhale.

5. Just 3–5 breaths will provide your brain, heart, and body with a refreshing and relaxing flood of oxygen.

"Oxygen feeds the cells and most people are starving for oxygen. No wonder so many of us feel tired so much of the time."
NINI BEEGAN

25

Wise Highs

THE LAUGHING CURE

Here's a great way to start your day:

1. Get out of bed. Stand up straight.

2. Place your hands on your hips. Keep your palms facing up. (Your fingertips will point to the rear.)

3. Laugh. Laugh some more. Keep laughing. Let your laughter generate more laughter until your whole body is laughing. You are one laughing being.

4. Keep laughing for several minutes. When you're ready, stop.

Now go out there and get 'em! The day belongs to you!

DID YOU KNOW?

Scientists and physicians are coming around to a conclusion that most people reached long ago: Laughing makes you feel better. Studies suggest that laughter actually decreases the body's levels of stress hormones and increases production of immunoglobulin (which helps fight infections) and so-called killer cells (which help the body fight viruses and cancers).

Note: A fringe benefit of this exercise is imagining your family or dormmates listening to you laugh. At first they'll think you've gone around the bend. Then they'll probably laugh, too. Can you imagine everybody in your house starting the day with two minutes of uproarious laughter?!? Ha, ha, ho, ho, hee, hee, hoo, hoo, ha, ha, ha!

ZEN POWER YELL

For those of you who are a bit too shy to start the day laughing your head off, here's another, more discreet way to greet the world:

1. Kneel down so you're sitting on your knees. Rest your butt on the heels of your feet. Your arms should be at your side.

2. Breathe deeply. After a few breaths, exhale and think *one.* Inhale again, then exhale and think *two.* Continue counting after each exhalation until you get to *five.*

3. As you inhale the sixth breath, clench your fists and cross your arms over your chest so your right fist is at your left shoulder and your left fist is at your right shoulder.

4. Keep counting your breaths until you get to *eight.* As soon as you exhale and think *eight,* breathe in deeply and JUMP FOR THE SKY! THROW YOUR ARMS OUT AND ROAR LIKE A LION!

If your parents ask you about the noise they keep hearing at 7:15 every morning, put on a quizzical expression and say "Noise? What noise?"

Breathing Highs

The Art of Breathing: Six Simple Lessons to Improve Performance, Health & Well-Being by Nancy Zi (Glendale, CA: Vivi Co., 2000). Written by a professional vocalist, this book is especially helpful if you're a singer, actor, or public speaker. Available with accompanying videotape.

Conscious Breathing: Breathwork for Health, Stress Release, and Personal Mastery by Gay Hendricks (New York: Bantam Books, 1995). Hendricks draws on 20-plus years of research and practice to show how you can breathe your way to improved physical and emotional well-being. Also by the author: "The Art of Breathing and Centering" audiocassette (Audio Renaissance, 1989).

Free Your Breath, Free Your Life by Dennis Lewis (Boston: Shambhala, 2004). The focus is using breathing exercises as a vehicle for self-discovery. Exercises and overall conscious breathing help you calm down, energize your body, gain confidence, manage stress, and more.

The Relaxation Response by Herbert Benson, M.D. (New York: Avon Books, 2000). This is the groundbreaking book, originally published in 1975, that demonstrated the immense physical and emotional benefits of deep breathing, meditation, and other relaxation techniques.

Chapter

3

Seeing the Light

Meditation Highs

Most teenagers' heads are full of mental chatter. Day in, day out, the gray matter keeps generating cerebral static: reminders, plans, hopes, regrets, rehearsals, memories, worries, resentments, reactions. The problem with such a cluttered consciousness is that it dwells in the past or the future. Awareness becomes time-bound: *in a minute; two hours from now; next month; last year.* Things are due, overdue, coming up. Rarely are they...*now.* In this moment. Or in no moment at all.

A mind full of debris and distractions leaves no room for *you*—for the core of consciousness that connects to all of time and space and spirit and life. Meditation stops time. It allows your consciousness to take a vacation from all those mental mutterings that cause anxiety but, deep down, don't really matter. Meditation clears the mind of confusion. It is purposeful "daydreaming" that allows you to get to know your true self.

We're so used to being caught up in the hurly-burly of school, work, family, relationships, conflicts, sports, and extracurricular activities; of thinking that we always have to be doing something "constructive"—building, creating, progressing, learning, earning, striving, thriving. While one can find great joy in working to better oneself and the world, too often it is done out of a sense of guilt or compulsion. In many ways, meditation is the greatest luxury you can

"When one devotes oneself to meditation, mental burdens, unnecessary worries, and wandering thoughts drop off one by one; life seems to run smoothly and pleasantly."

NYOGEN SENZAKI

give yourself: permission to do nothing, simply to *be*, to experience a true sense of who you are in order to lead a happier, healthier life.

Humans have been meditating for thousands of years. Some people meditate to show devotion to a god, guru, religion, or master. Others meditate for the benefits, which are many and real. Biofeedback monitoring reveals that meditation produces the alpha brain waves that indicate when a person has reached a relaxed state of being. Research also shows that meditation can:

Meditation Highs

- slow breathing and pulse rates
- lower blood pressure
- reduce stress
- alleviate anxiety, insomnia, and depression
- make you feel calm and alert
- improve creativity and mental focus
- enhance communication between the right and left hemispheres of the brain
- boost physical energy

The great thing about meditating is that you don't need lessons, money, or equipment (other than a mind) to do it.

Meditation itself isn't hard, but maintaining the discipline is. It's best if you start meditating with an instructor, friend, or group. This will help your discipline and motivation. As you become more experienced and comfortable, you may decide to meditate on your own.

"Health, a light body, freedom from cravings, a glowing skin, sonorous voice, fragrance of body: these signs indicate progress in the practice of meditation."
SHVETASHVATARA UPANISHAD

When to Meditate

Many people like to meditate first thing in the morning to start the day off right. Other people go straight from sleep to high gear and prefer to meditate later in the day, often before dinner.

It doesn't matter when you meditate, but try to do it at the same time(s) every day. Pick a time when you won't be disturbed. Inform siblings, parents, and/or roommates of your practice so they won't harass you with cries of "BREAKFAST!!!!" every three minutes. It's best if you don't meditate right after eating; a churning stomach makes it harder to become calm and focused.

Many people say they'd love to meditate but "can't find the time." Why is it that we *can* find the time to do all sorts of things that contribute little or nothing to our growth and well-being as humans, but we *can't* find the time to give ourselves one of life's greatest luxuries? Don't think of the time you spend meditating as "taking" 20 minutes of your day. Think of it as "giving" you 20 minutes of pure bliss. Think of it as 20 minutes during which you experience the most

Wise Highs

thrilling flights of spiritual experience. Think of it as something you *deserve.*

How long should you meditate? It depends. Some people meditate for as little as five minutes a day; others for 20 minutes or an hour. It's even possible to meditate for many hours or days at a time, taking occasional "rests." Fifteen to 20 minutes is a good length of time to start with. See how it feels. Then adjust accordingly.

People who don't meditate regularly sometimes get back into it when they have problems or stress in their lives. This would be like lifting weights the day before you need to carry something heavy: Too little, too late. Spiritual strength and balance, like physical strength and balance, are built up over time. The benefits of meditation come from doing it regularly—from practice and perseverance. Meditate when you are happy and healthy. Then, when problems do come your way, your spiritual conditioning will enable you to accept and/or surmount them.

Where to Meditate

If you can, create a spot in your room or house reserved exclusively for meditating. Make it comfortable, relaxing, and, er, meditative. You might want to put up a poster, painting, or photograph that inspires you or connotes something positive. Consider furnishing the space with plants or soft, billowing fabrics. Burn incense if you like. Avoid harsh lighting and extreme temperatures. Find a spot with minimal noise. If this poses a problem, use a white noise generator, a fan, or background tapes of soft music, birds singing, rainfall, or waves.

If you live in a place of natural beauty, you might want to meditate outdoors. Choose a location that is pleasant, calming, and spiritually healthy. Mountaintops, forests, fields, riverbanks, and beaches are all highly recommended. Landfills, train tracks, and toll plazas are not.

If your home or dormitory is like Grand Central Station, try a library or a deserted classroom before or after school. If you can't find a quiet spot, don't worry. As you get more experienced with meditating, you'll stop noticing the distractions and/or be able to let them pass through your mind. There are even meditations designed to improve your ability to acknowledge and accept pain, discomfort, and/or distraction.

WHO SHOULD MEDITATE?

People who want to feel relaxed and confident.

People who want to reduce stress in their lives.

People who want to soar beyond the everyday boundaries of life and experience.

People who want to experience planes of existence most people never reach.

People who want to get to know their true self.

People who worry a lot.

People who are always on the go.

People who feel tired and overworked.

People who are anxious or blue.

People who feel like they never have a minute to themselves.

How to Meditate

"Concentration" or "one-pointed" meditations involve focusing your attention on one thing. It can be your breathing, a mantra (a sound, word, or phrase you repeat silently to yourself), or an object. By concentrating on one thing, you still the distracting din of trivia and anxiety that usually occupies your mind. This leads to deep states of serenity and relaxation.

One of the purposes of meditation is to create harmony between your mind and your body. If you meditate in a posture that causes cramps, numbness, or strain, it won't work. Find a position that is comfortable...but not so comfortable that you fall asleep. Try different positions and/or chairs until you discover the one that works best. Here are the most common positions for meditating:

Meditation Highs

"Don't think you have to be solemn to meditate. To meditate well, you have to smile a lot."
THICH NHAT HHANH

Lying down (beware of nodding off)

Sitting on the floor against a wall (be sure it's not a door that somebody could open in the middle of your session)

Sitting on a chair (use a hard chair; no cushy couches, please)

"The quieter you become the more you can hear."
BABA RAM DASS

Lotus position (you may need to practice stretching exercises before being able to adopt this position)

Sitting cross-legged (a good compromise for the less pretzel-like; some people use a meditation pillow to sit on)

Wise Highs

"Meditation is not a means to an end. It is both the means and the end."

KRISHNAMURTI

Progressive Relaxation

Since it's difficult to meditate if your muscles are tied in knots and you feel achey, it's a good idea to begin each meditation session with what's called a *progressive relaxation* exercise. You can also practice these techniques anytime you feel tension and/or discomfort in your body, even if you don't meditate afterwards.

MIND OVER MUSCLE

1. Sit in a comfortable position or lie down.

2. Close your eyes and relax. (If seated, place your arms on your lap. Fold your hands loosely together. If lying down, place your hands along your sides.)

3. Breathe slowly and deeply from the diaphragm.*

4. Concentrate on the muscles at the top of your head. Think to yourself the word *relax* and consciously relax those muscles. (You may use any gentle or calming word such as *serene* or *restful*. Hard, harsh words like *dagger* or *screech* should be avoided.)

5. Once the top of your head is relaxed, bring your attention to your forehead and the area around your eyes. Continue to say *relax* as you consciously relax these muscles.

6. Now move to the muscles of your temples and ears. Relax them. Then your sinuses and nasal area. Once these areas are relaxed, go on to the back of your neck. Stay with each muscle until it is tension-free.

7. Continue to relax your shoulders, arms, hands, fingers, chest, abdomen...all the way down to the tips of your toes.

Note: You can take advantage of the fact that your mind and body will associate the feeling of being relaxed with whatever word you chose for this relaxation exercise (e.g., "relax," "peace," etc.). Next time you're in a stressful situation, practice deep breathing and silently say the word to yourself. Without moving a muscle, you'll feel calmer as your mind and body recall the state of relaxation associated with the word.

---

* See pages 17–18.

Variation for Flex-Timers

Meditation Highs

Begin as above by sitting or lying comfortably. Relax your arms. Take deep, slow breaths from your abdomen.

You're going to relax the muscles at the top of your head and all the way to those in your toes. Only, instead of repeating a word and using your mind to relax them, you're going to use the muscles themselves. Here's how:

1. Each time you concentrate on a muscle area, actually *tighten* those muscles. Hold the tension to a count of 5 and then release.

If you can't quite picture this, think of clenching your fist. Tighter and tighter. Feel the tension in your fist. Feel the strain in your forearm and hand. Now unclench your fist. Relax. Let the tension go. Notice how loose your hand feels.

2. Proceed through your body—clenching each muscle, holding to a count of 5, and then releasing and relaxing.

Start with one fist, then the other. Proceed to both fists. Clench your biceps. Squinch your forehead. Frown. Smile. Feel the strain created as you tense each muscle area for at least 5 seconds. Then enjoy the feeling of relaxation when you let go.

Purse and squeeze together your lips. Relax them. Close your eyes as tight as you can. Relax them. Tense your jaw. Let it go. Turn your head to the right to tighten your neck muscles. Hold. Relax. Now to the left. Hold. Relax. Roll it all the way forward. Hold. Relax. All the way back. Hold. Relax.

3. As you relax each muscle, visualize the tension leaving and being replaced by a warm, energizing white light.

4. Move along your body from top to bottom. Be as complete and creative as you can. You can clench your chin and tongue. Your shoulders, chest, and abdomen. Arch your back. Clench your buttocks and thighs. Keep the rest of your body relaxed while tensing each muscle group.

You'll learn a lot about your own body as you discover how to tighten various muscles.

Wise Highs

Breath Meditation

As you know if you've been paying attention, meditation involves focusing on one thing. While objects, words, and visualizations are often the locus of focus, many people like to meditate by concentrating on something repetitive and regular: *breathing*.

Breathing is very handy for meditating because it doesn't require any special equipment other than lungs. You can do it anywhere, anytime. And, as you become more aware of your breathing, you'll discover that this basic action can be a pathway to rich and unexplored worlds.

 UP YOUR NOSE

This is a great meditation for getting started, although it is not recommended for sinus sufferers.

1. Sit upright in a chair or on the floor.

2. Close your eyes.

3. Breathe fully and naturally through your nose.

4. Become aware of the air passing in and out of your nostrils.

That's all you have to do: pay attention to your breathing. If your mind drifts into "reality," just bring it back to the breath circulating in and out of your nose.

"Without mastering breathing nothing can be mastered."
G.I. GURDJIEFF

 IN AND OUT

1. Assume a comfortable position for meditating.

2. Close your eyes. Relax.

3. Concentrate on your breathing. Breathe naturally. Don't force long or deep breaths.

4. Inhale through your nose and think *in*.

5. Exhale through your nose or mouth and think *out*.

6. Begin to count each breath in your mind when you exhale. Exhale... *one*...inhale (if you wish you can think *and*)...exhale...*two*...and... *three*...and...*four*. Once you reach *four*, begin again with *one*.

If you get distracted and lose count, go back to *one*. Be aware of the "turning points" in your breathing cycle: the pauses between inhaling and exhaling, and exhaling and inhaling.

7. Focus on each breath. Become that breath. Let it hypnotize you. Visualize the number of each breath as the center of your being. Let each number gently dissolve into the next.

Meditation Highs

SWAMI SIVANANDA SAYS...

Indian physician, teacher, sage, and spiritual leader Swami Sivananda (1887–1983) spent much of his life in service and meditation. Here are just a few of his observations and insights:

"Meditation is an effort in the beginning. Later on it becomes habitual and gives bliss, joy and peace."

"Through regular practice of concentration and meditation you attain clarity of mind, increased grasping power, retentive memory, increased intelligence, confidence, peace, optimism and control of the senses."

"Regular meditation opens the avenues of intuitional knowledge, makes the mind calm and steady, awakens an ecstatic feeling, and brings the practitioner in contact with the source of his/her very being."

"Still the bubbling mind; herein lies freedom and bliss eternal."

"If you have controlled your mind you are the conqueror of the whole world."

"Meditation brings wisdom; lack of meditation leaves ignorance."
BUDDHA

Sound Meditation

When you say "meditation," a lot of people picture a bearded, white-robed, guru-looking guy sitting cross-legged in a field of psychedelic flowers chanting "Om. Om. Om." Even though this image is a caricature, "om-ing" is a widely practiced form of meditating. Religions and cultures throughout history have used sound as a means of spiritual expression and celebration. How else can you explain the fact that so many people sing in the shower?

In Buddhism, the syllables *om, ah,* and *hung* (pronounced *hoong,* with a soft *h*) have special meaning. Each sound expresses different aspects and healing qualities of the Buddha.

Wise Highs

- *Om* represents the enduring strength and beauty of our true nature—the Buddha body. Singing *Om* brings serenity, courage, and steadiness.
- *Ah* is the eternal expression and energy of reality—the Buddha speech. *Ah* is associated with energy and empowerment.
- *Hung* is the perfection of reality's oneness and connectedness—the Buddha mind. Singing *Hung* brings enlightenment and oneness with the infinity of all being.

You can meditate with these sounds to find peace and healing.

OOOOMMMM AHHHH HUUUUNNNNG

1. Choose a spot where you can chant or sing without feeling self-conscious.

2. Focus on your breathing.

3. When you breathe out, sing or chant your sound. Let it flow naturally. You can choose just one of the syllables and repeat it, or you can alternate between two or three. You can give equal emphasis to the sounds, or stress one more than others, depending on the healing you seek. For example:

Oooooommm. Oooooommm. Oooooommm.
Oooooommm. Oooooommm. Oooooommm.

—or—

Oooooommm. Ahhh. Huuuuuuuuuuuunnnnnnngggggg. Ooooooooooooo
oooommmmmmm. Ahhh. Huuuuuunngg.
Oooooommm. Ahhhhhhhhhhhhhhhhhhhhhhhhh. Huuuuuunnnnggg.

4. There's no *right* way to do this. You can chant the syllables at the same pitch, or you can vary the notes. You can sing softly or loudly—whatever feels most calming.

Note: If you feel inhibited about making a sound, that's *all the more reason to do it!* Think of the pleasure children get from babbling and vocalizing and talking to themselves. The older we get, the more inhibited many of us feel about using our voices for anything other than ordering a burger.

OOOOMMMM AHHHH ZZZZZZZZZ

What if you keep falling asleep when you're trying to meditate? Try meditating sitting up, without any back support. If you fall asleep in this position, you'll tip over and the THUNK you make will help you refocus.

If you find yourself dozing off frequently during attempts to meditate, you probably need more rest. Experiment with meditating at a different time (for example, before dinner instead of before bed) or in a different location (maybe in the laundry room instead of in your sleeping area). You might want to try meditating for just a few minutes; ten may be long enough to refresh you without lulling you to sleep.

AURAL FIXATION

TRY THIS!

An "aural" meditation is also a good way to deal with a stressful situation, or to steady your voice if you are nervous about speaking. To do this, first pick a mantra. You can use "om" or any other simple sound that can be said easily upon exhaling ("hum," "ah," "ime," "hoo," "ing," "hung," etc.).

1. Sit comfortably with your back straight.

2. Breathe deeply yet naturally through your nose. Focus on your breathing.

3. Visualize an image that symbolizes the situation about which you are anxious. For example, if you are nervous about speaking at an assembly, you could picture a black, cloud-like shape that represents the audience in a darkened room. Or, if a test has you tied up in knots, picture it as a stone tablet.

4. Once you've visualized your anxiety, repeat your mantra with every exhalation.

Imagine that your mantra is a flowing breeze or light of calmness and confidence. Every time you breathe out and recite your mantra, the symbol of your anxiety dissolves or disintegrates. So, the dark cloud evaporates and becomes a wondrously bright light; the stone tablet crumbles into dust which the wind blows away.

Every repetition of your mantra fills you with a feeling of security and self-assurance.

> "Neither comprehension nor learning can take place in an atmosphere of anxiety."
> FRANK SMITH

37

Meditating on Objects

Many people meditate by focusing on an object. The object could be the flame of a candle, a mandala,* a flower, a pinecone, a rock, a shell, a beautiful paperweight, or even something in nature such as a tree or waterfall.

 IT'S POLITE TO STARE

"Through meditation and by giving full attention to one thing at a time, we can learn to direct attention where we choose."
EKNATH EASWARAN

All you need to do is focus your attention on the object. If it's a small object, place it at eye level, 12 to 18 inches away from your eyes. If it's a larger object, you want it to fill your vision without over-whelming you.

Gaze at the object. Don't stare. Don't *will* the object into your consciousness. Just look at it. Notice everything you can about the object: color, texture, shadow, shape. Experience all of its qualities and properties as if for the first time. If your mind meanders, just refocus it on the object.

CANDLE CAUTIONS!!! In recent years there has been a dramatic rise in fires, injuries, and deaths caused by candles. Since nothing pulls you out of meditative bliss faster than an inferno in your bedroom, here are a few tips for candle safety:

• Make sure there is nothing near your candle that could burn. This may sound like a no-brainer, but a candle on a bedside table, for example, could set a lampshade above it on fire if it is too close. Especially watch out for curtains, bed linens, and any gasoline-soaked rags you may keep in your meditation space.

• Trim candle wicks to a quarter-inch.

• Place your candle securely so it can't tip over.

• If you're using a taper candle, make sure it won't fall out of its holder.

• Place a dish under your candle in case it springs a wax leak. While the wax itself may not start a fire, it could start fireworks with your parents if it leaks onto the carpet.

* See pages 118–119.

- Always blow out the candle if you are leaving the room or going beddy-bye.
- Do not use a water gun to extinguish a candle. Either blow it out or use a candle snuffer.

Dealing with the Wandering Mind

Virtually everyone who meditates experiences the Wandering Mind. It goes like this:

You're sitting in your meditation spot. Incense burns; a little fountain gurgles peacefully. Time to leave the confines of time and space. You begin your meditation and, after three whole breaths, your mind says Oh no! I left my math book in my locker!

Not a relaxing thought. You bring your attention back to your breathing and a couple of seconds later: HOW COULD DEBBY TELL SEAN THAT I LIKE HIM WHEN I TOLD HER IT WAS A SECRET????!!!!

You re-take your mind and focus on the air passing in and out through your nose. In. Out. In. Out. In. Out. You suddenly realize that for the last four minutes you've been carrying on a mental conversation with Debby.

If your mind seems determined to roam the range...let it. If your mind wanders, scolds, obsesses, worries, makes lists, holds conversations, and rehashes the day...let it. If your mind thinks *This is dumb; I'm bored; When am I going to feel anything?*...let it.

Simply let these thoughts pass through you. Don't get upset. Don't *force* yourself to concentrate. A wandering mind doesn't mean you're doing it "wrong." Just relax and return to your meditation.

Some people find it helpful to gently respond to their mind's meanderings by saying "Thank you," "Good-bye," "Relax," "Serene," or something similar whenever a distracting idea enters their head.

> "When you try to stop activity to achieve passivity, your very effort fills you with activity."
> SENG TS'AN

> "I was trying to daydream, but my mind kept wandering."
> STEVEN WRIGHT

Mindfulness Meditation

In mindfulness meditation, rather than ignoring or "banishing" the thoughts that go through your head, you observe them. Because

Wise Highs

you're in a state of peace and relaxation when you do this, you're able to witness your inner mental and emotional life without judgment or analysis.

You allow your thoughts and feelings to *be*. You don't censor, condemn, rationalize, or defend them. You simply witness and accept them. In so doing, you see more clearly what is on your mind and gain insight into your perceptions, fears, and feelings.

TRY THIS!

BUBBLE, BUBBLE, TOIL AND TROUBLE

The purpose of this meditation is to observe, without judgment, what's on your mind, and to let the thoughts leave your mind so you can experience peace and joy.

1. Assume your preferred meditation posture.

2. Close your eyes and relax into your breathing.

3. Imagine that you are sitting at the bottom of a deep pool of water. The water is warm, soothing, and full of light.

4. Each time you have a thought, feeling, or sensation, visualize it as a bubble. Let the bubble float to the surface and vanish.

5. As a new thought appears, see it as a bubble and let it, too, rise. If a whole bunch of thoughts come in rapid succession, they can float to the surface as a group of bubbles.

6. Don't think about your thoughts; don't criticize, evaluate, scrutinize, weigh, ponder, or argue with your thoughts. Just let them be. Let them float in front of, and away from, your mind's eye.

Variations for Landlubbers

Some people prefer not to imagine themselves underwater. (They don't want to get their hair wet, I suppose.) If this is the case for you…

…Imagine that you are sitting by a river. Your thoughts become leaves that slowly float downstream until they disappear from sight.
…Picture yourself sitting in a beautiful meadow. Your thoughts become bubbles that drift away on the wind until they vanish.
…See yourself sitting around a campfire. Thoughts rise as sparks or wisps of smoke.

Try these variations. Invent your own. Find the one that works best for you.

Meditation Highs

There are many different approaches to meditating, along with hundreds of books. Some you may find too "touchy-feely" or "New Age-y"; others may seem too "cult-like" or bound up in the adoration of a single guru. It's a good idea to shop around and become familiar with different practices. Other than the exercises and practices presented in this chapter, I'm not recommending any single approach—it's too personal a choice. Use these resources as a starting point for your own exploration.

Awakening the Buddha Within: Tibetan Wisdom for the Western World by Lama Surya Das (New York: Broadway Books, 1998). A definitive, nonsectarian guide to Buddhism as a practical and profound path to enlightenment, written by the most highly trained American lama in the Tibetan tradition. Offers a complete understanding of wisdom training (i.e., developing clear vision, insight, and inner understanding), ethics training (i.e., cultivating virtue, integrity, compassion, and self-discipline), and meditation training (i.e., mindfulness, concentration, and awareness of the present moment). If that sounds like heavy going, it isn't. The book is fun to read, with lots of anecdotes and stories. Very useful if you're wondering *Is there a God? What is the meaning of life? What is real? What is truth? What's for dinner?*

Wherever You Go, There You Are: Mindfulness Meditation in Everyday Life by Jon Kabat-Zinn (New York: Hyperion, 2005). Apart from having a great title, this best-selling book is a simple, straightforward, poetic introduction to Buddhist meditation practices.

Learning Meditation
www.learningmeditation.com

The Transcendental Meditation (TM) Program
www.tm.org • 1-888-LEARN-TM (1-888-532-7686)

> "By practicing meditation you will come to see that the true nature of the real you, the body of light, is everlasting bliss!"
>
> RAMA

Visualization

Visualization is a form of meditation that can help you overcome fear, anxiety, and negative thinking. If you're facing a stressful situation, you can visualize yourself handling it competently and confidently. This type of "positive imaging" is also used to treat illness, train athletes, overcome the fear of flying, and to alleviate incapacitating anxieties such as arachnaphobia (fear of spiders) and isoscelesphobia (fear of triangles).

Wise Highs

1. Do a relaxation exercise to release tension from your body.*

2. Close your eyes and picture a beautiful scene. It might be some-place you've been that you associate with total serenity and security, or someplace you've never been but would love to visit. Visualize the scene in all its beauty and detail: colors, textures, light, shadow, movement.

SEE IT, SKI IT

In the words of Camille Duvalle, world cham-pion water-skier: "I train myself mentally with visualization. The morning of a tournament, before I put my feet on the floor, I visualize myself making perfect runs with emphasis on technique, all the way through to what my personal best is in practice.... The more you work with this type of visualization, especially when you do it on a day-to-day basis, you'll actually begin to feel your muscles contracting at the appropriate times."

Don't just *see* the scene. *Hear* it: wind blowing, water flowing, birds singing, waves lapping. *Smell* it: saltwater air, perfumed fields, fresh-cut grass. *Feel* it: the warm sun, buoyant water, tin-gling sand.

3. As you relax into the beauty and peaceful-ness of the scene, say a positive affirmation to yourself: "I am at peace." "I feel carefree." "I can handle anything that comes my way."

Avoid negative statements such as "I don't want to feel shy and nervous." Instead, tell yourself "I can feel outgoing and confident in any social situation."

4. At the conclusion of your visualization, say "I will open my eyes and feel refreshed and calm."

And guess what? You will!

Athletes use visualization techniques for training and motivation. They picture themselves racing down the course, hitting the ball, acing the serve, or nailing the perfect three-and-a-quarter-double-reverse-ten-meter dive. Research shows that these visualizations work.

You can also use visualizations to deal with specific fears. For exam-ple, if you get very nervous when you have to speak or perform, visualize the situation. Picture yourself on stage. Say to yourself: *I feel confident. The audience admires me. They know what it's like to be in my shoes. They are my friends. My voice is strong. I am proud of my accomplishments. I have nothing to fear. I am a good person.*

---

* See "Mind Over Muscle," pages 32–33.

Meditation Highs

Visualization is also helpful for dealing with troubling emotions. Many people react to feelings of sadness or distress by trying to avoid them. This never works. Even if you manage to "forget" about the feeling by distracting yourself with work or play, the feeling is still there, eating away at you. The best way to let go of a feeling is to acknowledge its presence and embrace it.

1. Close your eyes. Visualize your sadness (or pain, guilt, shame, loneliness, or hopelessness) as an ominous dark cloud. Center it wherever you feel the most hurt. This might be in your heart, head, stomach—or someplace else. The cloud may feel heavy or suffocating. It may churn and billow. Acknowledge the cloud of sadness that engulfs you.

2. The sadness hurts. But you can feel it and stand your ground.

3. Now you are going to let go of your sadness. You are going to expel a part of it with every exhalation.

4. Breathe naturally. Every time you exhale, visualize the cloud escaping from your body like steam from a kettle. Soon, the entire cloud is outside of you. It drifts away. Slowly. Steadily. You watch it float into the distance. Farther and farther away. You can barely make it out. It becomes tinier and tinier. It is a hazy dot on the horizon. It...disappears.

5. Your sadness is out of sight. Out of mind. Out of body. You are no longer sad. Your hurt and tension have floated off into the far-distant sky. You feel relaxed. Calm. Light. At peace.

Variation: Light Meditation

1. Picture your sadness (or other feeling) as total darkness. It has overwhelmed your mind and body, blocking out all light. Feel the sadness. Let the darkness engulf you.

2. Now imagine a warm, healing light. It is the light of joy and hope and goodness. It is the light of love. This light could come from a higher power, from God, from the sun, from a thousand suns. It could come from above you, from all around you, from the atom at the center of your being. Place the light source wherever it feels most right.

WHY VISUALIZATION WORKS

Visualization tricks the brain. The picture you create is so "real" that your brain doesn't know that it's coming from your mind and imagination, rather than from external stimuli. So it "hears" the soothing waves and "sees" the sparkling water and "feels" the warm sun—and sends signals to your body telling it to relax. The same principle lies behind simulation. When pilots, astronauts, surgeons, and soldiers practice highly skilled operations with virtual reality simulators, the brain doesn't know it's all make-believe.

43

3. The light showers you with its warm, healing energy. It fills your entire body. As the rays touch each cell, visualize that cell turning into a beautiful, perfect blossom. All that is wondrous in life is in that blossom. It sparkles with the light of a million rainbows.

4. The sadness is gone. The darkness is gone. You are filled with light. You are light. The universe is light. You and the universe are one. You have nothing to fear. The world is a safe place. You are safe. Dwell in this feeling of warmth and security. Say to yourself: *My sadness is gone. I feel free. I can handle whatever comes my way.*

You can also visualize feelings, worries, fears, regrets, bad memories, and stressful events as smoke, shadows, weights, choking gases, frightening shapes, symbolic objects, chilling winds, or icy mists. Visualize a healing source that "matches" the image you have chosen for the feeling. This "antidote" could be a waterfall that washes the feeling away; a soothing nectar that slowly spreads through your body; a radiant fire that warms your chilled soul; a sweet-smelling breeze that fills you with fresh air; a pair of giant hands that gently holds and rocks you.

DOPE ON A ROPE

Perhaps you are obsessed with another person or you are involved in a destructive relationship. Perhaps your mind can't let go of an event in the past or a projection about the future. You are enslaved to these negative emotions. They drag you around by a rope or chain. At one end, it is tied around your neck. At the other end is the feeling or relationship from which you wish to cut free.

Imagine a source of power that casts a healing, laser-like beam. Ask this power to set you free. Visualize the laser. Train it on the chain of bondage. The chain starts to smolder and turn red. It falls from around your neck. The redness spreads along the entire chain. Soon, the entire length glows like a molten snake. It burns and steams until...it has consumed itself. It is gone, without a trace. You are free. You experience a sense of great relief.

THE HAPPY CURE

Want less stress in under a minute? I thought so. Here's what you need to do: Think "happy." Put a big smile on your face. Visualize how happy you look. Your eyes are sparkling. Your grin stretches from ear to ear. You're a human "smiley face." HAPPY! Tell yourself: *I'm HAPPY!!! I am just fine as fine can be!!!!* HAPP-YYYY!!!! I guarantee, this exercise is so silly you'll be laughing by the end of it.

Meditation Highs

Have you ever wanted to write, direct, and star in your own film? With visualization, you can create your own fantasies in the theater of your mind. And best of all, the floor is never sticky!

The first thing you need to do is create your own visualization tape. You can also have a friend record one, or you can read this visualization script (or your own) to each other. Whether you make a tape or do a live reading, be sure to allow enough time between phrases for you to picture the scene.

Set the mood. You may want to burn candles or incense. Put on some *restful* music or background sounds. Sit in a comfortable chair. (If you lie down, you're likely to fall asleep.) Focus on your breath. Relax into your breathing. Empty your mind. Feel how relaxed you are.

Ready? Here we go.

> You are on a beach...a tropical island beach...you gaze up and down the coastline...a crescent of palm trees arcs gently along the water's edge...emerald waves lick at the shore... sunlight dances upon the sea...the sand is white and fine as powder...warm under your bare feet...not a footprint can be seen...you are the first person to walk here since the beginning of time...

> The sky is a deep and infinite blue...a breeze that began in eternity washes over you...your hair blows in the wind...you hear the whisper of swaying palm fronds...the lapping of breaking waves...the chirping of birds...

> The sun embraces you in its warmth...your skin tingles...you dig your toes into the sand and feel the cool grains below the surface...

> You smell the perfumed air...sweet as gardenias...you breathe deeply and inhale the salt...the sun...the wind...the blue sky...

> You feel earth's gravity like a warm blanket...yet your insides are buoyant...you begin to run along the water's edge... through the white foam...darting over the squishy sand...you are a child...without a care in the world...you feel peaceful...at one with yourself...with the world...with all that is good and loving...

Wise Highs

Your strides lengthen...you pick up speed...it feels as if you could run forever...your toes skim the sand...barely touching the surface...the wind is in your face...you feel so free and powerful...you run faster...and faster...floating effortlessly between each step...you push off from the ground...extending your arms above your head...and are swept into the air...you are flying... truly flying...

You soar higher and higher...you see the plush satin sea...the swaying green trees...the entire lush island...ringed with a necklace of white sand...mountains shooting skyward from the interior...

You extend your arms to your side...like wings...you bank and swoop and glide on the wind...

You have never felt so safe and carefree in your life...

The currents of the wind carry you gently...in perfect silence...you feel lighter and lighter...warmer and warmer...calmer and calmer...you are floating on air...your consciousness melting...evaporating...diffusing...until...

All boundaries are erased...you are no longer aware of your body...you are part of the sky...and sun...the sea...the sand...you exist as warm eternal energy...in an ether of love and serenity...timeless...formless...floating...in perfect equilibrium...

After what may have been minutes... or millennia...a faint sound plays peek-a-boo with your consciousness...the sweet sound of birds singing...and it seems as if you have been hearing it all along...it calls you back to awareness...to your body...to a feeling of warmth...and one by one...like notes turning into a song...your senses return...and you are flying again...effortlessly...fearlessly...

You feel the rush of wind...the tingle of the sun...the thrill of swooping through the sky in perfect balance...

You see the blue and green of the sea...the glistening island...the sparkling waves breaking on its shore...the swaying tops of palm trees...

46

In long lazy spirals you descend...lower and lower...until you are flying over the beach...your body parallel to the sand...your arms extended in front of your head...you move your arms out to your side and your body gently rises and slows...and you are running in air...your toes kiss the sand... and you return to earth...

You run along the beach...leaping...splashing...laughing... seeing everything as if for the first time...the air is sweeter... the sea more dazzling...the breeze is softer...the trees more soothing...

You lie on the sand...and close your eyes...the sun shines above...and you bask in its warmth...the whole world spins... you experience what you thought only lived in dreams...

You rest...breathing deeply...you slowly count...***three***... ***two***...***one***...and open your eyes...

You stretch and sit up...and return.

Welcome back.

FIND OUT MORE

Creative Visualization: Use the Power of Your Imagination to Create What You Want in Your Life by Shakti Gawain (Novato, CA: New World Library, 2002). This book, along with its companion workbook of the same title, will show you how to use visualization techniques and imagination to break negative habits, improve self-esteem, find inner peace, and produce positive changes in your life.

Finding Flow by Mihaly Csikszentmihalyi (New York: Basic Books, 1998). If you've ever become so absorbed in a creative, athletic, intellectual, or social activity that you lose your awareness of self and time, you are experiencing "flow." Based on over two decades of scientific research, this book describes how to achieve flow and find meaning and happiness in your life.

"Ordinary people believe only in the possible. Extraordinary people visualize not what is possible or probable, but rather what is impossible. And by visualizing the impossible, they begin to see it as possible."
CHERIE CARTER-SCOTT

Self-Hypnosis

Wise Highs

Hypnosis comes from the Greek word for sleep. *(You are getting sleee-py.)* Self-hypnosis is a powerful way to reduce stress and make desired changes in your life.

With meditation, we reach a blissful, centered state free of life's burdens by focusing on an object. With self-hypnosis, we use the power of positive suggestion to change our behavior, attitudes, and/ or feelings.

You've probably experienced hypnotic trances without knowing it. For instance, if you've ever taken a long-distance drive during which you have no memory of passing certain towns or exits, you were in a hypnotic state. Daydreaming is also a form of self-hypnosis.

Self-hypnosis is safe. You will not do anything you wouldn't otherwise do. You won't embarrass yourself, blurt out secrets, uncover dark, repressed traumas, compromise your morals, or not be able to "get back." If you've seen a movie where someone was "hypnotized" into committing a villainous act, that's just Hollywood make-believe. If you've seen a hypnosis show where people do silly things on stage, the volunteers are usually extroverted hams who would do similar things even if they weren't hypnotized. People under a hypnotic trance do not behave unethically, illegally, or comically—unless they would behave that way in real life.

Under hypnosis, you create thoughts and images that your mind and body react to as if they were real. For example, when you watch a car chase or scary scene in a movie, your heart rate increases, your muscles contract, and you feel genuinely pumped or afraid. The events aren't truly happening to you, but your mind and body are fooled. When people are hypnotized and, through suggestion, believe that they are chasing someone, or sunning on a beach, or running a marathon, their body and brain respond as if the behaviors were actually taking place.

> "The mind is the limit. As long as the mind can envision the fact that you can do something, you can do it, as long as you really believe 100 percent."
>
> ARNOLD SCHWARZENEGGER

THE POWER OF THE MIND

These exercises demonstrate the power of suggestion. Try them with a friend who can witness your response.

Bowling Balls...

1. Stand up straight. Feet slightly apart. Close your eyes.

2. Imagine that you are holding a bowling ball in your right hand.

3. The bowling ball keeps getting bigger and heavier. Bigger and heavier. Imagine that it is weighing you down and pulling you over.

4. After several minutes, open your eyes. Are you still standing up straight? Or did you lean to the right? Ask your friend for corroboration.

...and Water Balloons

1. Stand up straight. Hold both your arms out to your sides at shoulder level. Keep your palms down. Close your eyes.

2. Imagine that someone is tying a water balloon to your right arm. Feel the strain. Now, a second water balloon is being tied to your arm. And a third! You can barely hold your arm up under so much weight.

3. Now, imagine that a helium-filled balloon is being tied to your left arm. Your arm feels light and buoyant. A second balloon is tied. And a third. It lifts your arm higher and higher into the air.

4. Open your eyes. Have your arms moved from level? Did your right arm sink and your left arm rise? What does your friend say?

FEEL YOURSELF BECOMING CALM...CALM AND RELAXED...DEEPER AND DEEPER

TRY THIS!

Self-hypnosis doesn't mean you're going to cluck like a chicken or jump around as if you had a thousand red ants in your underwear. Self-hypnosis is really just a deep form of visualization. You're going to achieve a very relaxed state of mind and give yourself affirmative suggestions.

Note: Before you begin, read the instructions all the way through. Think up the trigger words, phrases, suggestions, and special retreat you'll want to use for steps 6, 7, 8, and 9.

1. Find a place where you won't be disturbed. Sit in a comfortable chair or chaise lounge. Be sure your head, neck, arms, and hands are supported. Keep your arms and legs uncrossed. Wear loose clothing and remove any jewelry, contact lenses, glasses, or nose rings that might interfere with your relaxation.

2. Focus your eyes softly on a candle* or point in front of you.

---

* See "Candle Cautions," pages 38–39.

Wise Highs

3. Breathe slowly and naturally.

4. Do a relaxation exercise to release tension from your body.*

5. Imagine that with every breath in, a wave of relaxation washes over your body. With every breath out, your stress flows away.

6. Repeat the key phrases you have chosen to deepen your trance. You can use words such as *deep, heavy, drowsy, calm, relaxed, sinking, drifting, going,* etc. Let your mind say something like this, slowly and softly:

> I am going deeper and deeper...drifting and drowsy... deeper and deeper...feeling peaceful and calm...peaceful and calm...my eyelids are getting heavier and heavier...I am drifting deeper and deeper...heavier and heavier...

Keep repeating the phrases to yourself. You will feel more and more relaxed and comfortable.

7. You are now ready to go to your special retreat. Choose a place where you feel total peace, contentment, and security. It could be a clearing in a forest, a mountaintop, a beach, or a room from your childhood.

To reach this haven, you will count backwards from 10 to 0. Each "step" takes you deeper and deeper, closer and closer. You will feel more and more relaxed. When you reach *zero,* you are there. See, hear, touch, feel, and smell your special retreat with all of your senses.

8. Spend time in this place of total safety and relaxation. Deepen the hypnosis by repeating your key phrases: e.g., *peaceful and calm... going deeper and deeper.*

9. Now comes the suggestion. Say to yourself:

> Every time I hear the word _____ *[insert your trigger word],* I will return to this place of deep relaxation.

Repeat the suggestion at least three times. Later, as you go through your day, you can use your trigger word to recall the state of deep relaxation you experienced at the time you made the suggestion.

You can also create suggestions to help you deal with fears, minor injuries or illnesses, self-criticism, performance anxiety, low self-esteem, fatigue, and even habits you'd like to get rid of.**

---

* See "Mind Over Muscle," pages 32–33.
** See the tips on pages 52–53.

10. When you are ready to come out of your hypnotic trance, return by counting from one back up to ten. Say to yourself:

> On the count of ten, I will awaken and feel relaxed, alert, and renewed…**One**…I am becoming more alert…**Two**…more and more awake…**Three**…more and more refreshed…*[and so on to]*…**Nine**…my eyes are opening…**Ten**…I am wide awake and fully alert.

Meditation Highs

BE YOUR OWN HYPNOTIST

Put on some tranquil music or background sounds and then make a tape. Record yourself saying:

> I am feeling relaxed…I am breathing regularly and naturally… I am feeling more and more relaxed with every breath…In my mind I will count backwards from ten…When I reach one…I will feel completely relaxed…**Ten**…**Nine**…**Eight**…**Seven**… **Six**…**Five**…**Four**…**Three**…**Two**…**One**…I am completely re-laxed…I have a thousand red ants in my underwear…

Oops. Wrong suggestion.

At this point, you can make whatever positive suggestions you wish regarding a trigger word, or how you will feel or behave in certain situations, etc.

> "Every human mind is a great slumbering power until awakened by a keen desire and by definite resolution to do."
>
> EDGAR F. ROBERTS

COUNTDOWN

1. Lie down. (If you discover that you fall asleep if you lie down, do this exercise sitting in a chair.) Find a time and a place where you won't be disturbed or distracted. If there's a lot of noise in the back-ground, create some white noise: Turn on a fan, or take an old radio and tune to the static between stations.

2. Begin with a relaxation exercise.*

Now it's time to deepen your relaxation until you move into a hyp-notic state.

---

* See "Mind Over Muscle," pages 32–33.

Wise Highs

3. In your mind, count backwards from 100. With each count, imagine that you are getting more and more relaxed. You are drifting deeper and deeper.

Don't count quickly. You're not in a race. Dwell on each number for at least 2–3 seconds. You may want to link each count to your breathing.*

4. You are now in a deep state of relaxation and are ready to give yourself suggestions. You should prepare and memorize your suggestions ahead of time. Keep them succinct and positive. For example:

- "I am more confident in social situations."
- "I am getting along better with my mother."
- "I am working harder and improving my grades."

5. To conclude your session, think *At the count of three, I will be fully awake.* Then say to yourself:

One. I am beginning to move toward a waking state.

Two. I am more alert and ready to awaken.

Three. I am fully awake.

Remember, self-hypnosis takes practice, just like meditating. Don't expect to achieve a hypnotic state right off the bat. If you really want to become proficient at it, do it at the same time each day. When you first start, you'll probably think *Am I hypnotized yet? Is this it? Is this what I'm supposed to feel?* You won't know when you move into a hypnotic state, just as you don't know when you fall asleep. In fact, if you keep asking yourself *Am I asleep?* or *Am I hypnotized yet?,* you'll keep yourself from getting to that point. Only after you've awakened will you realize that you were asleep or in a hypnotic state.

"We cannot always control our thoughts, but we can control our words, and repetition impresses the subconscious, and we are then master of the situation."
FLORENCE SCOVEL SHINN

TIPS FOR HYPNOTIC AUTO-SUGGESTIONS AND POSITIVE AFFIRMATIONS

1. Think up and rehearse your suggestions prior to beginning a self-hypnosis session.

2. Keep your suggestions short. Do say *I will feel gratitude for all that is good in my life.* Don't say *I will count my blessings for having parents who love me even if they do nag too much, and even though I can't buy everything*

---

* For an alternative deepening procedure, imagine that you are floating to earth from a high place waaaay up in the sky. You can even combine this visualization with counting, picturing the numbers as your decreasing altitude.

I want I have a lot more money than most people on the planet, and life is really boring at times but at least my village isn't being bombed or tossed around by an earthquake, so I guess I should appreciate those things and not complain so much.

It's fine to combine a number of succinct suggestions. For example, if you get anxious every time you have a test, you could say *I will study every day. I will concentrate and absorb the information. I can learn everything I need to know. My mind is quick and bright. I will remember the material. I will breathe deeply when the teacher hands out the test. I will know how well prepared I am. I can see the test being returned to me with an A.*

3. Be positive. Instead of saying *I won't lose my temper,* say *I will be calm and in control.*

4. Visualize your suggestions. For example, if your suggestion is *I will give a terrific speech,* picture yourself giving it, standing proudly, the audience beaming, laughing, applauding, approving.

5. Don't use the word "try" e.g., *I will try to work harder and improve my grades*—as this suggests that you may not succeed. The whole idea of autosuggestion is that you *can* and *will* succeed.

FIND OUT MORE

Discovering the Power of Self Hypnosis: The Simple, Natural Mind-Body Approach to Change and Healing by Stanley Fisher, Ph.D. (New York: Newmarket Press, 2002). Describes ways to use self-hypnosis to deal with stress, anger, and disappointment; prepare for surgery; recover from illness; and alleviate such problems as performance anxiety, fears, insomnia, overeating, and smoking.

T'AI CHI CHUAN

If you've ever seen someone in a park moving his body in graceful slow motion, he's either bonkers or practicing T'ai Chi.

T'ai Chi is an ancient martial art based on the concept of *chi,* the vital life energy that circulates throughout the body.* T'ai Chi consists of over 100 *forms,* or sets of movements, designed to control

---

* See pages 135–136.

Wise Highs

and increase the flow of *chi* energy. While these "moving meditations" have combat applications, many practitioners use them not to fend off muggers, but to improve their posture, alignment, balance, coordination, and vitality. And, as I'm sure you know by now, anything that stirs up the ol' *chi* energy is a surefire way to alter your consciousness in amazing ways.

To learn T'ai Chi correctly, you really need to take instruction. Look in the Yellow Pages under "Martial Arts Instruction" or "Exercise and Physical Fitness Programs."

In the meantime, here's a very simple T'ai Chi exercise you can try.

 HORSE AROUND

1. Stand straight with your toes pointing forward and your feet shoulder-width apart.

2. Bend your knees forward until you resemble a person riding a horse. *Don't* do a deep knee bend. Don't say "Giddyap!" Keep your back straight.

3. Slowly lift your arms out in front of you. Pretend you're holding a giant beach ball at eye level. Your arms should describe a rounded arc. Your palms should face towards you. Keep your fingers spread, with the thumbs on top and curled inwards. The "ball" is so large that your hands cannot complete the circle. Your fingertips remain about six inches apart.

4. As you "ride the horse" and "carry the ball," visualize a circle described by your arms, fingers, the space between them, and your back. Now imagine that energy is flowing round and round in that circle—through your arms, out your fingertips, across the gap, and around your back.

5. Stare straight ahead between your fingers at a point on the wall or landscape.

6. Remain in this position for 10–15 minutes.

WHAT????!!!!

That's right. The *chi* energy will keep your arms up and your knees bent. Don't try to will your muscle power to do it. Instead, concentrate on the flow of energy. Visualize it.

This may be hard, and you may not be able to keep it up for the full time. (If you feel pain, stop immediately!) But don't worry if you can't do it at first. As you become more skilled at T'ai Chi, you'll be able to do this and many more exercises—and experience incredible highs.

Meditation Highs

The Complete Idiot's Guide to T'ai Chi & QiGong by Bill Douglas and Richard Yennie (Indianapolis, IN: MacMillan, 2002). You don't have to be an idiot to read this book, which shows you how to get started. You'll learn 64 basic postures and routines that can be done anywhere; even how to choose an instructor. There's also a companion series of videos available.

Yoga

Yoga is not a character from *Star Wars*. It's a meditative form of exercise that unites the body, mind, and soul. (In fact, "yoga" means *union.*) Because yoga focuses on the physical, emotional, and spiritual aspects of life, it's a great way to recharge your batteries, sharpen your mind, reduce stress, and discover more about yourself.

Yoga consists of slow, rhythmic poses that require a lot of concentration, balance, and flexibility to achieve. They are much harder than they look, and beginners need to exercise care to avoid straining their muscles, ligaments, or tendons. Overzealous teens have been known to knot themselves into pretzels from which they can't escape. Imagine the humiliation of friends coming over to salt you.

People who practice yoga are called *yogis* (but rarely to their face). Many yogis combine their exercises with abstinence, meditation, or

YOGA 101

Along with classes on anatomy and how to pronounce really long medical terms, some doctors-in-training at the School of Medicine at the University of California Los Angeles (UCLA) are learning yoga. School administrators hope that students who take yoga classes will be more open-minded in how they treat patients.

prayer to enhance the spiritual high. The most frequently practiced form of yoga in the western world is hatha yoga. Kundalini is another form of yoga that engages powerful energies in the body. When properly practiced, yoga has many benefits. It improves posture, coordination, circulation, and balance; it helps you to relax and concentrate; and it gives you strong, flexible muscles.

Wise Highs

The best way to get started with yoga is by taking a class, reading a book, or watching a video. Wear loose clothing and exercise on a surface that won't slip, such as a mat or carpet. Before long, you'll discover why so many people are yoga junkies. In the words of one teenage yogi:

"Whenever I want to forget my worries and escape into a more peaceful place, I pop my yoga instructional tape into the VCR and practice yoga postures and meditation. Yoga quiets the mind while strengthening the body and improving breath and circulation, among other benefits. Many people who don't know much about yoga think of it as a strange and even painful Eastern practice of bodily contortion. [Hey, that thing about teens turning into pretzels was just a joke!] On the contrary, yoga is a wonderful way to gently stretch and exercise the body. All you need is a small amount of space and a basic knowledge of how to practice yoga, which can be achieved through books, classes, videos, or even friends. I encourage anyone who is interested in a fulfilling mental and physical journey to learn yoga." **SARAH STILLMAN, 15**

SAY WHAT?

Many yoga poses have very descriptive names. For example, you might stretch your spine, back, and arms in the Cobra *(Bhujangasana)*, increase your flexibility in the Bridge *(Sethu Bandhasa),* or build strength in the Downward Facing Dog *(Adho Mukha Svanasana).*

FIND OUT MORE

I Love Yoga: A Source Book for Teens by Ellen Schwartz (Toronto: Tundra Books, 2003). Breathing, exercising, relaxation techniques, and yoga poses are described in a step-by-step format. Written especially for teens, this book is designed to help you deal with mood swings, succeed in school, and manage stress from any source.

The Little Yoga Book by Erika Dillman (New York: Warner Books, 1999). This illustrated mini-guide to hatha yoga will provide you with breathing exercises and workouts to improve your flexibility and stamina, soothe your mind and body, even help you work at the computer without getting muscle strain.

Yoga Journal
PO Box 51151
Boulder, CO 80322
1-800-600-YOGA (9642)
www.yogajournal.com
Published since 1975, *Yoga Journal* is the leading magazine on yoga and body-mind approaches to personal and spiritual health. In addition to providing information about yoga, the Web site will refer you to related books, videos, and audiotapes.

Out-of-Body Experiences

I have to admit that I have neither attempted nor undergone an out-of-body experience (OBE for short). But hey, if there's anything to this, it's got to be one of the ultimate highs. Believers claim they can visit distant friends and relatives, explore other countries, even travel back in time. Here's a book that's recommended by those in the know about astral projection. If you try it, let me know what happens. And whether they serve peanuts.

FIND OUT MORE

Out of Body Experiences: How to Have Them and What to Expect by Robert Peterson (Charlottesville, VA: Hampton Roads Publishing Co., 1997). Peterson believes that anyone can have an OBE. This anecdotal, accessible book is a good place to start learning about astral projection. The author also describes odd and startling aspects of OBEs that readers may not expect (like running into Santa high above Jamaica in the middle of July).

Chapter 4

Pumping Adrenaline

Sports, Exercise, and X-treme Highs

Physical highs come in several varieties: sports highs, exercise highs, and you'd-have-to-be-crazy-to-do-that highs. Let's start with sports highs.

Sports Highs

> "Sports do not build character. They reveal it."
>
> HEYWOOD HALE BROUN

When I was a wee lad growing up in suburbia, there was a television show called *ABC's Wide World of Sports*. Each episode began with a montage of sporty people engaged in various competitive activities such as the 100-yard dash, swimming, bobsledding, pole vaulting, auto racing, and the like. As these breathtaking examples of courage, skill, and endurance flew by on the screen, the announcer intoned dramatically about "the thrill of victory and the agony of defeat." And when he said "agony of defeat," you'd see race cars smashing into walls, skiers cartwheeling down mountains, errant javelins spearing shot-putters—that sort of thing. It gave me goosebumps.

Sports can get you high in a number of ways. For some people, the high comes from competing—and the thrill of victory. This is the case for these teens:

"I play golf. When I beat the guys I play with, I am so high that I want to dance in a circle like a little kid and say 'I beat you!'"

"I swim on the school's swim team. The feeling I have after I get out of the pool and find out that I broke a record, came in first, or even got a best time is exhilarating."

But winning isn't the only way to get a high from sports. Bonding with your teammates is another, as this teen knows firsthand:

"Rowing is my life. I wake up before dawn and am on the water when the sun comes up. I am closer to my crewmates than anyone else. They've seen all my moods and still love me. They are the most supportive and caring people I have ever met."

The human being is a social animal. We are designed to live, work, and play with others. When we're part of a team, *we* becomes more important than *I*. This type of human connecting is not only jolly good fun, but a powerful, transforming experience.* Why else would mud-covered men in shoulder pads pat each other's fannies in front of 40 million people to celebrate the fact that an oblong piece of pigskin found its way across a chalk line?

In addition to personal bests, bonding, and fanny-patting, sports offer another, more spiritual high. This is described by a fast-moving student-athlete who paused long enough to say:

"I run marathons and this takes me to a different zone—I am happy and in a world of my own."

This is the famous Zone you've heard about. Your body moves beyond pain and fatigue to become meditation in motion.** You draw your energy from the source of all life. Your mental focus is so intense you "lose" your mind. Endorphins and adrenaline course through your bloodstream. It is a place of perfect spiritual, mental, and physical balance. You are one with all.

Long-distance runners (and those engaged in other endurance sports such as cross-country skiing, cycling, swimming, and rowing) frequently enter the Zone. Part of the high is purely physical; it comes from the endorphins— the pleasure-producing, pain-relieving, mood-improving, memory-enhancing chemicals made in the brain during exercise. Because of

STUDYING "THE ZONE"

It's not just athletes who visit the Zone. University of Chicago professor Mihaly Csikszentmihalyi (pronounced *chick-sent-me-high*) has interviewed thousands of people—from chess masters to playwrights to sprinters—to learn about what he calls "flow," when the body and mind work in total harmony to achieve a goal. During a "flow state," you're totally absorbed in what you're doing and you do it just because you enjoy it, not because of any external rewards it might bring. If you want to know more about this, read Csikszentmihalyi's book *Finding Flow* (see page 47).

---

* For more about connecting, see Chapter 11.
** For more about meditation, look back at Chapter 3—especially if you skipped it.

this physical high, you can get addicted to running and other endurance sports. Many joggers report feeling depressed or out-of-sorts if they don't run for a few days.

While you're better off being addicted to running or rowing than to drugs, you don't want to become dependent on a daily endorphin high. To avoid this, vary your physical highs. Change sports from one season to the next. Enjoy team sports *and* individual sports; sports that require strength *and* sports that require endurance. Or, instead of playing sports, take ballet or swing dancing lessons, or learn yoga or a martial art.

Whatever you choose, you'll reap big benefits. And you'll probably find the high of sports so rewarding that alcohol and other drugs seem boring by comparison—or not worth trying. But don't take my word for it. Hear what your peers have to say:

"One way that I alter my consciousness without the use of drugs is through sports. It's essentially safe (depending on what sport it is), and it is definitely healthy. When my adrenaline starts pumping and I break for the touchdown run, or I beat a person by a hair when running, my mind changes. I become very single-minded and determined and start to feel very alive. It's that feeling of aliveness that I love." **GUILLERMO ZAVALA, 16**

"My name is Will and I have a way to keep off drugs. Weight training. I think this is the key. Martial arts also does it for me. I had the fortune to get into martial arts when I was six, way before I knew about drugs or girls or any of that stuff. All my friends who did drugs got help and got off and started doing martial arts and that was a real break for me, because I could help other people in my neighborhood. So that's why we stay together, 'cause we're off drugs and into martial arts, and it also gives us something to do when we need it or are bored. Weight training and martial arts are the best remedy for kids who need something to do besides drugs." **WILLIAM HALL, 17**

"I get a rush through sports. Without them I do not know where I would be. I am a rower on a local crew team and I love it. I enter this totally different mindset when I am practicing or racing. I have one goal and that is to be the best. If I chose to use alcohol and other drugs, I would not be able to do any of these things. It would be impossible to accomplish my goals.... Before a race there is this feeling of electricity in the air. Everyone comes together as a team. Being on this team is very important to me and losing the privilege to be on it because of alcohol and other drugs would be the end of the world for me." **ELIZABETH MCINTURFF, 17**

THE SURVEY SAYS...

We asked teenagers "How do you relieve stress, have fun, escape reality, and/or get high without alcohol or other drugs?" Many turn to sports. Here are some they enjoy:*

- biking
- bungee jumping
- hang gliding
- horseback riding
- inline skating
- karate
- kickboxing
- laser tag
- mountain climbing
- paintball
- ping-pong
- rock climbing
- sailing
- scuba diving
- skateboarding
- skiing
- skydiving
- surfing
- swimming
- tennis
- triathlon
- tubing
- tumbling
- weightlifting
- whitewater rafting
- working out
- wrestling
- X-treme skiing

> "Jogging is very beneficial. It's good for your legs and your feet. It's also very good for the ground. It makes it feel needed."
>
> CHARLES M. SCHULZ

Exercise Highs

I hate to break it to you, but studies show that teenagers are becoming less physically fit with each new generation. We all know the reason: remote controls. Modern labor-saving devices are turning us all into vegetables. At the rate things are going, we'll look back 50 years from now and admire couch potatoes for being so energetic!

It used to be that if you wanted a ham sandwich, you had to go out and find a pig. If you wanted to talk to your best friend, you had to hike six miles to see him. If you needed a fresh shirt for the school dance, you had to go down to the river to launder one.

Nowadays, most of us no longer have to chop wood to stay warm. Or haul water to take a bath. Or milk a cow for a glass of milk. Most of our basic survival needs can be met with little or no exertion on our part. So unless you play sports or have a job requiring physical labor, you may not be getting enough exercise. And even if you are active, you may not be getting enough *aerobic* exercise—the kind that speeds up your heart rate.

* From a survey of 2,000 students ages 11–18.

Wise Highs

Adults recognize the value of exercise. This is why they get into their cars to drive six blocks to the health club to run in place for half an hour. Regular exercise:

- increases lung capacity
- lowers blood pressure
- builds endurance
- burns fat and calories
- strengthens the heart
- boosts blood flow to the brain
- raises endorphin production
- increases alpha waves in the brain
- reduces the risk of heart attack
- lowers cholesterol
- lessens feelings of anxiety, helplessness, and depression
- wears out sneakers fast

LET'S GET PHYSICAL

Tired? Tense? Angry? Anxious? Irritated? Upset? Depressed? Distracted? Conflicted? Confused? Frustrated? Fed up? Or just in a plain old ROTTEN MOOD? Time to get physical. Go for a walk or run. Swim. Shoot some hoops. Be active. Breathe deeply. Cool down. You'll be amazed by how much better you feel.

Studies show that people who exercise regularly live longer, stay healthier, sleep better, and have more rewarding sex lives.* (Oh, so *now* you're paying attention.) Since exercise boosts energy, builds muscles, and tones the body, people who exercise are more likely to feel good about themselves. Increased alpha wave and endorphin production help you feel calm and happy. Improved lung capacity and blood flow reduce stress and keep your mind focused and alert. And, if you take an exercise class, you can enjoy the social high that comes from perspiring, groaning, and kick-boxing with 50 other like-minded individuals.

Now that we all know the benefits of exercise, why don't more teens do it? "BECAUSE WE DON'T HAVE THE TIME!" When you look into teens' lives, you discover that they *do* have time to watch reruns of *The Simpsons,* stare at their bedroom ceiling for half an hour, play video games, surf the Internet, and ogle underwear catalogs.

The full benefits of exercise come from an aerobic workout. While sports can be a lot of fun, standing around in the outfield for two hours (when you're not sitting on the bench) doesn't do much for your cardiovascular endurance. You want to chose an activity that gives the old ticker a vigorous workout. How do you know if it's vigorous enough? By striving for your *target heart rate.* Here's how to determine what it is.

---

* Married couples who start exercising report having sex more often and enjoying it more.

Start by figuring out your *maximum heart rate.* This is the fastest your heart should ever go—kind of like the red line on a tachometer. (Even though you're able to rev up this high, you wouldn't want to do it for very long.) To find your maximum heart rate, subtract your age from 220. For example, if you're 16:

220
–16
―――
204 beats per minute would be your maximum heart rate

The target range for a good aerobic workout is 70–85 percent of your maximum heart rate. Multiply 204 by .70 to find the low end of the range, and by .85 to find the high end:

204 x .70 = 143 beats per minute (rounded up)
204 x .85 = 173 beats per minute (rounded down)

To maximize the value of an aerobic workout, your heart rate needs to stay within 143–173 beats per minute for 20–30 minutes. You can check your heart rate by taking your pulse. (You don't have to count heartbeats for a whole minute. Instead, count for 10 seconds and multiply your number by 6.) The best places to feel your pulse are your wrist or carotid artery (that's the spot on the side of the neck that people in movies always check to see if someone's dead). If you have no pulse, consult your doctor.

The hardest thing about an exercise program is sticking to it. Here are ten tips that will maximize your chances for success:

1. Do it with friends. Some highly disciplined teens prefer solitary exercise (they get into the meditative, loneliness-of-the-long-distance-runner pleasure of it), but most are more likely to stick with an exercise program if they do it with friends. Chip in and buy an exercise tape (e.g., *Tae-Bo, Buns of Steel, Abs of Asbestos, Jar Jar Binks' Home Workout*). Meet regularly after school and you'll have your own aerobics class.

2. Pick something you like. There are so many activities to choose from—running, swimming, power walking, cross-country skiing, aerobics classes, alligator wrestling. Pick one that you *enjoy.*

Sports, Exercise, and X-treme Highs

STEP RIGHT UP

While achieving optimal fitness takes effort, even a few minutes of exercise a day will improve your health. In one study, scientists asked a group of sedentary college-age women to climb six flights of stairs. They started with one ascent per day and gradually worked their way up to six. Seven weeks later, the women who climbed stairs were in much better shape than a comparison group of women who did nothing of the kind. The climbers had lower heart rates and improved cholesterol counts, and they used oxygen more efficiently. These types of changes can drastically lower your risk of a heart attack as an adult.

3. Don't let competition ruin the fun. Exercise should give you a *workout,* not get you all *worked up.* While a fast-paced game of squash or tennis can get your heart pumping, don't choose a competitive sport if you're the type who turns a friendly game into a death match.

4. Exercise at a set time each day, or at set times on specific days during the week. It's much easier to get with the program if you schedule it into your life. If you're constantly trying to squeeze exercise in, it's going to get squeezed *out.*

5. Start slowly. You don't have to go out and run ten miles tomorrow. Aim to exercise three times a week for 20–30 minutes. Shoot for the *lower* end of your target heart rate range and then slowly work up. If all you can manage at first is once a week, that's still better than nunce a week.

6. Warm up. Think of yourself as a car on a cold day. You want to idle a bit and get the oil, er, blood flowing before you hit the gas. Always do some warm-up stretches.*

7. Cool down. When you stop suddenly after strenuous exercise, your heart continues to beat rapidly while the amount of blood reaching it drops suddenly. This can cause faintness, dizziness, nausea, irregular heartbeats, or even (in the most extreme cases) a heart attack. Never go from 100 mph to zero in no seconds flat. Always keep walking and moving. Do some cooldown stretches.**

8. Think positively. Instead of telling yourself *I'm going to stop being a lazy, disgusting slug,* say *I'm going to start taking better care of my body.*

9. Monitor your progress. You may want to keep a record in your journal or daily planner. Write down whatever you do each day, whether it's a 10-minute walk or a 10-mile bike ride.

10. Make it a habit. Promise yourself that you'll stay with your exercise program for three weeks. According to experts, that's how long it takes to form a new habit. Three weeks may seem like a loooong time, especially if you've been inert for the past three years, but the sooner you get started, the faster you'll succeed.

So you can find the best fit for keeping fit, here's the scoop on six popular exercise regimes:

* See page 68.
** See page 69.

EXERCISE	PROS	CONS
CALISTHENICS: General fitness exercises such as jumping jacks, sit-ups, deep knee bends, toe touching, finger lifts (see page 72) ,etc. *Best if done 30–45 minutes a day*	• Can be done almost anywhere • No equipment required • Perfect for people who like to work out on their own • Good for flexibility, strength, and cardio-vascular endurance (if you include jump-ing rope or running) • May be combined with other activities such as weight lifting, jogging, etc.	• Hard to spell • Not as effective as weights for building strength • May remind you of sadistic gym teachers
WEIGHT MACHINES AND FREE WEIGHTS: Repetitive lifting, push-ing, pulling, and crunch-ing builds strength, flexibility, and muscles *30–60 minutes 3 times a week*	• Possible to exercise virtually every muscle group • Easy to chart progress as you see steady improvement in amount you can lift • Done indoors; weatherproof • Chummy, supportive ambience in most gyms • Good way to meet people as long as you avoid lines like "Love your pecs!" • Improves body tone and image • Great for computer wonks who like to program the machines	• Painful when dropped on your toes • Often covered with other people's slimy sweat • Expensive to buy • Requires access to a gym or health club ($$$$$) • No cardiovascular gain unless combined with treadmill or stair climbing machines • Tends to attract people in skimpy outfits who stare at themselves in the mirrors

Sports, Exercise, and X-treme Highs

"Training...tones the spirit just as exercise conditions the body."
ARNOLD SCHWARZENEGGER

65

Wise Highs

EXERCISE	PROS	CONS
YOGA: Ancient Indian system of postures and movements designed to create mental and physical balance and well-being *Thrice weekly sessions at least 30 minutes in length*	• Rhymes with toga • Encourages body awareness • Improves flexibility • Excellent for posture and proper breathing techniques • Great for people who don't like or aren't good at sports • Reduces stress • Ideal for people who can't engage in strenuous physical activity	• Little benefit for cardiovascular endurance • Minimal effect on muscle strength • Requires classes or books to learn techniques
MARTIAL ARTS: Various Eastern approaches to self-defense (e.g., karate, judo, T'ai Chi) that involve different holds, kicks, and punches *Classes usually meet 2–3 times a week for 1–2 hours*	• More effective than squat thrusts for dealing with bullies • Trains the mind as well as the body • Terrific for self-esteem • Improves flexibility, strength, and cardiovascular stamina	• Outfits that look like pajamas • Lessons required • Demands a long-term, multi-year commitment • Ignorant people will ask you to chop boards in half
AEROBIC DANCE: Set to music, a fast-paced workout that combines calisthenics, running in place, martial arts moves, dance steps, etc. *Class schedules vary, but 1 hour 2–3 times a week is typical*	• It's FUN! • Can be done in a group with friends • Good for people who think they're unathletic • Depending on the routine, can improve balance, posture, flexibility, strength, body tone, and cardiovascular endurance • Almost limitless combinations of steps and moves keep boredom at bay	• Requires classes or video player and TV if done at home • Not good for people with foot, knee, or back problems • Collisions with other exercisers if you're not careful • High-impact aerobics may cause or contribute to shin splints, twisted ankles, pain in the knees or back • Leotard fatigue

EXERCISE	PROS	CONS
CARDIOVASCULAR WORKOUT: Activities such as running, stair climbing, swimming, cycling, or cross-country skiing that, when sustained, elevate the heart rate *30 minutes (5-minute warm-up, 20 minutes of aerobic activity, 5-minute cooldown) 3 times a week or more*	• Best exercise of all for conditioning your heart and lungs • Major endorphin flow produces happy, peaceful feelings • Good for people who don't like competition or who enjoy exercising on their own • Major benefit in minimal time • Increases endurance and strength • Easy to monitor progress by recording times and distances	• Requires warm-up and cooldown exercises to avoid injury • May have to be curtailed if you have an injury or physical limitation • Can be unpleasant in certain meteorological conditions (i.e., jogging during a blizzard)

WARNING!!! Because we love you and don't want you to hurt yourself or drop dead, we would include these cautions even if our lawyers said we didn't have to.

Physical exertion, especially if you're new to it, strains your body, muscles, and heart. You may have heard the expression *No pain, no gain.* Well, in terms of exercise, think *Pain—refrain!* If you're experiencing pain, or your muscles get stiff and sore, you're probably exercising incorrectly, not warming up or cooling down properly, or you have a physical condition which needs checking.

If you experience any of the following warning signs, stop exercising! Tell your parents or coach immediately. See a doctor.

• shortness of breath
• irregular heartbeat
• headache or pain in teeth, jaw, or ears
• nausea
• vomiting
• dizziness, light-headedness, or fainting
• chest pain
• elevated heart rate long after stopping exercise
• prolonged, excessive fatigue
• pain, stiffness, or "weird" sensations in joints, muscles, and ligaments

> "I don't think being an athlete is unfeminine. I think of it as a kind of grace."
> JACKIE JOYNER-KERSEE

Wise Highs

It's very important to do warm-up stretches before (and cooldown stretches after) vigorous exercise. Here are some suggestions for turning yourself into taffy. Ask your gym teacher, coach, or personal trainer-to-the-stars to teach you more.

Calf Stretch

1. Place your right foot directly behind your left foot, as if you were walking a tightrope.

2. Bend your left leg forward at the knee until you can no longer see your toes. Hold for a count of 2. (Hey, no lifting your right leg! Keep it straight. Imagine that your heels are glued to the ground. And, since you're not a basketball, do *not* bounce while holding the stretch.)

3. Switch legs and repeat.

Do this sequence 3 times.

Hamstring Stretch

1. Place your right foot straight out on something that's below the height of your hips. (No, not your younger brother.)

2. Lean your chest forward a bit. Keep your chin up. Hold for a count of 2. (It's *supposed* to feel that way. Why do you think they call it *stretching?!?*)

3. Switch legs and repeat.

Do this sequence 3 times.

STRETCH THOSE PROTEINS!

Your muscles are made up of microscopic fibers, which are themselves made up of proteins. When you stretch a muscle, these fibers lengthen one by one, though not all the fibers are affected; some stretch and some are just along for the ride. Through regular, progressive stretching, more fibers are recruited in the stretch and fewer tag along, resulting in a much more flexible muscle overall. Stretching also helps realign muscle fibers that are out of whack due to injury.

Here are some stretches for ending your workout. Ease into each stretch until you feel a light tension. Don't forget to breathe. Once the tension subsides, reintroduce it by further bending/leaning/ stretching/pulling. Breathe deeply and relax. Maintain each stretch for 10–20 seconds. Do *not* bounce.

Knee Hug

A great way to show your knees how much you love them.

1. Lie on your back with your knees slightly bent. Keep your heels touching the floor.

2. Reach under your upper right leg and place both hands behind your thigh. Gently hug your knee to your chest.

3. Pull your leg closer to your chest to "tighten" the stretch. Hold for 10–20 seconds.

4. Switch legs and repeat.

Do this sequence 4 times.

Quad Stretch

1. Stand on your left leg. (That alone is quite an accomplishment for some people!) Oh, okay, you can steady yourself by holding onto a chair back or railing.

2. Bend your right leg at the knee and reach behind your back with your *left* hand. Grab your right foot by the shin or instep.

3. Standing up straight, press your foot against your buttocks until you feel tension in your thigh.

4. Say buttocks 10 times without laughing.

5. Hold the stretch for 10–20 seconds.

6. Switch legs and repeat.

Do this sequence 4 times.

Calf Stretch

This warm-up stretch also makes a good cooldown stretch. Follow the instructions on page 68, only hold for a count of 20.

Sports, Exercise,
and X-treme Highs

"Those who think they have not time for bodily exercise will sooner or later have to find time for illness."
EDWARD STANLEY

Wise Highs

STEALTH EXERCISES

Sneak these into your daily routine and you'll feel more up and less down. No sweat!

- Instead of taking the bus or car pool, walk to school twice a week.
- When coming out of the subway, use the stairs instead of the escalator.
- Why mope when you can dance? Turn boring chores into swing routines. Gather your friends. Crank up the music. Hoof your way to a clean room or freshly vacuumed carpet.
- When you cut the grass, don't sit down on the job. Shun the garden tractor and use a push mower instead. For extra credit, use one *without* an engine.
- Turn tedious tasks into calisthenic drills. Rake some leaves…and do 20 jumping jacks. Rake some more leaves…20 squat thrusts. Keep raking…20 push-ups. (Your parents may think you've lost your mind, but that's just an added benefit.)
- Next time you take out the trash, turn it into a 100-yard dash.
- Run, don't walk. (Unless you're on a slippery pool deck.)
- Eschew (gesundheit!) elevators. Use the stairs instead.
- Take the long way 'round from one class to the next.
- Ride an exercise bike while watching TV.
- Take Fido for a *run* instead of a walk.
- Anytime you ride a bus, subway, trolley, taxi, rickshaw, gondola, buggy, or surrey with a fringe on top, get off a few blocks from your destination. Walk the rest of the way.

Relaxation Exercises

If you spend long hours sitting in class or working at a desk or computer, your neck, shoulders, and head may get tense and tired. This can lead to headaches, cricks, and fuzzy thinking. Following are a few simple stretches you can do anytime, anywhere to relieve tight muscles and restore mental alertness.*

---

* See Chapter 3: Meditation Highs for more relaxation exercises.

HEAD AND SHOULDERS

TRY THIS!

Sports, Exercise, and X-treme Highs

Heads Will Roll

1. Without removing your head from your neck, roll it clockwise in as wide and slow a rotation as you can.

2. Drop your chin as far as it will go at the bottom of the circle, and lift it as high as possible at the top.

3. After 3 complete circles, reverse direction and roll your head 3 times counterclockwise.

Heads Will Turn

1. *Slowly* turn your head from one side to the other 10 times.

2. Now that your neck is loosened up, *quickly* turn your head side to side 10 more times.

Shoulder Shrugs

1. Lift your shoulders as high as you can and then let them drop like a sack of potatoes. Your hands and arms should dangle by your sides.

2. Repeat 10 times.

3. Now lift and drop your shoulders alternately. Repeat 10 times.

"The time to relax is when you don't have time for it."
SIDNEY J. HARRIS

SAVE FACE

TRY THIS!

Most people don't usually think of their face and jaw when it comes to exercise. But let's face it, there are all sorts of pint-size muscles around your mouth, lips, eyes, and forehead that can become strained and cause headaches, stiffness of the neck, and eye fatigue. For the ultimate "facial," practice these exercises whenever you have a few free minutes. Do them by yourself in front of a mirror. Or face-to-face with your best friend!

Open Wide

1. Relax your face.

2. Open your mouth as wide as it will go.

3. Stick out your tongue.

4. Open your eyes as wide as you can and try to focus on the tip of your tongue.

71

Wise Highs

Eyes Wide Shut

1. Relax your face and close your eyes.

2. Scrunch up the muscles around your eyes. Hold for 10 seconds.

3. Relax the muscles and open your eyes wide. Hold for a count of 10.

Jaws

1. Close your mouth.

2. Gently move your jaw left to right 10 times.

Jaws II

1. Drop your jaw.

2. Open your mouth as wide as possible. Now close it.

3. Repeat 10 times.

ALEX'S FABULOUS FINGER LIFTS

The index finger is one of your most handy and expressive digits. It is indispensable when it comes to nose-picking and doorbell-pushing. It's the appendage of choice for scratching a mosquito bite and cleaning out your belly button. As a communication device, it's the preferred extremity for pointing, beckoning, and admonishing. When licked and held upright, it will identify the direction of the wind. Because of its importance, the index finger must be kept in tiptop shape.

1. Make two fists and extend both index fingers.

2. Hold your fists out in front of you approximately 12" apart and 12" from your face so the index fingers point up.

3. On the count of 1, bend both fingers at the second knuckle to make a right angle.

4. On the count of 2, bend both fingers all the way down so the pad of each fingertip touches the base.

5. On the count of 3, return both fingers to the halfway position.

6. On the count of 4, extend both fingers back to their original upright position.

7. Repeat this exercise 10 times or until you feel too silly to continue.

Thrill-Seeking and X-treme Sports

Sports, Exercise, and X-treme Highs

Ever since Galileo jumped off the Leaning Tower of Pizza with an apple and landed on Isaac Newton, human beings have been thrill-seekers. I mean, why do you think the monument to our greatest presidents is called Mount *Rushmore?*

The building block of all thrills is the *rush.* A rush slams you into the adrenaline red zone. It's a high–KICK; a surge of terror, joy, exhilaration, and freedom; a life-spike so intense you can only grab hold for a few seconds max.

There are falling rushes, flying rushes, whirling spinning looping rushes. Gliding rushes, diving rushes, swinging slamming sliding rushes. Some rushes require nothing more than an admission ticket (roller coasters); others a leap of faith (bungee jumping). Some require extensive training and practice (sky surfing); others none at all (watersliding). Some require a moment of courage (skydiving); others sustained strength and skill (whitewater kayaking).

Rushes get your heart pounding and your adrenaline pumping. This is the physical part of the rush—the *feeling* of flying or floating, of momentary "weightlessness" or the force of high G's. But every rush works on your head, too, as this daring teenager discovered:

THE KING OF RUSH

Anyone who remembers the 1970s (e.g., your parents) will always remember daredevil Evel Knievel. His spectacular motorcycle jumps (and even more spectacular crashes) were national media events. In his long, painful career, Knievel jumped over—or *almost* over—a tank of sharks, the fountains at Caesar's Palace in Las Vegas, the Snake River Canyon in Idaho, 13 Mack trucks, and cages containing rattlesnakes and mountain lions (he crashed into the rattlesnake cage once, and the snakes escaped into the crowd). In the process, he broke 35 different bones in his body.

"I have been cliff diving. It took me so much courage to actually walk off the platform. And when I finally surfaced, my confidence level went WAY up and I felt on top of the world. THAT is a rush."

When you push beyond your limits and conquer fear, your self-esteem soars and you ride courage's high. Confronting the possibility of death in a safe, risk-controlled way makes you realize how much there is to cherish in life.

Several sports and physical activities have a high thrill factor. Many also have a high bill (as in dollar) factor. Special equipment and training cost money, and often these sports/activities aren't things you can do just anywhere; if surfing is your thing, you have to go where the waves are. Starting on page 77, you'll find descriptions of resources specific to sports you may want to learn more about or try. For now, let's explore some no-cost and low-cost alternatives.

Cheap Thrills

Remember when you were a little kid and almost everything you did was thrilling? Like sliding down a banister or climbing the monkey bars or rolling down a grassy hill or skidding across a freshly-waxed floor in your stocking feet? Guess what: You're not too old to have fun for free. Here's how.

 UPSIDE-DOWN UPPERS

For a quick and easy high, stand on your head for 5 minutes. If you can do it "free-standing," great. If you need to rest your legs against a wall, equally great. The blood rushing to your head won't care.

TRY THIS! SEESAWS AND SWINGS

Just because you're a teenager doesn't mean you can't enjoy the pleasures of seesaws and playground swings. Of course we don't want you tossing six-year-olds onto the ground so you and your friends can have the swings, but perhaps we can *share*. So get on a swing, close your eyes, and go higher and higher and higher and higher.....

TRY THIS! JUMP FOR JOY

Along with its cousins skipping, hopping, leapfrogging, cartwheeling, and somersaulting, jumping is way too much fun to be abandoned as a childish pleasure. Claim your right to jump into adolescence and adulthood.

To perform a proper jump, put on your springiest sneakers. Crouch down. Bend at the knees and elbows. When you are suitably hunkered down, commence countdown: *10...9...8...7...6...5...4...3...2...1....Lift-off!* Use your legs to propel you into the air. Jolly jumpers choose this moment to extend their arms skyward and let out a shriek of delight. Continue to crouch and spring, crouch and spring, higher and higher. Jumping can be done as an individual pursuit, or as a group activity with like-minded jumping beans. You'll have a blast.

Once you have mastered basic jumping, you may wish to move on to trampolines.

SPIN CYCLE

TRY THIS!

Spinning is another delight too good to be reserved for the exclusive use of children. It's best done on a soft surface such as a beach, tumbling mat, or lush lawn.

Every proper spin begins with a moment of stillness. When you feel balanced, slowly commence spinning in a counterclockwise direction. Keep your feet in a small circle as you build up speed. Once you feel comfortably twirly, push off slightly so you leap into the air while you spin. Your feet will spread farther apart. Your arms will rise spontaneously like wings. Spin and spin until you can spin no more. Fall to the ground. The world will continue to spin. Guaranteed to give you a high!

ROLLER COASTERS

TRY THIS!

Mind Eraser, Cyclone, Hellevator, Serial Thriller, the Nightmare.... No, these aren't recent horror flicks. They're roller coasters.* In the race for customers and ticket sales, every amusement park wants to make its coaster faster, higher, longer, steeper, twistier, and more terrifying than the competition's. If you like to feel your teeth clatter, your heart drop to your stomach, and your eyeballs pop out the back of your skull; if you like being strapped, chained, buckled, and yoked into a harness while visions of death fly through your mind; if your idea of fun is an afternoon of inversions, loops, cobra rolls, and double hartline flips—then roller coasters are the high for you.

One of the best state-of-the-art rides is at Six Flags Magic Mountain in Valencia, California. This coaster hurls riders at speeds of 100 miles per hour, has a vertical drop of 415 feet, and generates a G-force of 4.5—greater than a space shuttle lift-off!

Tip: Go easy on the tacos, sodas, fries, pizza, and ice cream before you ride. You wouldn't want the people down below to get a lunch-chunk shower while waiting in line.

---

* Unlike the other activities in this section, roller coasters aren't free. But riding them is a lot cheaper than, say, skiing in the Alps.

Wise Highs

FIND OUT MORE

American Coaster Enthusiasts
3650 Annapolis Lane, Suite 107 • Minneapolis, MN 55447
www.ACEonline.org
The world's largest club of amusement ride enthusiasts. You'll find anything and everything having to do with coasters on their Web site. Check out the links, which will take you to lists, locations, and descriptions of hundreds of coasters; manufacturers; and coaster enthusiast organizations and publications.

Going to X-tremes

Bungee jumping. Paragliding. Bobsledding. Whitewater rafting. These are the sports that will thrill you to your soul and turn your parents' hair prematurely gray. Scan the next several pages, pick the sport(s) that interest you, then check out the resources listed. You can find out more about any of these activities by visiting your public library, surfing the Internet, consulting the Yellow Pages, watching television specials, talking to people who've been there/done that, or showing up at places that offer training or hold events.

What happens if, for example, you fall in love with hot-air ballooning but can't afford to indulge your passion? Try volunteering with a local club or group. Make yourself useful, ask intelligent questions, and prove that you're energetic and eager to learn. Maybe someday you'll be invited up, up and away. And even if you aren't, you'll know more about ballooning than you did before you volunteered.

BE CREATIVE

If traditional sports don't appeal to you and X-treme sports don't get you excited, why not make up your own sport? You can combine the high of physical activity with the high you get from creating something totally new. If you're looking for inspiration, try combining elements from different sports: maybe baseball and swimming, soccer and bowling, or cycling and archery (okay, maybe that last suggestion isn't such a good idea).

RING AROUND THE WEB

WebRing (www.webring.com) is a free Internet service that offers easy access to hundreds of thousands of member sites. The sites are organized by related interests into easy-to-travel Rings. Explore Rings that interest you by clicking on category links or searching within categories. I found dozens of sites for many of the sports listed here. To get started, click on "Recreation and Sports" in the main directory.

Air Highs

AEROBATIC FLYING

First Flight
www.firstflight.com
This virtual flight school provides online flying lessons and information about private pilot training.

BALLOONING

Balloon Federation of America
PO Box 400 • Indianola, IA 50125
(515) 961-8809 • www.bfa.net
All that's hot in hot air ballooning.

Balloon Life
9 Madeline Avenue • Westport, CT 06880
(203) 629-1241 • www.balloonlife.com
THE magazine for hot air balloonists and wannabes.

BUNGEE JUMPING

Bungee Jumping (Extreme Sports) by Jason Glaser (Mankato, MN: Capstone Press, 1999). The perfect book for people who like to jump off of high places with a giant rubber band tied to their ankles.

Bungee.com
www.bungee.com
The history of bungee jumping, hot jump sites, bungee masters, equipment, safety guidelines, and more.

GETTING SHOT OUT OF A CANNON

Would somebody *please* try this and let me know how it feels?

HANG GLIDING, PARAGLIDING

Hang Gliding Training Manual: Learning Hang Gliding Skills for Beginner to Intermediate Pilots by Dennis Pagen (Spring Mills, PA: Sport Aviation Publications, 1995). Pagen is "the Man" when it comes to books on air sports. In addition to hang gliding, he has written about ultralight flying, paragliding, and sailplanes.

A–Z of Paragliding
www.paragliding.net
International information on paragliding, competitions, festivals, lessons and events.

U.S. Hang Gliding and Paragliding Association
PO Box 1330 • Colorado Springs, CO 80901
(719) 632-8300 • www.ushpa.aero
Information on instructors, merchandise, and current news.

Wise Highs

SKYDIVING, SKY SURFING

Parachuting: The Skydiver's Handbook by Dan Poynter and Mike Turoff (Santa Barbara, CA: Para Publishing, 2003). This informative reference guide covers basic to advanced and emergency techniques and includes a list of skydiving centers.

Cloud Dancer
www.koyn.com/clouddancer
Koyn is a pioneer in freestyle skydiving. She was the 1992 World Champion and has published numerous videos and books on skydiving. Her site contains tons of useful articles and information on skydiving and sky surfing.

World Free Fall Convention
1659 Highway 104 • Quincy, IL 62305
(217) AAA-JUMP (217-222-5867) • www.freefall.com
Information on skydivers, skydiving events, competitions, training sites, and much more. Terrific links to other skydiving-related sites. Incredible photos.

SOARING

Soaring Society of America
PO Box 2100 • Hobbs, NM 88241-2100
(505) 392-1177 • www.ssa.org
Youth program listings, convention information, a news archive, first-person stories, links to great soaring sites, and more.

TRAPEZE

Learning to Fly: Trapeze: Reflections on Fear, Trust and the Joy of Letting Go by Sam Keen (New York: Broadway Books, 1999). A graduate of Harvard Divinity School, Keen always wanted to fly. At age 62, he enrolled in a trapeze class at the San Francisco School of Circus Arts! This inspiring book is about much more than swinging from a trapeze; it's about risk-taking, trust, strength, falling, and letting go. A metaphor for overcoming boundaries of the self and soaring through life.

Flying Trapeze Resource Page
www.damnhot.com/trapeze
Lists trapeze clubs, schools, resorts, and books. Includes articles and a great reference section and videoclips.

ULTRALIGHT FLYING

Ultralight Flying! Magazine
PO Box 6009, Dept. N • Chattanooga, TN 37401
(423) 629-5375 • www.ultralightflying.com
This monthly magazine is the oldest and largest publication dedicated solely to the sport of ultralight and microlight flying.

FALLING UP

When Didier (pronounced *dee-dee-yay*) Dahran jumped out of a plane in May 1993 over Boulac, France, he set a world record for surviving the longest fall...upward. Instead of plunging towards the earth, poor Didier was sucked into a freak cyclone current that propelled him in the opposite direction. He shot from an altitude of 1,000 feet to over 25,000 feet (just how much over we'll never know, since his altimeter jammed at its maximum reading). Two hours later, he was still in the jet stream. Finally his parachute collapsed and he began the long fall towards the ground; fortunately he was able to pull the cord for his emergency parachute before passing out. Didier ended up 30 miles from where he had started, but did not receive any frequent flyer miles.

United States Ultralight Association (USUA)
104 Carlisle Street • Gettysburg, PA 17325
(717) 339-0200 • www.usua.org
The USUA is the world's largest association dedicated to promoting, protecting, and representing ultralight and microlight aviation in the United States.

TRUE HIGHS
Ultra-Flights

Ultralights are those tiny airplanes you may have seen buzzing around like bees on steroids. They are made of lightweight tubular metal, thin steel cables, fabric, chewing gum, and a lawnmower engine.

Because ultralights are so...ultra-light, even a tiny engine allows you to take off in about 60 feet and climb practically straight up. With an ultralight, you can land in *no* feet. That would be considered a crash landing, so it's better to use up more runway. Speaking of runways, you don't need one with an ultralight. A farmer's field will do quite nicely, provided it's not planted with corn or cows.

Ultralights come in two versions: scary and *real* scary. If you've never seen an ultralight, it's like a go-kart with wings. There's no cockpit or cabin to protect you from crazed geese. When you're flying an ultralight, it's just you and all that space between you and the ground.

Ultralights are not to be confused with hang gliders, which are wings people strap on when they want to look like stealth bombers and run off cliffs. Ultralights are also not to be confused with gliders, which are humongous balsa wood model airplanes, except without the rubber bands. That's why gliders, in order to glide, have to be towed into the sky by planes with motors. Once they reach sufficient altitude, the gliders are released, at which point they fall like rocks. No, actually, this is where wings (the part of an airplane that helps you forget you have no business being up in the sky) come in handy.

You can probably tell from my technical expertise that I myself have flown ultralights. The great thing about ultralights is you don't need a pilot's license to fly them. All you need is a dearth of common sense. Some people buy an ultralight kit, put it together over a few beers, and take off. These people are known as *statistics*. It's much better to take lessons.

I took mine from a genuine American Airlines pilot. We met at an airport (a.k.a. a rutty grass strip next to some guy's house) in Culpeper, Virginia, a nice rural town in the foothills of the Blue Ridge Mountains. I took one look at the "airport" and said "Excuse me, what are those wires doing going across the runway?"

"Don't worry about them," the intrepid pilot said. "Just be sure you take off *before* them or *after* them." This, of course, is why he was

Wise Highs

the instructor and I was the student. Now that I knew not to fly *through* the wires, it was time for the pre-flight inspection. This is when you check to make sure that you have enough gas, the propeller is attached, and no chewing gum has come loose.

The training craft was a sleek two-seater that looked like Leonardo da Vinci's drawing of a flying machine. We put on our helmets, yelled "FORE!" and started the engine. I taxied to the end of the runway, choosing the longer but more scenic route by zigzagging from one side of the field to the other. Because your butt is about three inches off the ground, you keep a very sharp lookout for rocks and dozing porcupines.

I spent several exhilarating weeks learning to take off and land without running into power lines. Finally the day came when it was time to solo. As in flying alone. By yourself. Without an instructor to whom you can say "Your turn."

Now, let me tell you something about aerodynamics. If you've been flying a two-seater ultralight that weighs about three ounces, and there's been a 200-pound teacher by your side, and then that teacher turns into an empty seat, well, you're going to notice something like that. I think the wings did, too, which is why they were at a 45-degree angle to the ground for most of my first fright, er, flight.

After several successful (i.e., I didn't kill myself) "touch and go" landings in the training plane, it was time to take the one-seat aerobatic ultralight for a spin. Now *this* was one zippy little buzzer, the Ferrari Testarossa of ultralights. Before letting me take 'er up, though, my instructor said he needed to show me how to work the parachute.

"PARACHUTE?????!!!!!"

Yes, boys and girls, a parachute attaches to your seat. Well, not *your* seat. The seat you *put* your seat in. The rationale for this is as follows: Let's say some chewing gum comes loose and your plane breaks apart in flight, or a surface-to-air missile mistakes you for a B-2, or a flock of birds takes a shortcut through your wings. If you're wearing the parachute, how exactly do you jump free of the plane? I'll tell you. You don't.

If, however, the parachute is attached to the seat frame to which you're strapped, *and* if that parachute has an explosive charge to propel the canopy as it opens away from those parts of the plane that are either a) no longer there, b) breaking up in flight, or c) stuck on the beak of a bird, then you will fall gently to earth, safely strapped to your seat—or so the theory goes. I was not planning to put it to the test.

I mastered the concept of the parachute ("Push the red button") and taxied out for my first solo flight in this hot little baby with the wings on top. I pushed the throttle in, held the stick steady, and before I could say "Cremation, please" I was racing down the runway. I pulled back on the stick, the plane leaped into the sky, and the ground fell away. I leveled off at 3,000 feet, cruising at 80 mph.

I soon put the little spitfire through her paces. Time stood still as I looped and banked and dove and climbed. It was intoxicating (healthfully so, mind you!). I spied a herd of deer in a forest clearing. A gaggle of children ran after me, waving excitingly. The setting sun turned rivers and ponds into shimmering golden mirrors. As long shadows crept across the land and a soft, misty halo hovered over the blue mountain crests, I thought to myself "GET ME DOWN FROM HERE!!!!!"

It was soon time to head back to the airport. Now where *was* that airport? As I circled the field to make sure the wires hadn't moved, I saw my instructor polishing his other plane and looking very nonchalant, as if it hadn't occurred to him that I might land on his head. I entered the pattern, turned into final approach, reduced the throttle, pushed the stick forward, and mumbled *Please, God, if you get me through this in one piece I promise I'll floss every night.*

The ultralight descended straight and true, as if it were following a laser beam to the ground. We won't talk about that nasty gust of wind at the last moment that almost *did* make me land on my instructor's head. Suffice it to say that *any* landing from which you and your airplane walk away none the worse for wear is a good landing. So I lived to see another day. Although I still sometimes forget to floss.

I recommend ultralight flying to anyone seeking an adrenaline high. Be aware, though, that for several hours after flying, you're likely to burst out in spontaneous whoops of joy.

Land Highs

AUTO RACING

Auto Racing Daily
www.autoracingdaily.com
The latest auto racing news and blogs galore. It's all covered—from big-time races to local motorsports. Click on "start the newsfeed wizard" for up-to-the-minute racing stats and info.

Racingschools.com
www.racingschools.com
This is where you go to find a racing school near you.

> "I love to go driving with my dad at the track and feel like I am about to die. Going 120–130 (or however fast he goes)—it's insane. It's a rush to say the least."*
>
> ZIPPY STUDENT

---

* Please note that this high takes place at a *racetrack*. You can be sure that the father has taken driving lessons, the car has been carefully checked and equipped, and the driver and passenger wear shoulder harnesses and helmets. Driving this fast on a track is called a *rush*. Driving this fast on a highway is called a *fatality*.

Wise Highs

BMX AND MOUNTAIN BIKE RACING

BMX and mountain bike racing are great sports for people who like to pedal furiously around a hilly dirt track, perform amazing jumps and tricks, cut other riders off, crash, and see who gets to the finish line first. And for those who can do without the mud and dust, there are other cycling events that stick to the roads.

American Bicycle Association (ABA)
PO Box 718 • Chandler, AZ 85244
(480) 961-1903 • www.ababmx.com
The national sanctioning body for BMX racing, ABA establishes the rules of racing and organizes qualifying events for riders to advance to the next competitive level. The association also hosts championship competitions for amateurs and professional racers.

National Bicycle League
3958 Brown Park Drive, Suite D • Hilliard, OH 43026
1-800-886-BMX1 (2691) • www.nbl.org
NBL brings together local and state BMX associations, sanctioning over 3000 races per year. The league is dedicated to promoting a fun and healthy racing environment for riders.

USA Cycling, Inc.
One Olympic Plaza • Colorado Springs, CO 80909
(719) 866-4581 • www.usacycling.org
The national governing body for competitive cycling events sanctions cycling clubs, teams, and events across the country. From this site, you can access information about BMX, cyclo-cross, mountain biking, road racing, and track cycling.

BOBSLEDDING

International Bobsleigh Federation
www.fibt.com
The official site of the Fédération Internationale de Bobsleigh et de Tobogganing (FIBT), headquartered in Milan, Italy, covers everything you'd want to know about the sport, from the history of bobsledding to current news.

CIRCUS

Circus Center San Francisco
755 Frederick Street • San Francisco, CA 94117
(415) 759-8123 • www.circuscenter.org
Acrobatics, flying trapeze, juggling, contortion, teeterboarding, and more—learn it all at this respected school for aspiring circus performers. The Web site features lots of links to other circus and circus-related sites.

Clowns of America International Home Page
www.coai.org
Dedicated to the art of clowning. The COAI Web site is a gathering place for amateur and professional clowns.

GYMNASTICS

There aren't many sports that involve rings, vaults, bars, and horses. Or that require you to be part acrobat, daredevil, artist, and dancer. But gymnastics does. It's a great sport because it works every muscle in your body. You develop terrific timing and concentration and improve your flexibility, strength, and power. Plus you can whirl round and round in the air and do a flying dismount onto the lap of a spectator in the stands. Because gymnastics is a high-risk sport, it's essential that you learn from a coach or trainer and have a spotter.

The Gymnastics Almanac by Luan Peszek and James Holmes (Los Angeles: Lowell House, 1998). A great resource for gymnasts and gymnastics fans.

International Gymnast Online
www.intlgymnast.com
A Webzine dedicated to gymnastics.

USA Gymnastics
Pan Am Plaza • 201 South Capitol Avenue, Suite 300
Indianapolis, IN 46225
(317) 237-5050 • www.usa-gymnastics.org
As the national governing body for the sport, USA Gymnastics selects and trains athletes for the Olympics and World Championships. The official Web site features information on athletes, coaches, events, gymnastics history, team rosters, safety, men's and women's programs, and junior Olympic programs, plus links and more.

HORSEBACK RIDING

United States Equestrian Federation
4047 Iron Works Parkway • Lexington, KY 40511
(859) 258-2472 • www.usef.org
USEF is the national governing body for equestrian sports. Their mission is to inspire interest in equestrian competition and ensure the safety and kind treatment of horses.

United States Equestrian Team Foundation
1040 Pottersville Road • Gladstone, NJ 07934
(908) 234-1251 • www.uset.com
USET represents the U.S. in international competitions, including the Olympics. Programs are also offered for young riders to help improve their equitation skills.

ICE-SKATING

Figure Skating for Dummies by Kristi Yamaguchi *et al.* (Foster City, CA: IDG Books Worldwide, 1998). A primer for spectators and aspiring skaters, written by the 1992 Olympic gold medalist. Covers skating lingo, judging, equipment, competition, and how to skate. Of course, you'll probably need to hit the rink, too.

Speed on Skates by Barry Publow (Champaign, IL: Human Kinetics 1999). If, instead of spinning around in circles, you want to skate as fast as you can, this is the book for you. You'll learn basic techniques for both ice and in-line speed skating, as well as how to improve your performance, speed, flexibility, and stamina.

Ice Skating Institute of America
6000 Custer Road, Building 9 • Plano, TX 75023
(972) 735-8800 • www.skateisi.com
The ISIA oversees programs for hockey, freestyle, and figure skating for the beginner through advanced ice-skater. It also sponsors competitions, events, and exhibitions and provides scholarship assistance.

Sports, Exercise, and X-treme Highs

"It's a feeling of ice miles running under your blades, the wind splitting open to let you through, the earth whirling around you at the touch of your toe, and speed lifting you off the ice far from all things that can hold you down."
SONJA HENIE

United States Figure Skating Association
20 First Street • Colorado Springs, CO 80906
(719) 635-5200 • www.usfsa.org
The governing body for amateur figure skating in the United States, the USFSA is dedicated to advancing competitive figure skating by providing financial assistance, skating camps, and scientific research to skaters.

INLINE SKATING

Aggressive Skaters Association
5855 Green Valley Circle, Suite 308 • Culver City, CA 90230
(310) 410-3020 • www.asaskate.com
Fosters the growth of amateur and professional aggressive in-line skating by taking an active role in competitions, skate parks, events, and the newest gear.

Inline Skating Resource Center
www.iisa.org
Search for an instructor or places to skate, keep up with events and skating clubs, read guides to gear, and find links to other inline skating sites.

MARTIAL ARTS

If you search the Internet for "martial arts," you'll come up with thousands of sites. My AOL search engine groups them by categories—Aikido, Chung Moo Doe, Hwa Rang Do, Jeet Kune Do, Tae Kwon Do, Judo, Karate, Kickboxing, and more. The best thing is to dive right in and learn a bit about the different approaches, then choose the one(s) that sound most appealing and look into them in greater depth.

The following organizations and governing bodies promote their respective arts and sports and provide information on instruction, competitions, events, clinics, and educational programs.

Aikido Association of America
1016 West Belmont Avenue • Chicago, IL 60657
(773) 525-3141 • www.aaa-aikido.com

USA Karate Federation, Inc.
1300 Kenmore Boulevard • Akron, OH 44314
(330) 753-3114 • www.usakarate.org

U.S. Judo Association
21 North Union Boulevard • Colorado Springs, CO 80909
1-877-411-3409 • www.usja-judo.org

U.S. Tae Kwan Do Union
One Olympic Plaza, Suite 104C • Colorado Springs, CO 80909
(719) 866-4632 • www.usa-taekwondo.us

ROCK CLIMBING AND MOUNTAINEERING

Within Reach: My Everest Story by Mark Pfetzer and Jack Galvin (New York: E.P. Dutton, 2000). The youngest climber ever to attempt to ascend Mt. Everest, Pfetzer recounts his experience on the mountain at age 18.

American Alpine Club
710 10th Street, Suite 100 • Golden, CO 80401
(303) 384-0110 • www.americanalpineclub.org
Information and resources for rock climbing and mountaineering athletes.

Climbing Magazine
1260 Yellow Pine Avenue • Boulder, CO 80304
(303) 225-4628 • www.climbing.com
Amazing climbing experiences, photos, technical tips, interviews, news, and information about upcoming events.

The Mountain Zone
www.mountainzone.com
This site, affiliated with ESPN, features all sorts of information about mountain climbing, hiking, skiing, snowboarding, and other outdoor sports. You can find out about gear, safety, and upcoming events, or check out stories about daring climbs and expeditions.

SKATEBOARDING

Transworld Skateboarding Magazine
353 Airport Road • Oceanside, CA 92054
(760) 722-7777
www.skateboarding.com
News, photos, a buyer's guide, and trick tips.
See if your public library subscribes.

Tum Yeto
www.tumyeto.com
A kewl site with skate parks, news, events, photos, tips, ramp plans, classifieds, zines, chat rooms, and "Cool, Dumb Stuff."

SKIING, EXTREME SKIING, SNOWBOARDING

Search the Internet for "skiing" and see what happens. Without even trying, I came up with over 1,000 different sites. Plus you can find lots of books and magazines at your local public library, since skiing is one of the world's most popular sports.

The Good Skiing and Snowboarding Guide edited by Peter Hardy (New York: Overlook Press, updated often). "The essential guide to what's what and where's where" at ski resorts around the world. Any reference guide that tells you the price of hot chocolate in the lodge is bound to be good. Includes full-color maps, trail suggestions for various skill levels, accommodations, ski school info, and descriptions that give you a good sense of the "vibes" of the resort.

Skiing for Dummies by Allen St. John (Foster City, CA: IDG Books Worldwide, 1999). It can't beat dressing up in your long johns and hitting the slopes, but it makes for good reading by the fire.

Sports, Exercise, and X-treme Highs

"I love the sensation of being high up and away from all of life's complications."
BETH RODDEN, 19, ROCK CLIMBER

"You never conquer a mountain. You stand on the summit a few moments. Then the wind blows your footprints away."
ARLENE BLUM

Wise Highs

Extreme Team Advanced Ski Clinics
www.skiclinics.com
Information on ski clinics nationwide. AtPlay is the home of the X-Team (Extreme Team), which is in a lot of great ski films. You can also get a list of "heliskiing" resorts where the only way in (or out) is by helicopter.

First Tracks Online Ski Magazine
www.firsttracksonline.com
An online magazine with lots of competition reports and photos. Includes features on ski gear, resorts, weather, and techniques.`

Ski Central
www.skicentral.com
"The #1 search & index site for skiers & snowboarders" is a gateway to an ever-growing number of sites—news, articles, resort guides, ski reports, and snow cams; information on equipment, races, events, products, organizations, instruction, and trip planning; extreme skiing (with photos, resources, schools, and camps); and *much* more.

TRIATHLON

Triathloning for Ordinary Mortals by Steven Jonas (New York: W.W. Norton and Co., 1999). If you want the challenge of a swim-bike-run marathon, this book (written by a doctor who's a preventive medicine specialist and triathlete) will fill you in on the best ways to get started, train, increase endurance, and compete.

Ironman.com
www.ironmanlive.com
The official home of the Ironman competition.

Triathlete Magazine
328 Encinitas Boulevard, Suite 100 • Encinitas, CA 92024
(760) 634-4100 • www.triathletemag.com
A must-read for triathletes.

USA Triathlon
1365 Garden of the Gods Road, Suite 250 • Colorado Springs, CO 80907-3425
(719) 597-9090 • www.usatriathlon.org
The official governing body for the sport. Their site includes U.S. rankings, schedules, merchandise, travel information, membership information, and more.

WILDERNESS ADVENTURE AND SURVIVAL

On some days, going to school may feel like a survival exercise. But the ones we're talking about here are wilderness adventure programs. You know, the kind where you're given a match and two breadsticks and dropped in the middle of nowhere for three weeks. Actually, these programs are very safe and carefully planned. The instructors are well-trained, the gear and supplies are top-notch, and the planning is meticulous. Every year, thousands of teenagers develop a new respect for themselves and the environment by participating in these programs.

Geosmith
www.geosmith.com/wilderness
Links to wilderness survival schools and periodicals categorized by state.

Outward Bound
National Office, 100 Mystery Point Road • Garrison, NY 10524
1-866-467-7651 • www.outwardbound.org
Outward Bound is dedicated to conducting safe, adventure-based programs while instilling a sense of appreciation for the environment and respect for oneself.

Water Highs

SCUBA DIVING

"Scuba," sometimes spelled S.C.U.B.A. (see Hunter Johnson's story below), stands for Self-Contained Underwater Breathing Apparatus. Now you know!

All About Scuba
www.scuba.about.com
Articles for beginners, a scuba history timeline, info on how to get certified, and more.

TRUE HIGHS
What a Dive

by Hunter Johnson, 16

My name is Hunter and I live in North Texas. I am sixteen years old and I go to a small, conservative college preparatory school. I live a pretty normal teenage life, for this day and age. Sometimes I just feel that I need to get away from it all. When I was 13, I got certified in S.C.U.B.A. diving. So when I feel I need to get away, a friend of mine and I will go rent the necessary equipment, hop in my truck, and drive to Lake Travis in Austin or Possum Kingdom, which is a little over an hour drive. We spend most of the day underwater, completely cut off from everything.

S.C.U.B.A. diving during the day and drinking at night and then going diving again the next day is a very bad idea. S.C.U.B.A. diving causes nitrogen to build up in your bloodstream. Even though it is a very small amount, it is enough to really screw you up when you throw alcohol and drugs into the mix.

One time, I went on a S.C.U.B.A. trip to the Caribbean. It was so cool. I literally got high on a coral reef. I know it sounds corny, but this coral reef was so freaking cool. It was amazing to see all these

Wise Highs

different kinds of fish that I had never even heard of. The really cool part about diving is, when you get deep enough, nothing has any light on it and it all looks pretty bland, but when you bust out a high-powered flashlight, everything seems to come to life. I never thought there could be so many brilliant colors underwater.

Other things I like to do include hiking, mountain climbing, cycling, and bungee jumping. Bungee jumping is easy to learn; all you have to do is lean forward. One thing I really want to try when I get old enough is skydiving.

You might not like all that death-defying, adrenaline junkie stuff, but as long as you like to swim, you will love S.C.U.B.A. diving. The important thing is not to be afraid to try something new.

SAILING

Sailing for Dummies by Peter Isler and J.J. Isler (Foster City, CA: IDG Books Worldwide, 1997). Written by two world-class sailors, this funny, enjoyable guide covers everything you'd want to know about sailing without getting wet. You'll learn how to sail, tie knots, buy or rent a boat, navigate, repair leaks, rescue a "MAN OVERBOARD!!!!" and talk like a sailor ("Ahoy, landlubbers, tack to the port, no jibe!").

International Sailing Federation
www.sailing.org
Updates on worldwide sailing news, events, regattas, etc. An extensive, comprehensive site with lots of interesting information.

SURFING

Learn to Surf by James MacLaren (New York: The Lyons Press, 1997). A user-friendly book without any attitude, aimed at people who wouldn't recognize the difference between a surfboard and an ironing board. If you want to teach yourself to surf, this book will get you up on the board. Covers everything from riptides to reading waves, waxing to surfing etiquette.

Surfer Magazine
www.surfermag.com
This leading magazine is available at newsstands or by subscription. The Web site is fun to surf; find articles from the magazine, photo and video galleries, and links to tons of surfing-related sites.

National Scholastic Surfing Association
PO Box 495 • Huntington Beach, CA 92646
(714) 378-0899 • www.nssa.org
The NSSA's purpose is to "promote the sport of amateur surfing; provide top quality, structured events; and encourage the merits of academic achievement for the benefit of its members."

WAKEBOARDING, WATER SKIING

Wakeworld
www.wakeworld.com
News, articles, interviews with pros, event lists, and an online community of chat rooms, classifieds, and discussion boards will keep you up to date on everything in the wakeboarding world.

USA Water Ski (American Water Ski Association)
1251 Holy Cow Road • Polk City, FL 33868
(863) 324-4341 • www.usawaterski.org
The national governing body for organized water skiing in the United States. The site includes events, news, schools, clubs, competitions, and more, all organized into divisions (Wakeboard, Collegiate, Show Ski, Barefoot, Ski Racing, Kneeboard, Disabled), plus links to dozens of other waterskiing-related sites.

WHITEWATER RAFTING, KAYAKING

The Complete Whitewater Rafter by Jeff Bennett (New York: McGraw-Hill, 1996). An entertaining guide to river running. Covers equipment, safety and rescue, underwater currents, wave patterns, river classifications, whitewater photography, paddling techniques—even the history of rafting.

American Canoe Association
7432 Alban Station Boulevard, Suite B-232 • Springfield, VA 22150
(703) 451-0141 • www.acanet.org
Founded in 1880, the ACA is the nation's largest and most active nonprofit paddle sports organization. Its purpose is to promote the "health, social and personal benefits of canoeing, kayaking, and rafting." The Web site features information on membership, conservation, safety, instruction, and events.

American Whitewater
PO Box 1540 • Cullowhee, NC 28723
1-866-BOAT-4-AW (262-8429) • www.americanwhitewater.org
The "Who, What & Where of American Whitewater." All about whitewater safety, races, rodeos, festivals, river access, and conservation.

WINDSURFING

American Windsurfing Industry Association
www.awia.org
Information about gear, lessons, and travel. Includes a glossary of windsurfing terms.

U.S. Windsurfing Association
PO Box 99 • Chelsea, MI 48118
1-877-386-8708 • www.uswindsurfing.org
The national governing body of the sport provides information on how and where to windsurf, plus competition news.

Sports, Exercise, and X-treme Highs

"In the summer my friends and I go water skiing and once I was on a ski board and I flipped the board over and actually landed. And when I slalom and make a big cut it always makes me feel good."

STUDENT AT A WAKE

Chapter 5

Food for Thought
Healthy Eating Highs

We all know there's a connection between what we eat and our physical health. But did you know there's also a connection between food and mood?

Some foods make us jumpy, others make us grumpy.
Some foods make us sleepy, others make us weepy.
Some foods make us stinky, others make us drink-y.

And some foods, apparently, make us write terrible poems.

Many teenagers have poor eating habits. They skip meals, binge on junk food, eat too fast, and go on yo-yo diets.* My own theory for why poor eating habits don't ruin teens' lives is that they have a lot of compensating factors going for them. For example:

- Many teens play sports and get a lot of exercise, so they burn up all those junk food calories.**

- Many teens eat foods that drop energy levels, but because teens have so much energy to begin with, they don't fall asleep in the middle of band practice.

---

* I'm not talking here about teens with actual eating disorders such as bulimia or anorexia nervosa. These go way beyond poor eating habits and usually require professional help.
** But they're also establishing eating habits that may come back to haunt them later in life, when they're not as physically active. (You've been warned!)

- Many teens eat foods that can make them feel anxious and down in the dumps, but interests, activities, and the support of their friends keep them from going totally to pieces.

Still, some teens are running on only three cylinders. And why go through life on three when you could be using all eight? If you want to experience the high of feeling fit and having a well-tuned body that resists stress and disease, I have two words for you: *exercise* and *nutrition.*

You may hear those words, make a face, and say "Yucch." Some teens seem to think that well-balanced diets are for wusses. As for exercise, you know what they say: If you ever feel the urge to exercise, just lie down and it will pass.*

I don't know why nutrition gets such a bad rap. Maybe it's because people are sore that pizza and French fries aren't considered food groups. But a well-balanced diet is one of the best ways to feel stoked, energetic, and unstressed. Let's look at ways you can use food to calm down and perk up.

Healthy Eating Highs

"Food is our common ground, a universal experience."

JAMES BEARD

The High of Clear Thinking

What you eat affects the amount of oxygen that reaches your brain, the ability of your brain cells to transmit messages, and the levels of various chemicals that enhance or inhibit mental processes. Inadequate nutrition can lead to memory loss, fuzzy thinking, poor concentration, impaired reasoning, loss of motivation, and hastened aging in the brain. It can affect your mood, intelligence, personality, school performance, self-esteem, and social life long before any physical effects are apparent. Here's how to eat smart.

START THE DAY WITH BREAKFAST

Skipping breakfast deprives the brain of the glucose it needs to function. And a brain without glucose is like a car without fuel: No go. *Eating breakfast is the single most important thing you can do to keep your mental functioning in tip-top shape.* In fact, research with children shows that eating breakfast increases motivation and interest in learning and improves school attendance.

If you've been skipping breakfast, it can take as long as two weeks to change your hunger cycle so you wake up hungry and want food.

"All happiness depends on a leisurely breakfast."

JOHN GUNTHER

---

* Or read Chapter 4: Sports, Exercise, and X-treme Highs.

Wise Highs

This is because people who skip breakfast tend to overeat at other meals and snack late into the night. So they wake up full.

Don't eat *too* big a breakfast, though. A large breakfast will make you sleepy. Go easy on the fat. A lot of fat slows your digestion, which can impede the flow of oxygen to your brain and lead to lethargy. It's also a good idea to avoid high-sugar breakfasts like coffee and doughnuts or pastry. Too many carbohydrates, you'll feel sleepy; too little protein, you'll be hungry again.

You may be thinking *What's left? SEAWEED?*

How about a bagel with low-fat cream cheese and some fruit? Or oatmeal and a banana? Cereal with milk is a good breakfast, as long as the cereal is high in fiber and low in fat and sugar. Here are a few more nutritious breakfasts that will feed your brain and fuel your body:

- a fruit-juice sweetened breakfast bar with a piece of fruit
- an individual-sized carton of 100% fruit juice and an English muffin with peanut butter
- nonfat yogurt topped with fresh fruit
- toast with melted low-fat cheese and a fresh fruit salad
- hot cereal sprinkled with cinnamon and raisins, with a glass of orange juice
- melon wedges with a scoop of low-fat cottage cheese
- whole-wheat or oat-bran pancakes with a fresh-fruit topping

There's no law that says you can only eat "breakfast foods" for breakfast. What about last night's leftovers? Heated-up pasta or rice can be yummy first thing in the morning.

CALLING ALL FLAKES

If you're like most people, you sometimes sit at the breakfast table and feel the weight of the world on your shoulders. Riddled with anxiety, you stare at your bowl of cereal, contemplate the stress-filled day that lies ahead, and wonder *How come corn flakes floating in milk tend to move toward each other?* (What, you haven't noticed?) Once two flakes get less than an inch apart, they usually "embrace."

Now, you may just assume that the flakes have a thing for each other. You know, some sort of Chex appeal. But scientists who have studied this phenomenon (they must not be very *busy* scientists) have come up with other explanations.

Healthy Eating Highs

Researchers from Kellogg's, who should know a thing or two about the mating habits of cereal, believe that it's due to *surface tension.* Each flake presses on the surface of the milk. This creates a tiny depression or valley around the perimeter of each flake. (Picture the dip a stone would make around itself if placed on a stretched piece of plastic wrap.) So the flakes are swimming around, minding their own business, wondering whether they're next up for that great small intestine in the sky, when suddenly one flake moves within an inch of another. Their two "valleys" link, forming a basin in the surface of the milk. And the flakes slide toward each other.

Of course, it's also possible that other factors such as temperature, breezes, currents from stirring or pouring the milk, and even bumping the table could play a role. But I think this is enough science for one day.

EAT LIGHTER, MORE FREQUENT MEALS

TRY THIS!

High-fat, heavy meals can make you feel sleepy and stuffed (and put on the pounds). It's better to eat a hearty breakfast, a moderate lunch, and a light dinner.

If you get hungry between meals, go ahead and snack, as long as the snacks contain a combination of proteins and carbohydrates. Most of the carbohydrates should come from grains, fruits, and vegetables, *not* from sugar and sweets. Here are ideas for healthy snacks:

- air-popped popcorn or low-fat microwave popcorn, sprinkled with a dash of garlic powder or Parmesan cheese
- raw vegetables with a dip made from low-fat plain yogurt, low-fat cottage cheese, or a low-fat salad dressing
- pretzels (low-salt varieties are available)
- frozen fruit-juice bars or fruit smoothies
- mini pizzas made with English muffins, pita bread, or bagels, tomato sauce, and part-skim mozzarella cheese
- quesadillas made with low-fat cheese and salsa
- nonfat or low-fat frozen yogurt topped with bananas or berries
- graham crackers or fruit-juice-sweetened granola bars
- rice cakes or bagels with low-fat cream cheese, peanut butter, or 100% fruit spread

FISHY BUT TRUE

Next time you're feeling crabby or floundering in the sea of life, instead of carping on the unfairness of everything, try a dish of fish. Studies show that eating fish can make you healthier and happier. Our bodies depend on something food scientists call omega-3 fatty acids but you and I can call *fish fat.* Research shows that these fats reduce the risk of heart disease, stimulate proper neurological development in infants, ease the pain of rheumatoid arthritis, slow the development of certain tumors, and alleviate symptoms of depression.

93

Wise Highs

Whether you chew Fred Flintstone or take your vitamins in some other form, it's crucial that you get the minimum daily requirements of these nutrients. Even mild vitamin deficiencies can lead to irritability, anxiety, apathy, impaired mental function, depression, confusion, reduced attention span, fatigue, aggressiveness, mood swings, lethargy, and sleepiness. Severe deprivations can cause dementia and psychosis. Yikes!

The B family of vitamins is especially important. There's little B1, and B2 (which is also the name of a bomber), and niacin and B6 and B12 and folic acid. One study found that children who supplemented their diets with B1 to make up for deficiencies scored higher on memory and intelligence tests after one year.

TRY THIS!

EAT A CROWBAR

Most active women and many teens have an iron deficiency. This doesn't mean they're neglecting the wrinkles in their clothes; it means they're not getting enough of this important nutrient. Iron deficiency can impair your immune system, sap your energy, and make you irritable. Iron is essential to brain function. Children who don't get enough iron are more likely to have or develop learning difficulties, and to suffer from apathy, poor concentration, and shortened attention span. This can affect your thinking and learning—which can affect your WHOLE LIFE!

The best sources of iron are oysters, liver, tofu, and beef heart. Right now, you're probably thinking *No wonder people are iron deficient!* Let's move on to some foods you might actually eat. How about kidney beans, black beans, and refried beans? They contain healthy amounts of iron. Lean beef and hamburger are also good sources. Not to mention acorn squash, tuna packed in water, green peas, and chicken. Even strawberries and tomato juice will get you ironed.

PLEASE PASS THE MUD PIE

It's not unusual for people to eat paper, plaster, hair, paint, gravel, ice, and other bizarre substances that have no food value. This syndrome, called *pica,* may have psychological or emotional causes. But in many cases, it's due to the body's instinctive awareness that it's not getting enough of certain minerals. This is especially true in the case of eating clay to make up for iron deficiency. If you or someone you love isn't just making mud pies, but is actually *eating* them, check it out with a doctor.

TRY THIS!

Healthy Eating Highs

The nutrition police won't come after you for the occasional drippy, gooey, cheesy, greasy burger, fries, and shake. But if most of your meals consist of fast food, chances are you're getting too much fat and not enough vitamins and minerals. Try limiting your fast-food dining to two or three times a week—no more. When you do give in, follow these guidelines:

1. Choose grilled or broiled chicken over burgers.

2. Lean, grilled, or broiled meats are better selections than fried.

3. Skip the fattening extras like cheese, bacon, mayonnaise, guacamole, sour cream, and/or tartar sauce.

4. Choose soft taco shells (they're lower in fat than fried hard ones).

5. Avoid anything called "super," "double," "extra," or "deluxe." These catchy terms often mean "extra fat and sodium."

6. Beware of hidden fat and high levels of sodium in salad dressings.

7. Avoid fried foods like French fries and fish sandwiches.

8. Skip the meat toppings and extra cheese on pizza. Plain cheese, pineapple, or fresh vegetables are healthier choices.

9. Don't load a healthy baked potato with mounds of sour cream, butter, cheese, salt, and/or bacon bits. Pile on steamed vegetables instead.

LENTO ALIMENTO

In response to the ubiquitous presence of fast food, the Slow Food movement has emerged with a philosophy based on the principle that food (and life) is to be tasted and enjoyed, rather than merely consumed. While fast food demands standardization and efficiency, Slow Food advocates superior food quality, with a particular emphasis on regional differences. The organization hosts conferences, dinners, and other events and produces several publications about fine food and drink. Based in Italy (where else?), the group has members all over the world. For more information, visit the Web site (www.slowfood.com).

FIND OUT MORE

"Fast Food Facts." Published by the consumer division of the Minnesota Attorney General's Office, this free brochure gives you the calorie, fat, sodium, and cholesterol counts of popular menu items at national fast-food chains. Call or email: 1-800-657-3787 • consumer.ag@state.mn.us

Food Facts
www.foodfacts.info
Search for information about specific restaurants and menu items.

Wise Highs

If you sometimes feel like a steam kettle with the spout at the wrong end, it may be due to excessive consumption of gas-producing foods. Try avoiding the following one at a time and see if the air quality improves:

THE VIRTUOSO

For most people, passing gas is, at best, a source of juvenile humor. But one talented Frenchman turned flatulence into a lucrative show business career. Joseph Pujol, better known as Le Petomane, brought art to the fa— er, passing of gas. Gifted with remarkable control over his abdominal muscles, Le Petomane achieved tremendous feats of flatulence; in a typical performance he might play tunes with his posterior, blow out candles, and—hold on to your hat—smoke a cigarette through a flexible tube. Le Petomane sold out theaters wherever he went and died a rich, happy man in 1945.

apples (raw)
avocados
beans (black, garbanzo, kidney, lima, navy)
broccoli
Brussels sprouts
cabbage
cantaloupe
cauliflower
corn
cucumbers
green peppers
honeydew melon

kohlrabi
leeks
lentils
onions
peas
pimientos
radishes
rutabagas
sauerkraut
scallions
shallots
soybeans
turnips
watermelon

The Scoop on Caffeine

I hate to break it to all you latte lovers, but caffeine is a drug—a stimulant. While you may think of a cup of coffee as a relaxing time-out, caffeine actually depletes your body of B vitamins and provokes a stress response.* This is why, after that initial jolt of vim and vigor, you experience a drop in energy. And need another cup of coffee to perk you up again.

Anytime a drug causes you to feel "good" and then, as the feeling wears off, you need more of that drug in order to not feel "bad," you have the potential for a cycle of dependency.** If you need further proof that caffeine is a drug, try quitting cold turkey. You'll probably get a headache. This withdrawal symptom is your body's way of saying "WHERE'S MY CAFFEINE?!?"

What else does caffeine do to your body? Plenty. Some of it's good, but most of it isn't.

---

* For more on stress, see Chapter 1: Serenity Highs.
** Of course, there are many wonderful life-saving drugs on which people are "dependent." I'm talking about the other kinds of drugs.

- Caffeine stimulates brain activity by inhibiting the production of adenosine. Adenosine is a neurotransmitter whose job is to keep a check on neural activity. By inhibiting the inhibitor, caffeine arouses the brain—kind of like two negatives making a positive.

- Caffeine increases your heart rate. Four cups of strong coffee can boost your heart rate as much as 20 beats per minute.

- Caffeine speeds up breathing. Xanthines, the class of compounds to which caffeine belongs, relax the smooth muscles in the tubes that bring air into the lungs. While xanthines have been used to treat asthma, side effects (e.g., upset stomach, restlessness) make it less desirable than other available treatments.

- Coffee (regular and decaf) can irritate the protective mucous lining of the stomach, causing acid secretion and heartburn.

- Caffeine is a diuretic, which means it stimulates urine production.

- Caffeine can have a slight positive effect on physical endurance. But, since caffeine also increases water loss, people who exercise with caffeine in their system may become dehydrated, especially in hot weather. Plus, if exercise increases your heart rate, and caffeine increases your heart rate, you're placing extra stress on your heart.

- Caffeine increases the amount of adrenaline in the body. When you're stressed, your body produces adrenaline; drinking caffeine adds even more stress to your system.

- At relatively high doses (5–6 cups of strong coffee), caffeine has been shown to trigger panic attacks in people. If you're already full of anxiety, a cup of coffee may make you feel worse, not better.

> ### DEATH BY COFFEE?
>
> Fatal overdoses of caffeine, while *extremely rare,* can and do happen. Symptoms of caffeine poisoning include nausea, confusion, vomiting, panic attacks, and rapid or irregular heart rate. Some people have convulsions or become delirious. A 50-pound child could exhibit toxic effects by drinking seven cups of strong coffee, or by taking four caffeine pills such as Vivarin or Caffedrine. Newspapers recently reported the death of a student who took too many caffeine pills to stay awake while cramming for exams.

Would you like to know even more about caffeine? I thought so! Here are a few fun facts:

- Caffeine is the most widely used drug on the planet. (Alcohol is second.) Tea and coffee are the most popular drinks on earth.

Wise Highs

- Caffeine belongs to a family of mostly poisonous substances called alkaloids. Other members of this family include strychnine, hemlock, nicotine, morphine, and mescaline.

- A four-ounce chocolate bar contains just about as much caffeine as a cup of percolator-brewed coffee.

- The International Olympic Committee lists caffeine as a "doping agent" which, like steroids, can provide an artificial performance boost. Numerous athletes have been disqualified or banned from competition after high levels of caffeine were discovered in their blood.

- Recognizing the performance-enhancing properties of caffeine, many professional bike racers insert caffeine suppositories before a race. While this avoids the risk of an upset stomach from drinking caffeine-rich liquids, it could keep their butts up all night.

A SPEEDY HISTORY OF CAFFEINE

According to legend, tea was discovered by Chinese emperor Shen Nung in 2737 B.C. Supposedly the emperor was boiling water over an outdoor campfire when some scorched leaves from a nearby shrub fell into the water. Shen Nung decided to drink the brew rather than throw it away. Liking its aroma and taste, he continued to make the concoction and, over time, came to believe it had medicinal value. Buddhist priests brought the practice of drinking tea from China to Japan around A.D. 600; by the 1500s, people drank tea widely in Europe.

Coffee was first grown in the sixth century in Yemen. As with tea, its powerful stimulant properties were recognized and desired. In fact, ancient tales suggest that early users believed the jolt they got from coffee beans was the result of divine intervention. One often-heard legend describes an Ethiopian shepherd named Kaldi who noticed that his herd of goats got all jazzed up whenever they chewed the berries of a particular native bush. Soon Kaldi started chewing the berries himself to stay alert during those long, tedious hours of goat herding. A weary monk passing by on his way to Mecca noticed Kaldi and his goats cavorting and thought *Man, I got to get me some of them berries,* and soon his fellow monks were berry happy. Eventually people discovered that if they roasted and ground the seeds, soaked them in hot water, and drank the resulting brew instead of chewing the berries, they got a greater buzz.

By the 1600s, coffee houses had spread all over Europe. From the beginning, these establishments were known for their scholarly, intellectual, and political conversation. Meanwhile, in the not-yet-but-soon-to-be United States of the mid-1700s, tea was much more widely consumed than coffee. That all changed when the British levied high taxes on tea imported by the colonies. To protest, the colonists dumped 342 chests of tea in the harbor, and many switched to drinking coffee. By the mid-20th century, coffee consumption averaged 20 pounds per person per year (which may be why *homo sapiens* are also referred to as *human beans*).

Since then, coffee consumption has dropped to about 10 pounds per person per year. More than 50 percent of Americans drink two or more cups of coffee a day; of these coffee drinkers, almost half consume five or more cups a day. While Americans may be drinking less coffee than they did several decades ago, they're getting more caffeine from soft drinks and chocolate.

Healthy Eating Highs

BE A QUITTER

TRY THIS!

It *is* possible to quit caffeine, and if you do, you'll be amazed at how great you feel in a couple of weeks. Javaholics, once they get caffeine out of their systems, report that they sleep better and have more energy. They have less stress and heartburn, fewer headaches and muscle aches. They no longer get a contact jolt every time they walk past a coffee shop.

If you'd like to feel good naturally, cut out the caffeine. Try these tips for saying no way to au lait:

1. Do it slowly (so you won't get headaches). If you drink several cups of coffee every day, cut back by one cup on your first day. A few days later, cut back by another cup. Continue until you give up your last cup.

2. Switch to decaf. If you're someone for whom life without a daily-double-mocha-hazelnut-espresso-cappuccino-with-cinnamon-on-top isn't worth living, you don't have to give up coffee. Just give up *caffeinated* coffee. Start by making a brew that's half caf and half decaf. Over the next week, gradually increase the decaf proportion until you end up with 100 percent decaf. (Even decaf has some caffeine in it, but hey, let's not be fanatics.)

Wise Highs

3. Substitute other liquids. For people who drink a lot of coffee, the ritual of having something to drink is as habit-forming as caffeine itself. Instead of taking a coffee break, take a juice break. Or a sparkling water break. Or a piece-of-fruit break. Or a pickle break.

4. Beware of caffeine in hiding. Many beverages, foods, even over-the-counter drugs contain significant amounts of caffeine. Check out the chart.

HOW MUCH CAFFEINE? *

PRODUCT	Serving size	Milligrams of caffeine
COFFEES		
Brewed	8 oz.	135
Instant	8 oz.	95
Maxwell House Cappuccino, Mocha	8 oz.	60–65
General Foods International Coffee, Swiss Mocha	8 oz.	55
Decaffeinated	8 oz.	5
TEAS		
Celestial Seasonings Iced Lemon Ginseng Tea	16 oz.	100
Tea, leaf or bag	8 oz.	50
Snapple Iced Tea, all varieties	16 oz.	48
Lipton Tea	8 oz.	35–40
Lipton Iced Tea, assorted varieties	16 oz.	18–40
Tea, green	8 oz.	30
Nestea Pure Lemon Sweetened Iced Tea	16 oz.	22
Tea, instant	8 oz.	15
Celestial Seasonings Herbal Tea, all varieties	8 oz.	0
Lipton Soothing Moments Peppermint Tea	8 oz.	0
SOFT DRINKS		
Mountain Dew	12 oz.	55
Surge	12 oz.	47

* Copyright 1998 CSPI. Reprinted/Adapted from *Nutrition Action Healthletter* (1875 Connecticut Ave., N.W., Suite 300, Washington, DC 20009-5728. $24.00 for 10 issues).

PRODUCT	Serving size	Milligrams of caffeine
Diet Coke	12 oz.	45
Coca-Cola	12 oz.	40
Dr. Pepper, regular or diet	12 oz.	41
Sunkist Orange Soda	12 oz.	40
Pepsi-Cola	12 oz.	37
Barq's Root Beer	12 oz.	23
7-Up or Diet 7-Up	12 oz.	0
Minute Maid Orange Soda	12 oz.	0
Sprite or Diet Sprite	12 oz.	0
FROZEN DESSERTS		
Ben & Jerry's No Fat Coffee Fudge Frozen Yogurt	1 cup	85
Häagen-Dazs Coffee Ice Cream	1 cup	58
Starbucks Frappuccino Bar	1 bar	15
Healthy Choice Cappuccino Chocolate Chunk Ice Cream	1 cup	8
YOGURTS		
Dannon Coffee Yogurt	8 oz.	45
Yoplait Cafe Au Lait Yogurt	6 oz.	5
Dannon Light Cappuccino Yogurt	8 oz.	< 1
CHOCOLATES OR CANDIES		
Hershey's Special Dark Chocolate Bar	1.5 oz.	31
Hershey Bar (milk chocolate)	1.5 oz.	10
Cocoa or hot chocolate	8 oz.	5
OVER-THE-COUNTER DRUGS		
NoDoz, maximum strength; Vivarin	1 tablet	200
Excedrin	2 tablets	130
NoDoz, regular strength	1 tablet	100
Anacin	2 tablets	64

Sugar Shock

Wise Highs

According to our survey of 2,000 teens, the #1 method they use to get high without alcohol or other drugs is eating sugar. They scarf sugar when they're stressed or want to get an energy buzz.

When they're feeling loco, they gulp some cocoa.
When everything's a bore, they have a s'more.
When they're hurt, they devour frozen yogurt.
When life ain't dandy, they binge on candy.
When they're on the brink, they have a drink—of sugary, caffeinated soda.*

HIDDEN SUGARS

Dextrose, fructose, glucose, lactose, maltose, sucrose, sorbitol, Manitol, Malitol, Xylitol… all are sneaky names for the sugars hidden in many foods. If they're listed several times on a food label, or if they're listed first or second, that product is probably high in sugar.

P.S. Brown sugar is *not* "better for you" than white sugar. Brown sugar is white sugar—with added molasses.

Sugar is so widely used for "mood control" that you see TV characters turning to ice cream for companionship or to soothe a broken heart.

In 1840, the average American consumed four teaspoons of sugar daily. Today the average American consumes *over ten times* that amount—43 teaspoons a day. And it's not just candy and ice cream and sodas and cakes and pies that are crammed with sugar. Check out the ingredients in cereals, ketchup, and tons of other food products. You'll find sugar everywhere.

The reason people turn to sugar is that it's a natural tranquilizer. While you may experience an initial power surge from snarfing something sweet, *your body* says "Hey, what's with all the sugar?" and secretes insulin to decrease the sugar content in your blood. This lowers your energy level and induces a feeling of relaxation.

> "Where there is sugar, there are bound to be ants."
> MALAY PROVERB

There's nothing wrong with "ice cream therapy." It's a lot less risky than turning to alcohol or smoking or high-speed driving every time you're upset. But "sugar moments" should be used sparingly. You don't want to rely on sweets every time you feel sad, upset, lonely, or tired. You may get a temporary burst of energy or a feeling of calm, but it will quickly wear off, at which point you'll look for another sugar fix. This cycle could lead to eating disorders, weight gain, tooth decay, and a host of other problems that will make you feel even worse. Also, people who eat a lot of sweets tend to take in fewer vitamins and minerals (and more fat and calories) than is healthy.

---

* A 12-ounce glass of regular cola contains eight *tablespoons* of sugar.

Are You Eating Too Much Sugar?

Ask yourself the following questions and pick the answers that best describe your eating habits.

Healthy Eating Highs

How often do you...	never	1–2 times a week	once a day	several times a day
...eat pre-sweetened cereal?	❏	❏	❏	❏
...drink sodas, punch, lemonade, chocolate milk, or fruit drinks?	❏	❏	❏	❏
...eat candy or chew gum with sugar in it?	❏	❏	❏	❏
...add sugar to iced tea or coffee?	❏	❏	❏	❏
...eat sugary snacks and desserts like cookies, cakes, or brownies?	❏	❏	❏	❏

How often did you check "once a day" or "several times a day"? What does that tell you?

CAN CHOCOLATE MAKE YOU HIGH?

Many teens chow down on chocolate when they're feeling depressed or anxious. They claim that it gives them a sense of happiness and well-being.

There are at least three possible scientific explanations for this:

1. The moderate level of caffeine in chocolate may induce a feeling of relaxation.

2. When you consume sugar, a chemical called tryptophan goes to the brain, where it is converted into another chemical called serotonin. Serotonin is a natural opiate that stimulates the pleasure centers in the brain. This causes people to feel calm and relaxed.

Wise Highs

3. Researchers have recently discovered that a compound in chocolate is very similar to one in the brain that interacts with THC receptors. THC is the psychoactive compound in marijuana. Thus, it's possible that chocolate activates the THC receptors in a manner similar to THC, producing a mild pleasurable feeling.

Don't think you can get stoned from chocolate bars, though. You'd have to eat 25 pounds to get the effect of a typical dose of marijuana.

TRY THIS! CUT BACK ON SWEETS

If you feel you're consuming too much sugar, it's time to cut back. Here's how:

- Ask the family member who does the grocery shopping not to buy sweet snacks (you won't eat them if you don't have them).

- Choose brands with less added sugar, or none at all.*

- Eliminate soft drinks from your diet. If you crave something fizzy, try carbonated water; flavor it by squeezing in the juice of fresh fruits like lemons or limes.

- Beware of fruit-flavored beverages, punches, or lemonade—they're usually loaded with sugar. Drink 100% fruit juice instead. You'll quench your thirst and add vitamins to your diet at the same time.

- Have lots of naturally sugar-free snacks handy for between-meal grazing.

- Fresh fruit, sliced vegetables, and air-popped popcorn (unbuttered) are satisfying alternatives to sweets and junk food.

---

* Watch for hidden sugars. See page 102 and start reading labels.

FIND OUT MORE

Food and Mood: The Complete Guide to Eating Well and Feeling Your Best by Elizabeth Somer (New York: Owl Books, 1999). This practical, easy-to-understand guide describes the connections between what you eat and how you think and feel. You'll learn all about food and depression, stress, poor sleep, mental functioning, memory, cravings, and winter blues.

Healthy Eating Highs

A Good Night's Sleep

According to Mary Carskadon, a sleep specialist in the department of psychiatry and human behavior at Brown University, 15-year-olds need 9.2 hours of sleep a night—which probably makes you say *Holy sheet! I'm lucky to get seven hours of sleep!*

Most teenagers are sleep deprived...and no wonder. They have to get up early (often skipping breakfast to eke out a few more min-  utes of sleep); they race through the day in high gear, spend hours on homework, carve out a *few* minutes for fun and friends, and then collapse into bed late at night. And, if they smoke (tsk, tsk), drink lots of coffee or soda, eat a big meal at dinner, have a late-night sugar-laden munchie, and/or feel stressed out, the sleep they get is not going to recharge their batteries.

Teenage sleepyheads are more likely to be irritable, forgetful, inattentive, intolerant, and depressed. Because they're sooooo tired, they often give up sports, hobbies, and socializing. Insomniacs (people who have trouble sleeping) have more accidents, bounce back more slowly from stress, and get sick more often. This is not the stuff of pleasant dreams.

There's no magic number of hours every teen needs to sleep. It varies from person to person. Some teens wake up refreshed after six hours of sleep; others need nine or ten to get back in the saddle again.

If you're not getting enough sleep, or you feel tired no matter how much sleep you get, this could be the result of:

- medical problems (e.g., asthma, hypertension, sinusitis)
- too much caffeine or sugar in your system
- alcohol or other drug abuse

HOW SLEEPY ARE YOU?

According to a survey by the National Sleep Foundation, many young people don't get the sleep they need. Parents report that 60 percent of children under the age of 18 complained of feeling tired during the day, and 15 percent admitted to falling asleep at school. Teenagers are more likely to complain of being tired during the day than are younger children (23 percent of teenagers vs. 11 percent of younger children).

Wise Highs

- indigestion or gas from pigging out at dinner, or eating spicy or gas-producing foods
- stressful events in your life (e.g., SATs, big paper due, illness or death of a close friend or relative, alcoholic parent)
- emotional problems (e.g., worries, guilt, interpersonal conflicts, identity issues)
- environmental disturbances (e.g., an unfamiliar bed or room, too much noise or light, temperature of room too hot or cold, roommate who snores or throws pillows at you in his or her sleep)
- large man-eating bugs in your bed

NATURE'S SLEEPING PILL

If you want a safe, natural, healthy way to make yourself sleepy at night, try eating a banana one to two hours before bedtime. Or an apple. Or any other high-carbohydrate, low-protein snack—such as toast and jam, air-popped popcorn, or a baked potato with non-fat sour cream. If you're not sensitive to sugar, try a fat-free dessert sweet, a low-fat oatmeal-raisin cookie, even a dish of sherbet. (Avoid anything with chocolate because it contains caffeine.) Keep your snack small, since consuming a lot of food or liquid right before bed can keep you up or in the bathroom throughout the night.

Why does this work? Because a high-carbohydrate, low-protein "nightcap" raises the levels of tryptophan in the brain, which in turn increases the amount of serotonin. Serotonin has been shown to help people fall asleep 50 percent faster, and improve the quality and duration of sleep.

ZZZZZZZZZZZZZZZZZZ

Any of the following suggestions may help you sleep better. Experiment with them. See which ones make a difference. You don't have to do them all, but chances are the more you do, the better you'll sleep.

1. Be physically active during the day.

2. Nix on tobacco and alcohol.

3. Avoid caffeine.

4. Make breakfast (or lunch) your biggest meal of the day. Keep dinner light.

5. Be sure to have some protein for dinner.

6. Spicy is dicey. Avoid hot, spicy dishes at supper. These can cause indigestion or heartburn.

7. Gas is a pass. It's hard to sleep soundly when you feel like a hot air balloon. Stay away from gas-producing foods, especially after lunch.

8. Just say no to MSG (monosodium glutamate). This seasoning, often found in Chinese food, can disturb your sleep. And if that isn't reason enough to avoid it, how about the name itself: *glutamate?* Yicch!

9. Don't gulp your food. Swallowing a lot of air can make you feel uncomfortable all night.

10. Refrain from doing homework or other daytime things in bed. Condition your body to associate bed with *sleeeeeeeeeeeeeeeeeeeeeeeep.*

11. Maintain regular sleeping patterns. Try to get up and go to bed at the same times each day.

12. Create a bedtime ritual. (When you were little, your parents did this for you when they put you in the tub, got you into your jammies, read you a story, and kissed you on the tip of your nose.)

13. Before going beddy-bye, watch a comedy or read something funny. Laughter releases endorphins which promote a sense of well-being.

14. Don't read page-turner mysteries at bedtime.

15. Take a hot shower or bath before bed.

16. Have a high-carb, low-protein snack one or two hours prior to sleepy-time.

17. Make yourself a cup of warm milk right before you toddle off to slumberland.

18. Always check under the bed for monsters.

Healthy Eating Highs

"One hour's sleep before midnight is worth two after."

PROVERB

"The key to getting ahead is setting aside eight hours a day for work and eight hours a day for sleep—and making sure they're not the same hours."

GENE BROWN

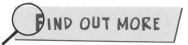

FIND OUT MORE

Get a Good Night's Sleep: Understand Your Sleeplessness—and Banish It Forever! by Frank Joe Bruno (Foster City, CA: IDG Books Worldwide, 1997). A step-by-step program in a carry-along size.

Sleep Home Pages
www.sleephomepages.org
Discussions, publications, newsletters, research, links, and more.

Chapter 6

The Eyes Have It
Visual Highs

Your eyes are for more than studying, watching videos, surfing the Internet, sneaking peeks at someone you have a crush on, staring into the refrigerator, rolling when your parents are lecturing you, and looking both ways before you cross the street. For fun, inexpensive, surprising highs, you can always play with your eyes. And you don't even have to take them out of your head.

The Power of Perception

"Many eyes go through the meadow, but few see the flowers in it."
RALPH WALDO EMERSON

In the movies, when directors want to show that a character is in an altered state, they monkey with the way things *look*. The audience is made to see things from the character's point of view (POV, for all you aspiring screenwriters). Everything appears fuzzy and out-of-focus. Colors become unreal, lights pulse, images multiply, shapes swim and morph. Filmmakers do this because they recognize the extent to which vision affects and reflects our state of consciousness.

You can use the power of perception to see the world in new ways. Here are some great natural "eyes" you can try.

LOOK FOR SOMETHING NEW

Visual Highs

Try to see *five new things* every time you return to a familiar place.

Take one of your classrooms at school. You know it inside out...or do you? You know the blackboards and windows, the maps and charts and bulletin boards, the rows of desks, the flag over the door, the clock that seems to take forever to count 43 minutes—all of these elements are etched in your visual memory.

But there are *thousands* of other things in that room you've never seen. *Look for them.* You'll discover a world of hidden details: scratches, scuffs, and chipped paint; floor tiles, woodwork, and tiny nails; maybe a cobweb or a dust mote. With new eyes, you'll notice how things are put together; how light and shadow move across the room. You'll discover how much of your world you never see—even though it's right in front of your eyes.

CATCH A SNAPDRAGON

A snapdragon is a small object shaped like a pyramid. You can buy one for a few bucks in many museum or novelty stores. If you look at something through the small end of a snapdragon, it will multiply the image 24 times. As you twist or rotate the device, the images become designs.

You can try this in your room at home; in restaurants, gyms, movie theaters and stores; even on familiar routes you drive once a week. You can also look for *differences* between the seasons, or between night and day.

LOOK FOR PATTERNS

Our eyes tend to focus on the most obvious aspects of whatever image or landscape we're looking at. We'll see a mass of trees and think *forest.* We'll see the plane we're walking on and think *floor.* But these images are composed of abstract *patterns.*

- Next time you look at a floor, don't see it as a floor. Instead, see it as a pattern of tiles, squares, or pieces of wood.

- Next time you're riding down a suburban highway, instead of looking at the fast-food joints and malls and parking lots, focus on the electric wires that parallel the highway. Forget that they're wires. See them as lines that have rhythm and pulse and tension as they swoop and cross and stretch over the road.

- Look for patterns in trees, windows, fences, brickwork, paths, and lampposts.

"Every closed eye is not sleeping, and every open eye is not seeing."
BILL COSBY

Wise Highs

○ Instead of looking at storefronts as you walk along a down-town street, look at the tops of buildings.

If you seek out patterns you'd otherwise miss, you'll not only see the environment in new ways. You'll hone your powers of observation. This is very useful if you want to be an artist, writer, or witness to a crime.

THEN AND NOW

Pick a favorite spot. It could be a porch swing, a bench in the park, an outdoor café, a comfy chair in your living room. Go there first thing in the morning. Sip a cup of decaf, herbal tea, or cocoa. Look around. Experience the setting through your eyes. *See* how the space feels. Is it warm and cozy? Bright and airy? Do the colors glow? Does sunlight play in the room?

Return to the same place late in the afternoon, at sunset, or after dark. Does it feel different? Do you feel different? Since it's the exact same spot, any difference you notice is due to changes in what you see—changes in light.

TOPSY-TURVY

Visual perception is linked to gravity—to the way the human body experiences the physical world. The sky is always above, the ground below. Our eyes know what's up, what's down, and where things "should" be.

Challenge the visual status quo by looking at the world upside down through your legs. This is especially effective if you're outdoors and can invert an entire landscape. Notice what happens to the horizon. How do colors and shapes change? Where do your eyes want to rest?

FINGERS IN THE EYES

Here's a powerful way to alter consciousness that is practiced by many monks and shamans. It's quick and easy, and you're never without the requisite equipment.

"Our sight is the most perfect and most delight-ful of all our senses. It fills the mind with the largest variety of ideas, converses with its objects at the greatest distance, and continues the longest in action without being tired or satiated."

JOSEPH ADDISON

First, make sure your hands and face are clean. Then sit in a comfortable chair. Close your eyes and *gently* rub your eyeballs by pressing lightly with your fingertips near the inside corners of your eyes. Do this for about 5 seconds. You'll see colored spots and shapes. These are called phosphenes. Experiment by varying the pressure and location of your fingertips—but always massage *very lightly.* Enjoy the show.

Visual Highs

Watery Variation

Close your eyes in the shower. Turn your face towards the shower head so the water falls on your closed eyelids. (Be sure the pressure is gentle.) You'll see stars.

STARE-WAY TO HEAVEN

TRY THIS!

Take a visual trip by staring at people, objects, or landscapes.

Sit opposite a friend so you're 3–5 feet apart. Adjust the lighting so it's adequate for seeing your friend's face but not harsh or overly bright. (A lamp with a shade that throws off a warm glow is ideal.) Gaze at your friend's face. Don't strain your eyes. Relax them. Defocus. Let yourself see double. Try not to blink. Let your friend's face go in and out of focus. Before long, your friend's face will change right before your eyes into a visage you won't recognize.

Next time it's raining, look up and stare at the sky. If you're driving in a snowstorm, stare at the snow as it comes towards you (as long as you're not behind the wheel!). Stare at the stars. Stare at waves breaking on the shore.

Staring is the visual equivalent to repeating the same word over and over. For example, repeat the word *noodle.* After a while, it loses its meaning and sounds different. Same thing with staring. After a while, the object looks different and turns into something else.*

DON'T BLINK

Stand behind a window or sturdy screen. Have an accomplice stand on the other side of the barrier and throw a Nerf ball or similar *soft* and *lightweight* object at your face. (That's right, kiddies; do *not* throw a brick.) Try not to blink. It'll probably be impossible, since blinking is a reflex designed to protect your eyes.

* Objects are often used as a focus for meditation. See page 38.

Wise Highs

A metronome is a gadget that produces a steady yet adjustable beat. You can buy one at almost any musical instruments store—or maybe you can borrow one from the music room at your school. Musicians use metro-nomes to keep time when they're practicing. You can also use a met-ronome to hypnotize yourself.* Here's how:

1. Set the metronome at a medium speed—maybe 1 beat per second for starters. If it's too fast, you won't be able to keep up with it; if it's too slow, you'll get bored between beats.

WRINKLE WREDUCTION

It's hard to believe, but someday you, too, will have wrinkles around your eyes, also known as crow's feet. Why? Because there are no oil glands located around the eyes to keep the skin moist and springy, and because every facial expression you make—from smiles to frowns to quizzical looks—affects your eyes. It's not too soon to start using a moisturizer. Someday you'll thank me for this suggestion.

2. Release the hand and stare at it as it swings back and forth. Readjust the speed faster or slower until the beat seems "right."

3. Continue to watch the hand sway from side to side. Back and forth. Left, right, left, right. Back 'n' forth. Back 'n' forth. You're getting sleepy. Your eyelids are getting heavy. Heavier and heavier. You are going deeper. Deeper and heavier. Deeper and heavier. You can barely keep your eyes open. You feel them closing. Closing. You are drifting deeper and deeper. Deeper and deeper....

At this point, you're ready to give yourself positive auto-suggestions.**

Unlike regular bulbs that fade out when turned off, strobe lights go off immediately. So the rapid flashing is much more contrasty and intense.

You can find strobes at electronics stores, party supplies stores, and theater-lighting stores, and at many gift and novelty shops. Once you have one, find a room that you can make *totally* dark. Place the strobe at eye level anywhere from 3–10 feet away from where you'll sit. Set the strobe so it flashes between 8–25 times per second. If you can't count that fast, see if the strobe has a timing indicator. ***Tip:*** For most people, the "best" visual images reportedly occur at 10 flashes per second.

---

* For more about self-hypnosis, see pages 48–53.
** For tips, see pages 52–53.

Turn off the room lights. *Close your eyes* and "stare" right at the strobe. You'll begin to see all sorts of wild visual images. Experiment by varying the speed of the strobe. Does it change the nature of the images you see?

Visual Highs

If you want to stare directly at the strobe with your eyes open, place a red gel (piece of plastic) in front of the bulb. As you zone out, you may see a weird glow floating above the strobe or in the space between you and the strobe. Focus on this form. See what happens.

You can also make your own strobe. Get a lamp that throws a bright, white light in one direction (like a spotlight). Place a fan in front of the light and turn it on to *slow.* The blade will create the strobe effect as it rotates in front of the light.

Get some friends together and dance or move while the light flashes. The strobe effect will make it look like you aren't moving at all.

CAUTION!!! Rapidly flashing lights (like strobes) can cause seizures in people who have photosensitive epilepsy. This condition is very rare—epilepsy is estimated to affect between 1 and 2 percent of the population, and only about 5 percent of people with epilepsy are photosensitive—but be aware.

FIND YOUR BLIND SPOT

Did you know that everyone has a blind spot? There are no receptors at the point on your retina where the optic nerve leaves the eye to go to the brain. Since this spot is not sensitive to light, images hitting it are invisible to the eye.

Try this experiment to see where your blind spot is. Hold this page about 12" in front of you. Close your left eye. Through your right eye, look steadily at the dot on the left. Now move the page slowly toward your face, then away from it. At one point, the right hand dot disappears completely. It's here that the image falls exactly on your blind spot.

Wise Highs

Binocular Vision

Binocular vision doesn't require binoculars. In fact, unless you have a visual impairment, you use this type of vision every day without thinking about it. Binocular vision means that both of your eyes work together as a team—simultaneously, equally, smoothly, and accurately. This gives you stereo vision (two separate images from two eyes are combined into a single image in the brain) and depth perception (seeing in 3D).

Here's a quick way to test your binocular vision (and get ready for two amusing visual exercises).

1. Hold this page at arm's length in front of your face. Focus on the dot.

●

2. Touch your free thumb to the end of your nose.

3. Slowly move your thumb straight out from your nose. Stay focused on the dot. Soon you should see 2 thumbs framing 1 dot.

4. Now switch your focus to your thumb. You should see 2 dots framing 1 thumb.

Did it work? Then your binocular vision is in great shape—and you're ready for "Wag the Dog" and "Three Thumbs Up." What if it didn't work? Try again. Be sure to focus first on the dot, then on your thumb. Still didn't work? You might want to have an eye exam. Ask your optometrist or ophthalmologist to check your binocular vision.

EVIL EYES?

Since ancient times, cultures worldwide have believed in the "Evil Eye," the superstition that people can inflict misfortune on others—either intentionally or accidentally—merely by looking at them with jealousy or malice. Young children, the elderly, and animals were thought to be most vulnerable to the Evil Eye. People wore elaborate eye makeup or brooches in the shapes of eyes or certain animals to protect themselves; newborn children were kept under wraps and away from prying eyes.

WAG THE DOG

1. Make 2 fists and hold them 6–8" in front of your face.

2. Extend your index fingers. Touch them tip to tip.

3. Look at the spot where the two fingers touch. Instead of focusing on the point of intersection, relax and defocus your eyes, almost as if you were letting them cross (but don't actually cross them). A hot dog (or, more accurately, a cocktail sausage) will appear between your index fingers.

4. Move your hands closer to your eyes and the sausage will grow. Move it away from your eyes and the sausage will shrink until it looks like a bean. Pull your fingers apart and the sausage will float in midair. Fun!

Advanced Hot-Dogging

This time, don't make any fists. Simply hold your hands 6–8" in front of your face, palms toward you. Touch the 4 fingertips of one hand with the 4 of the other. Look at the intersections as you did above, defocus your eyes, and voilà, you'll see 4 cocktail sausages (enough for a party).

For more fun with hot dogs, move your hands closer to and farther from your face; pull your fingers apart to "float the dog"; wiggle individual fingers up and down and in front of others; make pyramids and shapes with your interlocked fingers.

This is a great activity when you're by yourself and want a little pick-me-up. Why, in just a few short minutes, I saw not only hot-dogs between my fingers, but kidney beans, heart-shaped Valentine candies, three carrots, and a flying peanut shell.

THREE THUMBS UP

1. Hold your arms out in front of you. Make 2 fists.

2. Extend your thumbs so they point up and are approximately 2" apart. *Tip:* It's best if the background behind your thumbs is neutral.

3. Instead of staring at your thumbs, relax and defocus your eyes. Once you do this successfully, 2 new thumbs will appear between the outside 2, for a grand total of 4.

Wise Highs

4. Slowly move your "real" thumbs together until the 2 inner ones overlap to form a single third thumb.

This new thumb will seem to throb and glow and flicker as if it were more "real" than the others. And, if your third thumb is anything like mine, it'll look like a cross between E.T. and the Singing Nun.

Variation for Penny-Pinchers

Place a couple of pennies 2" apart on a flat surface. By relaxing your eyes, you'll soon see 4 pennies. Play with your focus and distance from the pennies until the 2 inner pennies merge into 1. If you focus on this "make-believe" penny, it will soon become more luminous than the coins on either side.

That which *isn't* becomes more "real" than that which *is*. Hmmmm…

3D Vision
www.vision3d.com
Tips on how to see in 3D, information on visual health and visual therapy, a "3D Gallery" of Magic Eye images (the 3D pictures hidden within 2D patterns that were all the rage in the 1990s), and more. A Cool Medical Site of the Week winner.

The Language of Color

You probably already know that color can affect your mood. Some colors are discomforting while others are soothing. This is because different colors have different wavelengths and vibrate at different frequencies.

HEALING LIGHT

Scientists have discovered that exposure to red light can cause brain-wave abnormalities in epileptics, and that jaundice in newborn babies can be cured if they are exposed to blue light. Red clothes have been shown to raise blood pressure; blue clothes lower it.

Blue calms and cools. College students tested in a blue room were more likely to say they were happy and calm than students tested in red, yellow, or neutral rooms.

Red stimulates and warms. In one study, students gambling under red lights took greater risks than students under blue lights. Red can also feel oppressive and confining.

Pink soothes and tranquilizes. After a prison holding cell was painted pink, prisoners became less aggressive and hostile.

Green may increase stress, induce fatigue, and encourage passivity.

Brown and beige appear to have a calming influence. In a room, they create feelings of security and intimacy.

Yellow has been associated with everything from diminished boredom to increased irritability. Some people find yellows very cheering.

White communicates innocence, purity, and spirituality. A white environment can be calming and restorative or, if too harsh, cold and irritating.

Visual Highs

We also tend to associate certain characteristics with colors. We say that someone leads a "colorful" life, is "in the pink" or "seeing red." A grumpy person is in a "black mood"; a sad person is "blue." A novice is "green"; a coward is "yellow." But there's no need to fly into a purple rage about this. Instead, use color to your advantage. Experiment to learn which colors you look and feel best in.

Like musical pitches, colors can harmonize or clash with each other. Some colors are more easily seen than others, just as some notes are more easily heard. This is why crossing guards wear orange rather than gray belts. And why we look or feel good in some colors and not others.

MONKEY SEE, MONKEY DO

Scientists are convinced that monkeys have color vision. How did they find that out? They showed monkeys red squares and green squares, always placing the monkeys' food under the red square. Once the monkeys learned where the food was, they always went straight to the red square when hungry, suggesting they can distinguish between red and green.

COLOR YOUR WORLD

TRY THIS!

Paint your room in warm, soothing colors. Or, if your parents and/or budget won't allow you to paint your room 14 times until you find the right mood-altering color, use fabric. It's a great way to completely change the character of a room, create an intimate, exotic feeling, even hide unsightly stains, cracks, and peeling paint. You can get large amounts of fabric relatively inexpensively. And many fabric stores will let you take a bolt or sample home to see how it looks in place.

"It's a good thing that when God created the rainbow, He didn't consult a decorator or He would still be picking colors."
SAM LEVENSON

Wise Highs

FIND OUT MORE

The Complete Color Directory: A Practical Guide to Using Color in Your Home by Alice Westgate (New York: Watson-Guptill, 1999). Advice and guidance on light and texture, how to choose color, what the various colors mean and how they work together, and more. Includes perforated color swatches you can bring with you to the paint store.

Mandalas

"It is looking at things for a long time that ripens you and gives you a deeper understanding."

VINCENT VAN GOGH

Mandalas are circular drawings people use as a visual focus when they meditate. The word "mandala" means "holy circle" in Sanskrit. Mandalas are symbols of the belief that the universe flows outward from a single source of life energy. You can see countless examples of this divine symmetry in snowflakes, spiderwebs, starfish, and flower petals; or in the way a solar system orbits around a sun, or atoms spin around a nucleus.

Virtually every culture embraces the mandala form in its sacred art, religious and ceremonial rituals, and/or symbols of power and protection. The idea is that when you focus on a mandala, you become one with all life, all spirits, all divine energies. Not a bad thing to do on a rainy afternoon.

TRY THIS!

MANDALA MEDITATION

Choose or create a mandala. Visit the library and look through books until you find one that interests you. Or make your own mandala (more about that in a minute).

If you stare at something for 15 minutes a day, you're going to end up on rather intimate terms with it. Therefore, it's important that you *like* your mandala, that it *means* something to you. There aren't any hard-and-fast rules for mandalas. Some patterns are simple; others are complex. You may want to start with a relatively basic one for a few weeks and then try one that is more complicated.

Once you've found your mandala, go to a calm, quiet spot. Sit comfortably with your mandala clearly visible in front of you. (Prop it up on a bookstand or easel, or tape it to a wall.) Relax your eyes and focus on the image. Gently stare at the center of the mandala while letting your consciousness take in the entire pattern. Your mind may drift to your history test and the friend you're mad at and other daily distractions. If this happens, simply bring your consciousness back to the mandala.

After a few minutes of focusing on the center of the circle, let your eyes meander over the entire mandala. After several more minutes, close your eyes. Keep "looking" at the mandala through your "third eye." This "eye," located on your forehead above the bridge of your nose, is supposed to be a portal to consciousness. If you lose "sight" of the mandala, open your eyes to remember the image, then close them again. Focus your "third eye" on the mandala until it *becomes* the mandala, radiating its healing and cleansing power throughout your body.*

Make Your Own Mandala

Think of an image or symbol with special meaning to you. It could be an object, a number, a letter of the alphabet. Or maybe it's a tree or a bird. It might represent something you love or aspire to; a place of particular beauty or serenity.

You can use virtually any medium to create your design: paint, watercolors, ink, pastels, charcoal, crayons, collage, mosaic. Experiment with different colors. If your drawing skills leave something to be desired, you might want to consider a preexisting work of art, illustration, or photograph. For extra protection and portability, frame or laminate your mandala.

Mandalas can be 3D as well. Find an object you like—a beautifully patterned glass paperweight, a pinecone, a pottery vase. Or create your own 3D mandala by arranging leaves, shells, pebbles, crystals, or colored glass into a circular design. You may want to do it on a tray or glue it to a base so you can move it easily.

"Sight is a faculty; seeing is an art."
GEORGE P. MARSH

 **FIND OUT MORE**

Creating Mandalas for Insight, Healing, and Self-Expression by Susanne F. Fincher (Boston: Shambhala Publications, 1991). A practical guide to mandala drawing for personal growth, stress reduction, and creative expression.

Clare Goodwin's Mandala Page
www.abgoodwin.com
Artist Clare Goodwin paints personal mandala portraits and leads workshops on mandalas. Her site includes information on mandalas, a mandala glossary, a mandala of the week, and a terrific collection of links.

* For more about meditation, see Chapter 3: Meditation Highs.

When Seeing Isn't Believing: Visual Illusions

Your eyes tell you that one block is taller than another. Your ruler tells you otherwise. Which is the reality?

Look at a distant tree. If you close your eyes, can you be sure it's still there?

What is real? What you *believe* you see, even if it's false? Or what you *don't* see, even if you believe it to be true?

If what really *is* doesn't appear to be, is it?

Optical illusions play games with reality. To turn some of your assumptions about reality upside down, let's look at a selection of favorites.

Figure 1: Which Is Tallest?

Which of the three blocks is tallest? The one in the back? Actually, all three are exactly the same size. (Go ahead, measure.) It's the perspective of the background that creates the illusion.

> "All that we see
> or dream
> Is but a dream
> within a dream."
> EDGAR ALLAN POE

> "No object is mysterious.
> The mystery is your eye."
> ELIZABETH BOWEN

Figure 2: The Necker Cube

This is an illusion of object reversibility. The cube flip-flops so that one moment, you see the bottom from below; the next, you see the top from above.

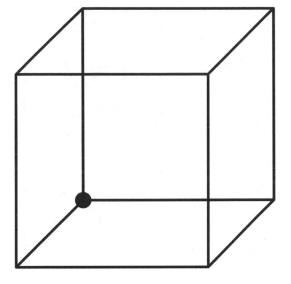

Figure 3: Heads or Goblet?

This is a figure-ground illusion. Do you see a white goblet against a black background? Or two black silhouetted heads against a white background?

121

"The map is not
the territory."
ALFRED KORZBYBSKI

Figure 4: Zöllner Illusion

Which, if any, of the long diagonal lines are parallel? None? Look again. They're all parallel. It's the short cross-hatching that throws off the eye.

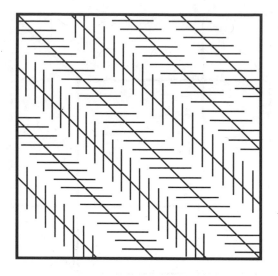

Figure 5: Hermann Grid Illusion

Stare at this grid of black squares. (I know it's not polite to stare, but do it anyway.) As you scan the matrix, do you notice anything going on in the white crosses between the squares? Like dark, circular, fingerprinty smudges at the intersections of the white strips? Most people see these blobules.

"A rose is a rose is a rose."
GERTRUDE STEIN

Figure 6: Lyin' Lines

Which line is longer, the vertical one or the horizontal one? (Nyah, nyah, fooled you.)

"The foolish reject what they see, not what they think; the wise reject what they think, not what they see."
HUANG PO

Figure 7: Find the Pit

Which avocado has the pit? The one on the left? Correct. The one on the right? Also correct. (These are the kind of test questions we like.) The two avocado halves are identical except for their placement on the page. Without your being aware of it, your eyes made an assumption about the direction of the light source, and this determined where you saw the pit. If you turn this page upside down, the pit should "jump" into the other half.

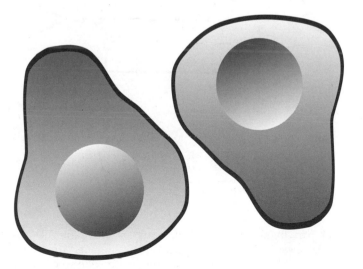

Wise Highs

Figure 8: The Kanizsa Figure

Most people see the edges of the triangle, even though they don't exist. But the notches in the circles create the illusion. Nannies sometimes see the lower disks as babies' prams. Hungry people sometimes see the disks as wheels of Brie cheese.

Figure 9: Müller-Lyer Illusion

Which of the two lines is longer? A, you say? Gotcha. They're equal in length. (And if that's what you said, I bet it's not because they look equal to you, but because you figured they had to be equal or there'd be no illusion.)

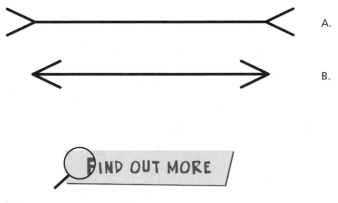

A.

B.

FIND OUT MORE

IllusionWorks
illusionworks.com
Sponsored in part by the Shimojo Laboratory at the California Institute of Technology, this award-winning site bills itself as "the most comprehensive collection of optical and sensory illusions on the world-wide web." Look here for interactive demonstrations, scientific explanations, puzzles, 3D graphics, suggested reading, links, and lots of illusions.

Fascinating Fractals

To put it *very* simply, a fractal is a complex geometric shape that exhibits self-similarity. An identical motif repeats itself over and over again, getting progressively smaller. Any part of a fractal is similar to a larger or smaller part when magnified or reduced.

Fractals are found everywhere in nature. A coastline is a fractal; each bay has smaller bays, and those have even smaller bays, and so on to microscopic levels. A goosedown feather is a fractal; a galaxy of stars is a fractal. Fractal equations have been used to explain all sorts of natural phenomena, from the differentiation of embryonic cells to the way weather travels around the Earth.

Math- and computer-savvy artists have created programs that graph fractal sequences. They use color and animation to create beautiful, hypnotic abstract images. Some people believe that these images can alter consciousness and connect you to the great, mysterious beyond.

> "Vision is the art of seeing things invisible."
> JONATHAN SWIFT

FIND OUT MORE

You can find fractals in books, on videos, as software (CD-ROMs; fractal-generating programs), and on the Internet. Visit your local library or software emporium; do a search for fractals on any search engine, or start with a Web ring.

Fractals Web Rings
www.fractalus.com/ifl
Lots of links to sites with fractals (static and animated), fractal-generating programs you can download (including some freeware), FAQs (Frequently Asked Questions files), and much more. Try not to get lost.

Visual Music

If you've ever been to a planetarium or Laserium show, you've experienced visual music. Colorful images (including fractals and special effects) combine with lush, multi-layered, multi-textured music to create a feast for the eyes and ears.

Other forms of visual music are found in the films *Fantasia*, *Fantasia 2000* (formatted for Imax theaters), and *2001: A Space Odyssey*. Some people think that music videos qualify as visual music; others don't. It probably depends on the video. Those videos

Wise Highs

that use animation, imagery, and special effects come closer to being visual music than those that feature the performers of the songs.

Check out a local show or watch a videotape. Or, if you want, you can listen to music and let your mind create its own images. Jonn Serrie, Steven Halpern, and Constance Demby are just a few composer/performers whose music has accompanied planetarium shows and image-rich videos. Of course, you can listen to any music that paints pictures in your mind. It's best if the music doesn't have words.

If you're online and you love music, you've probably already discovered MP3s—digitized songs you can download to your computer's hard drive and play whenever you want. And you've probably found a free plug-in or two that also lets you see the music. Waves, forms, colors, and other visual effects are controlled by the music and synchronized to the beat. Watching the twisting, twirling, flashing, pulsing, fluid full-screen images is a definite high.

FIND OUT MORE

Illuminations. An award-winning video by Ken Jenkins, with music by Iasos, Constance Demby, Jonn Serrie, and Charles Thaxton. Check your local library or New Age bookstore, or contact Immediate Future Productions, 312A Auburn Street, San Rafael, CA 94901; (415) 485-4491.

MP3 for Dummies by Andy Rathbone (Foster City, CA: IDG Books Worldwide, 2001). Turn your computer into a jukebox or promote your own recordings over the Internet. This friendly guide shows you step-by-step how to find, download, and play MP3 files—and how to upload your songs to MP3 sites.

MP3.com
www.mp3.com
A huge library of songs for desktop DJs, plus links to software sites.

WinAmp
www.winamp.com
Download the popular MP3 player, grab some songs, and find the latest plug-ins including state-of-the-art "eye candy."

Help for Tired Eyes

Sleepy peepers? Distorted vision? Stiff neck? Sounds like you've been spending too much time glued to your computer. Or maybe you've been overdoing some of the activities in this chapter. Either way:

- Close your eyes. Splash your face and closed eyes with cold water. Soak a washcloth in warm water and place it over your eyelids. Alternate the cold and warm treatments.

- Lie down. Close your eyes and place (cool) wet teabags or slices of cucumber over your eyelids. Your eyes will soon become rejuvenated, and you'll have a head start if you wish to have tea and cucumber sandwiches.

Visual Highs

LAZY EIGHTS   TRY THIS!

Try this to reduce eye fatigue and help circulate oxygen north of the neck.

1. Sit up straight in a chair. Keep your feet flat on the floor. Relax your arms and place your hands in your lap. Close your eyes and pretend that your nose is a pencil. (Not that it *looks* like a pencil, that it *is* a pencil.)

2. Move your pencil, er, nose so you "draw" a large figure-8 in the air in front of you. Do this as one smooth, fluid, continuous motion. Repeat three times, then stop in the center of the 8.

3. Now trace the same figure-8 *backwards*. Repeat three times, then stop in the center.

4. Now turn the figure-8 on its side and draw a large version with your nose. Repeat three times, then stop in the center.

5. Draw three more sideways figure-8s, this time smaller.

Repeat steps 2–5 until you feel more relaxed or your head falls off, whichever comes first.

Note: If you want to look like one of those bobbing dachshunds people put on their dashboard, you can trace the number 1.

Wise Highs

"When the sun is shining I can do anything; no mountain is too high, no trouble too difficult to overcome."
WILMA RUDOLPH

Lighten Up

Do gray, rainy days put you in the doldrums? During the winter months, do you sleep more? Do you feel lethargic, depressed, or irritable? Do you lose interest in friends and activities? Binge on sweets and carbohydrates? Gain weight? Have a hard time concentrating?

And then, when spring rolls around, does the old vim-and-vigor reappear? Does your appetite return to normal? Do you shed the weight you gained?

If any of this sounds familiar, you may have SAD: Seasonal Affective Disorder.

The farther north you live from the equator, the greater your chances of experiencing SAD during winter. Why? Because the days are shorter and there's less sunlight during winter. Scientists have discovered that the amount of sunlight that hits the retina of the eye can have a powerful influence on how alert and happy we feel. It all has to do with the effect this light has on the production of chemicals in the brain such as melatonin, serotonin, and dopamine that affect mood, and on our sleep and eating patterns.

Visual Highs

The important thing is that 75 percent of SAD sufferers feel better simply by exposure to a special "light box" for anywhere from a half-hour to a couple of hours a day. The light box consists of fluorescent tubes or incandescent bulbs with a shiny reflector behind them that magnifies the amount of light emitted. So you can read or work while getting your therapy, the lights come in several different models, ranging from a "desk lamp" style to a visor you wear and can walk around in. (That'll get you a few stares on the subway.) You can get light boxes through mail order companies that advertise in natural health or alternative medicine publications. Your local natural foods store would also be a good resource.

Most SAD sufferers report that their symptoms go away within 2–14 days after beginning their therapy. While the lights appear to be safe and, unlike the sun, don't emit any harmful rays, some people may experience headaches, eyestrain, or trouble sleeping. These side effects are usually alleviated by shortening exposure time or sitting farther away from the lights.

CAUTION!!! Because certain medications can heighten sensitivity to light, and some people are hypersensitive to light, always check with your doctor before beginning light therapy. He or she can also advise you on other treatments for depression such as medication, aerobic exercise, stress management, and diet.

FIND OUT MORE

Winter Blues: Everything You Need to Know to Beat Seasonal Affective Disorder by Norman E. Rosenthal, M.D. (New York: Guilford Press, 2005). The author led the team of researchers that first described SAD. This book has a self-test to check your own seasonal mood swings, advice, coping tips, and resources. It covers the basic winter blues, too. You don't have to have full-blown SAD to read it.

The Society for Light Treatment and Biological Rhythms
www.sltbr.org
Information on SAD, jet lag, sleep disorders, nonseasonal depression, and other conditions, plus treatments including light therapy.

Chapter

7

Coming to Your Senses

Sensuous Highs

"There is no way in which to understand the world without first detecting it through the radar-net of our senses."

DIANE ACKERMAN

We tend to think of the senses as *receptors*. But they are also our most vital *expressors*. Our eyes not only take in visual messages but also convey our deepest emotions; they are windows to our soul for anyone looking in. We hear through our ears—but in listening to others, we extend support and comfort. We experience the physical world through touch—yet, with the tiniest of gestures, *our* touch conveys affection, pride, compassion, or anger. Our mouths and tongues serve as taste receptors—and as transmitters of wisdom, solace, and corny jokes. Our nose allows us to inhale the awesome array of odors in the world—and it is through our noses that we expel millions of mucous molecules into the air, thus grossing people out. (Oh, all right, so the analogy falls down a bit when it comes to smell.)

Our senses provide us with some of the greatest highs a person can experience: viewing a sunset over the ocean, tasting a delectable gourmet meal, listening to an inspiring piece of music, inhaling the sweet fragrance of a flower, touching someone we love. So...come to your senses.

Cats Know Where It's At

Sensuous Highs

Cats are sensuous critters. They love to be stroked. Their senses of hearing, sight, and smell are very sharp. This allows them to distinguish between different people's footsteps, to see in the dark, and to detect if their owner has been unfaithful by consorting with other cats.

Wouldn't you love to be a cat? Here's an exercise that will increase your sensitivity to your own senses.

THE CAT'S MEOW — TRY THIS!

1. Place some pillows or cushions on the floor. Curl up on them as if you were a cat. "Go to sleep" by closing your eyes. Inhale slowly and deeply.

2. Become aware of *touch*. Feel the heaviness of your body. Feel the cushions. Notice which parts of your body you are most aware of.

3. Become aware of *sound*. Concentrate on opening your ears. Listen for sounds you might not otherwise have noticed. Do you hear more than you thought you would?

4. Become aware of *smell*. Breathe deeply. How many odors and fragrances do you smell?

5. Become aware of *sight*. Open your eyes. What do you see? If you're curled up on the floor, you're looking at the world sideways and from a low perspective. Do you see things you never noticed before?

6. Now roll over onto your knees. Keep them tight to your chest, your head and shoulders low to the ground, like a cat ready to pounce.

7. Straighten your arms and rock forward until you are on all fours.

8. Arch your back toward the ceiling—like a cat that has its dander up.

9. Now make a reverse arch, lowering your back as close to the floor as you can get it.

10. Slowly return to a sitting position. Take in the world before getting up. Try not to purr.

> "The mind is like a richly woven tapestry in which the colors are distilled from the experiences of the senses, and the design drawn from the convolutions of the intellect."
>
> CARSON MCCULLERS

> "Nothing can cure the soul but the senses, just as nothing can cure the senses but the soul."
>
> OSCAR WILDE

Wise Highs

"There are strange flowers of reason to match each error of the senses."

LOUIS ARAGON

Another way to appreciate and refresh your sensory awareness is to deprive yourself of one or more of your senses.*

- **Blindfold yourself** so all light and vision are blocked. Spend at least an hour blindfolded. How does this affect your other senses? Do they become more acute? Are you more aware of sounds, smells, or textures? *Important:* Unless you're doing this in a safe and familiar space (such as your bedroom), be sure you have a friend with you at all times who can act as a "lookout."

- **Wear mittens for a day.** This will distort and constrain your sense of touch. In addition, it will show you how essential your fingers and hands are to nearly every task you perform.

- **Screen out all sound.** This is almost impossible to do unless you happen to have access to a soundproofed chamber. But you can alter your perception of sound by wearing earplugs, headphones, and a couple of knit caps that roll down over your ears. Of course, you'll look like a dork, but it's all in the interest of science. (You can also dip your ears underwater next time you take a bath or are in a swimming pool.) With your sense of sound distorted, are your other senses altered? If you tickle yourself, does it feel different?

The Power of Touch

"Touch is the meaning of being human."

ANDREA DWORKIN

Babies usually stop crying within seconds of being picked up. Toddlers crawl into their parents' bed for cuddling. Kindergartners feel grown-up when they go for a walk and hold Mommy's hand. Dad's arm around your shoulder makes you feel proud and secure.

Kids instinctively sense the language and emotional benefits of touching and being touched. But by the time they become teenagers, many of them have lost touch with being touched. They don't give or get as many hugs and kisses as when they were small. Boys especially may internalize messages from society that say "real men don't touch."

---

* For more on deprivation, see pages 166–168.

Getting out of touch with touch can be hazardous to your physical and emotional health. In fact, researchers have found that people with pets have fewer stress-related diseases than petless people. This may very well be due to the relaxation and sensuous comfort derived from nuzzling and petting an animal.

Bring touch back into your life. I'm not suggesting that you start stroking people on the subway. Rather, become aware of the role of touch in your relationships. Is your family physically affectionate? Do you hug or kiss your friends? If you're a boy, do you have to engage in stealth touching with your friends (such as backslaps and noogies) rather than giving and getting genuine hugs and handshakes?

In many cultures, teenagers of both genders routinely greet their friends (of both genders) with hugs and kisses. They walk arm-in-arm. In America, touch has become so sexualized that we tend to repress our instinctive need for physical connection. Don't let America's juvenile attitudes towards touching and sensuality inhibit your enjoyment and expression of this sense.

Sensuous Highs

TOUCHING FACTS

Psychologist Sidney Jourard compared the frequency with which couples in different countries touch each other. He observed them in cafés and found the highest rates in Puerto Rico (180 times per hour) and Paris (110 times per hour). In contrast, couples in the United States touch each other only *two times* per hour. Jourard also discovered that French parents and children touch each other three times more often than American parents and children.

KISSING PALMS

TRY THIS!

Try this with a family member or close friend.

1. Sit opposite each other.

2. Make a "palmist's kiss." Hold up your hands and press your right palm to your partner's left palm. Press your left palm to his or her right palm.

3. Close your eyes. Picture the warm, positive, life-affirming energy flowing between your palms, flooding through your bodies, cleansing you of all fear.

4. Interlock your fingers and squeeze. You'll experience an intense feeling of warmth, safety and emotional closeness.

5. Open your eyes and marvel at how such a simple moment of contact can produce such a rush of intimacy and unspoken communication.

"A light, tender, sensitive touch is worth a ton of brawn."
PETER THOMSON

133

Wise Highs

WHY DO PEOPLE CLOSE THEIR EYES WHEN THEY KISS?

No doubt you have spent a considerable amount of time pondering this question—perhaps even while kissing someone. In his book, *What Are Hyenas Laughing At, Anyway?* David Feldman presents answers readers sent in when he posed this puzzling question. Here are a few theories:

1. The Intensify-the-Pleasure-by-Screening-Out-Distractions Theory. Kissing is not a visual activity. Rather, it engages our senses of touch, taste, and sound. Closing one's eyes during a kiss intensifies the pleasure by blocking out extraneous visual distractions such as trash cans, dust mites, or passing cars. This theory is supported by the fact that people close their eyes when receiving a massage. Many individuals also shut their oculi when listening to music or savoring a delicacy to heighten the sensations of sound and taste.

2. The Cross-Eyed Theory. This hypothesis is based on two assumptions:

    a. Looking at someone from a distance of a quarter-inch is disconcerting; a gorgeous lover will mutate into a Cyclops or deranged beast. (Or, to put it another way, staring at the zit on someone's forehead is a sure way to spoil a romantic moment.)

    b. The distance between a pair of kissers is too close for comfort. The eye cannot focus without straining itself.

3. The I'm-Kissing-You-but-Thinking-of-Someone-Else Theory. Sometimes there's a gap between reality and fantasy. According to this theory, we close our eyes when kissing so we can better imagine the person of our dreams... while kissing the person in our arms.

My own belief is that there is some truth to all of these theories. But I could be wrong. I'd better go do some research.

Here's the Rub: Massage

Massage is one of life's greatest pleasures. We tend to think of massage in terms of its effects on the body—releasing tension, reducing soreness, relaxing muscles. But it also works on the mind and spirit.

When we give or receive a massage, we establish a communication of caring with another human being. If we're the giver, our concentration and consideration fill us with positive energy, a calm sense of well-being, and the satisfaction that we're causing another human being to purr with pleasure. If we're the receiver, we feel accepted, valued, and kneaded.

Many teens cite massage as a means of reducing stress and zoning out from reality. They do it with friends, siblings, family members, or boyfriends/girlfriends. The great thing about giving and receiving massages is that it's free, you don't need any special equipment, and you can do it almost anywhere.

Of course, here's where some of you will run up against your own and/or society's inhibitions. I admit that inviting your mates on the football team over for an afternoon of massage may raise some eyebrows. And you may not know anyone you'd feel comfortable exchanging massages with. Time and new relationships may open up possibilities for you.

Or get a professional massage. Look in the Yellow Pages under Massage—Therapeutic. Also, many cities have institutes of massage therapy, where people learn to become expert masseurs or masseuses. These schools often offer massages at bargain rates (as low as $10–$15 an hour) if you're willing to be massaged by students. Don't worry; by the time they're permitted to practice on the general public, they're already pretty good.

There are many different types of massage. Here are a few examples:

Sensuous Highs

Swedish massage is what most people picture when they hear the word "massage": paws of steel rubbing, kneading, and pressing the muscles of some oil-coated, towel-clad guinea pig. One of the primary purposes of Swedish massage is to enhance circulation. While the heart pumps blood to the body's extremities, the blood returns to the heart by muscle action. Therefore—and this is today's anatomy lesson—having your muscles rubbed in the direction of blood flowing to the heart is good for your circulation. Since the lymph system also relies on muscle action, Swedish massage stimulates the body's ability to eliminate various acids and metabolic wastes. By relaxing nerves and stretching ligaments and tendons, this form of massage is often recommended for stress reduction.

> ## HEALING TOUCH
>
> Hundreds of studies show the importance of touch. In one, premature babies who were massaged three times a day for ten days gained weight 47 percent faster and left the hospital six days sooner than preemies who weren't given massages. Other studies show the value of massage in treating such conditions as asthma, depression, stress, cancer, bulimia, diabetes, and heart disease.

Shiatsu ("finger pressure") is a Japanese form of massage designed to open the flow of *chi* in the body's meridians. Chinese and Japanese medicine are based on the belief that there are 12 main meridians (energy channels) in the body. You may have heard of two: *yin* and *yang*. Each meridian relates to different organs and functions in the body. The energy flowing between these meridians is known as *chi*.

When *chi* flows easily, we feel relaxed and balanced. But when *chi* is blocked, we suffer from mental, emotional, or physical disorders.

Reflexology and **acupressure** are based on the belief that the body contains points that are related (via meridians) to other parts of the body. (Acupressure uses the same points and meridians as acupuncture; you're just using fingers instead of needles.) Manipulation of these points affects the corresponding organ or function and can reduce stress, relieve pain and minor ailments, eliminate toxins, and improve circulation.

Other types of massage include myotherapy, polarity therapy, myofascial release, craniosacral therapy, Reiki, Trager Psychophysical Integration, Hakomi, Jin Shin Do, Pfrimmer deep muscle therapy, Alexander Technique, and the Feldenkrais Method.

Aromatherapy is often combined with massage.* The application of fragrant oils to the body allows the masseur to apply more pressure. Proponents of aromatherapy claim that the various scents have therapeutic value themselves. At the very least, pleasantly scented oils are a good defense against masseurs with B.O.

> "Touch is the landscape of what is possible."
>
> KATE GREEN

GIVE A BACK MASSAGE

First, you'll need a quiet, soothing space for the massage. Keep the lighting low. Make sure the room is at a comfortable temperature— not too hot or cold.

Since it's unlikely that you'll have a massage table lying about (ironing boards are *not* good substitutes), have the victim, er, the person getting the massage lie face down on a bed or the floor. If you use a bed, make sure it's not too squishy. If you use the floor, soften it with some blankets or a camping mattress.

Put some massage oil in your hands. You may want to microwave it briefly before you begin to warm it up. (If the person has a shirt on, forget the oil.)

If you're wondering why you're the massag-er instead of the massag-ee, remember that 'tis better to give than to receive. Now we may begin with the proper attitude.

> "We are what we are, the spirit afterwards, but first the touch."
>
> CHARLOTTE MEW

---

* For more about aromatherapy, see page 142.

1. Place your paws on each side of your partner's spine at waist level. Gently move them up the back without pressing on the spine. Separate your hands and sweep them across the shoulders. Send them southward down your partner's sides and return them to the base of the spine. Repeat 5 times.

Note: Be alert to physical and auditory cues from your massage partner: Shrieks mean your hands are cold; twitches and uncontrollable laughter mean he/she is ticklish; moans mean he/she either loves what you're doing or has a stomachache.

2. Place your thumbs on each side of the base of your partner's spine. No, you're not going to hitchhike up his/her back, you're going to make gentle circles with the tips of your thumbs. Pressing lightly, let your thumbs do the walking as they climb the spine. When you reach the shoulders, sweep your hands back down to your partner's waist. Repeat 3 times.

3. Now concentrate on your partner's shoulders. Place your hands over the shoulder muscles. Push up with the balls of your hands while clenching the flesh with your fingers. Pretend that you're kneading pizza dough. Repeat 10 times.

Note: If your partner's muscles are tense, he/she may say "OUCH!!!" This is a signal that you should lighten up.

4. Conclude the rubdown with 5 10 spinal sweeps as described in step 1.

5. Ignore your partner's pleas to please don't stop.

There are many excellent books and videos that will teach you how to give a massage. (No instruction is necessary for receiving one.) The best thing to do is go to a library or bookstore and check them out for yourself. Since they cover the entire body, and some of the drawings or photos are of *uncovered* individuals, these books/videos range from PG to R. I hesitate to recommend any one in particular, since I don't want to get letters from outraged adults scolding me for suggesting that teenagers buy a book with somebody's naked butt in it.

Natural Healers
www.naturalhealers.com
This educational resource lets you search by state to find a massage therapy school near you.

Sensuous Highs

"When one is out of touch with oneself, one cannot touch others."
ANNE MORROW LINDBERGH

"If you push hard on the world, the world pushes back on you. If you touch the world gently, the world will touch you gently in return."
PAUL G. HEWITT

Wise Highs

Reflexology is an ancient healing art that combines massage and pressure to relieve stress and treat various types of illness. Reflexologists believe that certain spots on the feet and hands correspond to other parts of the body. For example, massaging the big toes benefits the head; massaging the heels benefits the lower back; massaging the whole foot has a soothing, relaxing effect on the entire body.

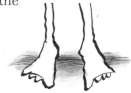

To experience reflexology, you'll want to visit a professionally trained and qualified practitioner. Meanwhile, you can treat your feet to a do-it-yourself massage.

1. Wash your feet in warm, soapy water. Dry them thoroughly (don't miss between your toes).

2. Work a small amount of lotion or cream into your hands. (Peppermint foot cream is especially nice.)

3. Firmly massage your feet. Start at your toe tips, work the joints, then gradually inch your way up (tops, bottoms, sides). Massage your ankles and, if you want, your calf muscles.

Take your time. You might play some soothing, relaxing music and dim the lights a little. See if you feel less stressed when you're through. Your feet will thank you.

GET ROLFED

Rolfing (not to be confused with ralphing) was developed in the 1950s by Ida Rolf. This form of massage is based on the belief that our muscles retain memories of stressful events in our lives. Thus, our bodies reflect the emotional and physical hurts and traumas we suffered as children. These "memories" can cause present-day pain, discomfort, and illness.

Rolfers work on muscles and tissues deep in your body, taking up to 10 one-hour sessions to stretch and restore your muscles to their proper state. Because Rolfing "massages" long-buried feelings such as guilt, hurt, rejection, or fear, the process can be intensely emotional. But the high comes when you experience not only physical relief, but also the lifting of heavy emotional and spiritual burdens you may not have even realized you were shouldering.

FIND OUT MORE

Sensuous Highs

The Rolf Institute of Structural Integration
5055 Chaparral Court, Suite 103 • Boulder, CO 80301
1-800-530-8875 • www.rolf.org
Visit the Web site to learn the history of Rolfing, how to find a Rolfer or Rolfing workshop, and more.

Taste

For teens on the go, food is something you gulp when you pull in for a pit stop. And eating is something you do while watching TV, reading, or working on your homework. But throughout history, the experience of eating and savoring food has been one of the most primal, sensuous rituals known to humankind. I mean, can you imagine anything more mouthwatering than a radish melting on your tongue?

All the tastes you love and all the ones you don't are made up of four fundamental qualities your tongue detects: *sweet, sour, bitter,* and *salty.* But your sense of flavor in food depends on more than your tongue. Your senses of smell and sight also influence the way foods taste to you. Don't believe it? Try eating your favorite food while holding your nose. Or add green food coloring to your scrambled eggs. Gross!

Food can be so much more than just fuel if you pay attention to the tastes, textures, and smells of what you eat.

"Eating is heaven."
KOREAN PROVERB

"The cherry tomato is a wonderful invention, producing, as it does, a satisfactory explosive squish when bitten."
MISS MANNERS

GO S-L-O-W

TRY THIS!

No, you don't have to chew every bite 1,000 times. But at least a few times a week, try to slow down and really *experience* the sensation of taste. If you go out to a fine restaurant, pay attention to the varied and different tastes in each dish. Certain recipes treat your taste buds to a multi-layered trip of many distinct flavors. Eat slowly. Chew thoughtfully. Savor every bite.*

"Noodles are not only amusing but delicious."
JULIA CHILD

---

* See also "Lento Alimento" on page 95.

Wise Highs

Nutty Variation

Next time you eat a peanut M&M, see how long you can draw out the experience. Let the candy coating s-l-o-w-l-y melt in your mouth (not in your hand). Caress the chocolate with your tongue. Linger over its sweet succulence. How long can you hold out before you bite into the peanut? Let your lingua loiter on its salty, hard surface. When you finally crack the nut, don't swallow it right away. Instead, grind it down into tiny pieces until it's just one squishy gob of peanut gloop. Yummy!

QUIET DIET

Eat a meal with another person or a group of friends *without* talking. See how this changes the experience. Are you more aware of the sounds of eating? The taste? The feel?

Gourmet Variations

- Close your eyes for part of the meal.
- Eat the entire meal with your hands.
- Have participants feed each other.
- Pick one item, like mashed potatoes or ice cream, to eat without hands or utensils. (Check that no adults are in sight.)

Let's Sweat

We all know that the main reason people sweat is to support the deodorant manufacturing industry. But sweating also helps to purify and regulate the body. Perspiration evaporating on the skin cools the body in hot weather. Sweating also eliminates unwanted chemicals, drugs, and toxins. This saves wear and tear on the liver and kidneys. Excess sodium, for example, is eliminated through sweat, which is why perspiration tastes so salty when you lick your armpit.

Sweat bathing is a popular and important ritual in many cultures. Many Native American tribes use sweat lodges as part of their religious and spiritual traditions. In Finland, the *sauna* (which means "sweat like a pig" in Finnish) is a widely practiced social activity. While we think of sauna-taking as a recreational pastime, the Finns hold the custom in reverence. This stems from ancient beliefs that fire is holy and should be worshipped.

There are two types of heat: wet and dry. You can experiment and see which you like best.

Sensuous Highs

For wet heat, get thee to a steam room. Because steam is more efficient than air in conducting heat to your body, you would feel very, very hot in a 115°F (47°C) steam room. In a sauna, however, where the humidity is much lower, you would be able to stand temperatures as high as 210°F (98°C).

In America, saunas are usually wood-paneled rooms with an electric stove. This creates a very dry heat. In authentic Finnish saunas, the heat comes from a real wood fire in a stove. Rocks on the stove are sprinkled with water to produce steam. This low-tech but highly effective system allows you to alternate between wet and dry heat. At the conclusion of their sauna, the Finns take a nice, refreshing plunge into cold water. *Brrrrrrr!*

CAUTION!!! Because sweat bathing can have a dramatic effect on cardiovascular function, people with heart or circulatory conditions should always consult their doctor before taking a steam bath or sauna.

Tips: For your first roasting, start gently. You may feel like a boiled lobster, but don't worry; your blood is *not* going to boil. In fact, your internal temperature rises only slightly. It's your skin temperature that soars. Over time, you'll be able to enjoy hotter temperatures for longer periods. Be sure to drink a lot of water before and after you enter so you don't get dehydrated. If possible, conclude with a cold shower or dip.

The sensuous pleasure you experience while body baking is ample reward for taking a sweat bath. Turning yourself into toast will also reduce tension, relax muscles, soothe your soul, help you sleep, and keep you tingling all day.

DID YOU KNOW?

In extreme heat or strenuous physical activity, a person may sweat up to four liters of fluid in an hour.

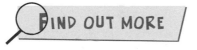

FIND OUT MORE

Sweat
www.cyberbohemia.com
Mikkel Aaland spent three years traveling the world, researching and enjoying Finnish saunas, Russian banias, Turkish hammans, and American Indian sweatlodges. His Web site contains lengthy excerpts from his fascinating book, *Sweat* (Santa Barbara, CA: Capra Press, 1978).

Aromatherapy

People use essential oils to relax, boost energy, reduce anxiety, improve sleep, prevent colds, and heal insect bites. These oils come from various plants, fruits, and herbs. When inhaled, they act on the brain and nervous system by stimulating the olfactory nerves. Oils can also be added to bathwater, burned, and massaged into the skin. Studies suggest that the active ingredients of oils, when applied directly to the body, are absorbed into tissues and the bloodstream.

For example, oil of lavender shows up in the urine of guinea pigs within an hour of being massaged into their skin. (It is unclear whether the pigs received Swedish or Shiatsu massages.)

There are many different types of essential oils: eucalyptus, myrrh, peppermint, cedarwood, frankincense, basil, chamomile, jasmine, patchouli (which sounds like a sneeze), rosemary, camphor, juniper, hyssop, melissa, neroli, ylang ylang, and 10W-40. Only the last is recommended for cars. Oils aren't cheap, because they must be 100 percent pure and free of additives like Cancer-Producing Red Dye #4791328. But a little drop'll dew ya, so you can probably fit it into your self-care budget.

Tip: Try before you buy. Visit your local health care store, natural foods store, co-op, or bath and body store and check out the samples. For starters, it's believed that rosemary aids concentration, peppermint has a positive effect on mental energy, and lavender can help you relax and unwind. You can also create your own blended fragrances.

BEST SMELLERS

The male silkworm moth, which is only an inch long, can detect the scent of a female moth up to 6.8 miles away. If you translate that into human dimensions, it would be the same as a six-foot-tall man smelling his girlfriend's perfume at a distance of nearly 500 miles!

"The sense of smell has the strongest memory of all the senses."

JANE SEYMOUR

FIND OUT MORE

The Complete Book of Essential Oils and Aromatherapy: Over 600 Natural, Non-Toxic and Fragrant Recipes to Create Health, Beauty, and a Safe Home Environment by Valerie Ann Worwood (Novato, CA: New World Library, 1991). Describes how to use these ancient oils for physical, mental, and environmental health; contains more than 500 recipes for using essential oils instead of commercial health, beauty, and cleaning products (which are often toxic). Other books by the author include *The Fragrant Mind, The Fragrant Pharmacy, The Fragrant Heavens, Seasons of Aromatherapy, Aromatherapy for the Healthy Child,* and *Scents and Scentuality.* I couldn't tell you whether these are "scratch 'n' sniff" books.

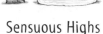

GET INCENSED

Sensuous Highs

Incense was the earliest form of "perfume." To give your room an exotic, mood-altering ambience, burn some incense. It comes in all sorts of "flavors," from fruity to woodsy, spicy to garden-y. Be sure to use an incense holder so the ashes have someplace to fall and the glowing tip won't burn anything.

Pamper Yourself

Once upon a time, people (usually women) went to spas to lose weight. Today people go to spas for all kinds of reasons—to relax, slow down, be treated like royalty, start exercising, eat better, make lifestyle changes, or just try something new (like being covered from head to toe in green algae paste). Chances are you can't afford a week at a spa in Switzerland or even an afternoon at a local day spa. But that doesn't mean you can't pamper yourself.

GIVE YOURSELF A FACIAL

Pure, sybaritic luxury to enjoy at home or a friend's house, facials are also perfect slumber party activities. Here's what you'll need to give your face a relaxing, invigorating high:

- boiling water
- dried herbs or rose petals
- a large bowl or basin
- clean towels
- 1 cup cornmeal
- 1/4 cup honey
- a small mixing bowl and spoon
- a facial mask that matches your skin type (you can buy these in drugstores and at cosmetics counters)
- two cucumber slices (chilled, please)

Here's what to do:

1. Secure your hair so it doesn't fall all over your face.

2. Pour a quart of boiling water into a large bowl or basin. Toss in some rose petals or fragrant dried herbs. *Don't stick your head in the boiling water!*

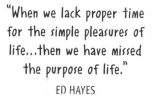

"When we lack proper time for the simple pleasures of life...then we have missed the purpose of life."
ED HAYES

Wise Highs

3. Create a tent by draping a towel over your head. Bend over the basin and steam your face for 10 minutes.

4. Mix a cup of cornmeal with a quarter cup of honey. You'll get an oatmeal-like paste.

5. Apply the mixture to your face. Continue stroking it over your face for 5 minutes, as if giving your skin a gentle rubdown. *Don't get any in your eyes.*

6. Rinse your face and pat it dry with a towel.

7. Apply the facial mask, following the package directions.

8. Lie down on a bed or sit in a comfy chair. Place a chilled cucumber slice on each of your closed eyelids. Relax for 15–20 minutes, or however long the mask directions say. Ignore any obnoxious remarks from siblings who want to know what you're doing.

9. Rinse your face with lukewarm water and pat it until it's nearly dry.

10. Apply your favorite moisturizer.

 ## A HAIR-RAISING EXPERIENCE

It's easy to forget, as you go about your busy life, that your locks may feel neglected and taken for granted. When's the last time you said "Thank you, hair, for being on my head"? Hair likes to get high, too. Treat your tresses to a super conditioning and get a contact high in the process. Here what you'll need:

- olive oil
- essential oil
- large plastic bag
- shampoo
- a towel or two

1. Douse your mane. Dry it gently with a towel until it's damp but not dripping.

2. Pour 1 (if you have short hair) to 3 (long hair) teaspoons of olive oil into your hand. Mix in a few drops of essential oil (lavender or jasmine are good for relaxing; peppermint or eucalyptus will give you energy).

3. Work the mixture of oils into your hair and scalp.

4. Massage your scalp by moving your fingertips in small circles. Work your way from your forehead to the back of your neck. Take your time; you should spend from 3–5 minutes doing this.

5. Place a plastic bag over your hair.* Wrap a towel around it.

6. Now relax. Chill. Veg out. Do nothing. Practice deep breathing.** Have a cup of herbal tea.

7. After 20 minutes, shampoo your hair thoroughly until it no longer looks like seaweed in salad dressing. Rinse, rinse, rinse 'til it's squeaky clean.

Sensuous Highs

Natural Home Spa by Sian Rees (New York: Sterling Publications, 1999). Do-it-yourself relaxation therapies, massages, pick-me-ups, and recipes for masks, moisturizers, conditioners, toners, and more.

About.com Spas
spas.about.com
Lots of information and links from the helpful human guides at about.com.

"It isn't the great big pleasures that count the most, it's making a great deal out of the little ones."

JEAN WEBSTER

GET NAKED

TRY THIS!

If God hadn't meant us to be naked, we'd all be born wearing khakis. Children under five are natural nudists. But birthday suits don't fit every occasion. So, in the interests of culture ("Nobody goes to church naked, dear"), etiquette ("Grandpa's more comfortable when you're dressed"), or practicality ("You might get splinters in your behind"), we come to be clothed from an early age.

Since we're so used to wearing clothes, you can get quite a sensuous high simply by taking them off. Of course, this is where that old saying "There's a time and a place for everything" applies. Nudity is not appreciated at the mall or the skating rink. But if you can get buck naked at the right time in the right place, go for it. Skinny-dip in a lake or ocean at night. Stand outside in the rain. Run through a field. Lie out in the sun. Walk around your room in the buff. Doff the duds and experience the freedom and novelty of the unattired life.

---

* That's *hair,* not head. Placing a plastic bag over your head will cause you to suffocate. Please do not make this mistake, since I don't want to receive nasty letters from parents of suffocated readers.
** See Chapter 2: Breathing Highs.

Chapter
8

Blue Skies, Cow Pies
Nature Highs

Do you remember when you were a little kid and a patch of soil kept you entertained for hours? Can you recall fields of fireflies on hot summer nights? Thunderstorms that took you beyond terror? Did you ever float with the clouds on a windy fall day? Dance through leaves? Tumble down hills? Burrow into snowdrifts? Chase butterflies until you collapsed dizzy on the warm earth, your head spinning; earth, sky, body, soul—all boundaries erased?

Now that you're older, when's the last time you watched a sunset? (It doesn't count if you were stuck in a traffic jam.) Or fell asleep to the lapping of waves?

Have you ever gazed upon the world from the top of a mountain? Or hiked deep into a canyon gorge?

Do you ever wake up to the sounds of birds—and that's *all* you can hear?

How often does the wind rush through your soul?

Those of you who live in Outer Boondockia or other places of natural beauty know all about nature's highs. You probably listen to the caw of a seagull or the whisper of a breeze and think *Man, what I wouldn't give for a weekend in the city!*

But if you live in the city or suburbs, you may feel cut off from nature. If you hear birds singing, it's over the din of honking horns and banging trash cans. If you see lightning in the sky, it's against a backdrop of skyscrapers, billboards, and neon signs. And even if you

> "Nature has been for me, for as long as I remember, a source of solace, inspiration, adventure, and delight; a home, a teacher, a companion."
> LORRAINE ANDERSON

live in the country, you may be so busy racing from home to school to sports to band to chores to the mall to the library to friends' houses that if you do notice the full moon, it's from the bus coming back from an away game.

Nature Highs

Why Nature?

Human beings need nature. We *are* nature. Nature reminds us of our place in the universe—that we came from the *garden* of Eden, not the *shopping mall* of Eden. Nature keeps us humble and puts things in perspective. Silly worries, petty grudges, and materialistic cravings become insignificant in the face of nature's mysteries and magnificence. Inhale the sweet fragrance of spring and try to stay angry at the person who dumped your books. Listen to the roar of a million-year-old waterfall and ask yourself if the zit on your nose really matters.

When you commune with nature, you become aware of the vastness and inexplicability of the cosmos. You reconnect with the primordial ooze from which we all came. You return to your roots, to your childhood.

Ah, wilderness. Purple mountain majesty. Fire-breathing sunsets. Ants crawling up your pants.

There's nothing quite like lying under the stars in a sleeping bag. As the campfire spits orange confetti into the night and the crisp mountain air fills your lungs, you lie awake wondering *Is that couple in the Winnebago ever going to turn off the TV?!?!?*

My definition of nature does not include mobile hotel rooms with bumper stickers saying "We're spending our children's inheritance." Nor does it include satellite dishes, air conditioning, ATVs, SUVs, or VCRs. If you can't leave technology behind, go camp out in a shopping center parking lot.

> "Health comes from learning to live in vibrant harmony with ourselves, with the natural world, and with one another."
> JOHN ROBBINS

THE BUZZ ON MOSQUITOES

To me, nature can best be summed up in two words: *mosquito repellent.* Which brings us to the question that has plagued nature lovers since the dawn of Sterno cans: "How come mosquitoes bite some people more than others?"

Scientists have given this question a lot of thought. After careful research, they concluded "Who knows?"

Actually, it seems to have to do with smell. Yours. Everybody has a different smell, depending on the soaps, perfumes, or deodorants they use, their body chemistry, and what they ate for lunch. Mosquitoes have a very good sense of smell. (This was determined by a study in which scientists asked blind-folded mosquitoes to identify 18 different items by smell—e.g., anchovies, rose petals, gorgonzola cheese.) They can detect differences in human odors and clearly prefer some over others. People who get bitten more than their fair share are more odorifically attractive to mosquitoes. Since insect repellents work by either masking attractive odors or generating repulsive ones, further research into the aromatic likes and dislikes of mosquitoes will allow scientists to create better insect repellents.

But until this happens, if your boyfriend or girlfriend should ask "Why do the mosquitoes always go after *me?*" the correct response is "Because you're so sweet."

"I like to take my dog for a walk, because it makes me happy to be outside."
STROLLING STUDENT

"I like to go outside on my back porch, watch the sunset, and just think about my life."
MELLOW STUDENT

THE SURVEY SAYS...

We asked teenagers "How do you relieve stress, have fun, escape reality, and/or get high without alcohol or other drugs?" Many turn to nature. Here are some of the things they do:*

look at the sky
watch clouds
watch the sun rise
watch a sunset
gaze at the stars
get fresh air
birdwatch
smell flowers
sit by the ocean
listen to the rain
sing in the rain
walk through puddles
sit outside on the front porch
    and listen to a heavy storm
hike in the woods
go to the beach

go horseback riding
go camping
go tubing
go up in a hot air balloon
climb trees
have a friendly snowball fight
stand on top of a mountain
lie on a raft in a lake
float in a pool
sunbathe
be alone in nature

* From a survey of 2,000 students ages 11–18.

STOP AND SMELL THE ROSES

TRY THIS!

Try not to rush through the day without checking up on nature. Even if you live in the city, try to sit on a bench for a couple of minutes and watch some clouds. Listen for birds. Sit in a park. Admire a flower bed. (And please leave the flowers in it.) Rub some petals between your fingers. Sniff. Speaking of sniffing, inhale a deep breath of crisp winter air. Smell spring. Breathe in freshly cut grass. *Ahhhh-choooo.* Go outside at night and look for the moon.

TAKE A HIKE

TRY THIS!

Whether you embark on a marathon trek from Maine to Georgia, stroll through the majestic redwoods of Marin County's Muir Woods, or take a quick walk around a pond, a hike in the woods will put you in an alternative world where you can be alone with your thoughts. And if you get lonely, you can always chat up a squirrel.

FIND OUT MORE

Hiking and Backpacking: A Trailside Guide by Karen Berger (New York: W.W. Norton & Company, 2003). A great book full of practical tips on gear, first aid, planning, camping, food selection, finding your way, and not leaving a trail of litter in your wake.

American Hiking Society
www.americanhiking.org
An organization dedicated to protecting America's hiking trails. The Web site includes a "Trail Finder" to help you find trails in your area.

TRUE HIGHS
Chatahoochee Challenge

by Carter Coe, 17

One way to get a rush without using drugs is by experiencing nature and the great outdoors. I mountain bike, hike, and off-road. These activities are fun and exhilarating. I live in Atlanta, which is not a very outdoorsy city, but there are many wonderful opportunities for

Nature Highs

"We will have to give up taking things for granted, even the apparently simple things."
J.D. BERNAL

"Hiking through the Appalachian Mountains makes me feel at peace."
HIGH SCHOOL HIKER

Wise Highs

me around the Chatahoochee River. I can experience great mountain biking and beautiful hiking trails. I also off-road in my 1989 Jeep Cherokee. This can become a very expensive hobby, but it is very enjoyable for thrill-seekers. All three of these activities bring me heart-pounding excitement and they are not damaging to my health. It's amazing the beauty you can find in our world while mountain biking, hiking, or off-roading.

SLEEP UNDER THE STARS

Don't forget to count 'em. If you see a falling star, chase it to the wall at the edge of the universe—and climb over.

Bonus: Depending on where you live, what time of year it is, and other factors beyond your control, you might luck out and see the Northern Lights (a.k.a. aurora borealis). They have a scientific explanation (something about the interaction of electrons and protons, solar activity, and the Earth's magnetic poles), but you won't care if you happen to catch these magical dancing lights. Shimmering and flashing across the sky in arcs, folds, waves, and luminous curtains, touched with red, purple, and green, they'll take your breath away.

> "No sight is more provocative of awe than is the night sky."
> LLEWELYN POWYS

GO CAMPING

Let's hear it for camping. The pleasure of carrying a 50-pound backpack while portaging a canoe. The thrill of answering nature's call in the great outdoors (and hoping nothing bites you on the butt). The joy of being awakened in the middle of the night by hungry bears. The bliss of dousing yourself with bug repellant. The satisfaction of sleeping on the cold, hard ground. It kind of makes you wonder why people moved into caves in the first place. Or invented plumbing.

> "Nothing is more beautiful than the loveliness of the woods before sunrise."
> GEORGE WASHINGTON CARVER

On the other hand, you do get to hear birds bright 'n' early every morning. (Verrrry early.) And food cooked over a campfire (even beans in a can) tastes better than dinner at a four-star restaurant. And stories told under the stars are more memorable than great works of literature. And it's ever so bracing to bathe in an icy stream.

People either love camping or they hate it. Some can't wait to leave civilization far behind; others shudder at the thought. If you've never gone camping, give it a try. Meanwhile, you can practice this camp song, sung to the tune of "Singin' in the Rain":

> *I'm campin' in the rain, just campin' in the rain.*
> *The tent and the campfire are soggy again.*
> *The clouds in the sky are making me cry*
> *My waterlogged shoes may never get dry.*

Nature Highs

TRUE HIGHS
Secret Places

by Jason Burks, 16

I alter my consciousness when I witness a beautiful sight, like the sunset over Yosemite Park, or the waves crashing over the western beaches in California. The sights and sounds create such a high in my mind that nothing else matters and all my worries are forgotten. My wish would be to stay in these wonderful treasures of nature forever, never having to care about what the next day brings.

The memories I have of sitting alone on deserted beaches are enough to make me yearn to be there again. Peace and relaxation are found only in these secret places nestled in my mind. This is what I do instead of drugs, because the more I sit with nature, the better I feel.

> "What I like about camping is you can get really dirty. Either you're all by yourself, so no one else sees you, or everyone you're with is just as dirty as you are, so nobody cares."
> FORMER BOY SCOUT

FIND OUT MORE

Woodall's Camping Guides (Highland Park, IL: Woodall Publishing, Inc., published annually). These respected guidebooks will help you find a campsite anywhere in North America. Government and privately owned facilities are listed, described, and rated. Includes information on fees, handicapped accessibility, pet friendliness, attractions, and more. Regional versions (New York & New England, Mid-Atlantic, Far West, etc.) are available. Check out the publisher's Web site (www.woodalls.com).

Family.com
family.go.com (do a search for camping)
All sorts of useful advice, whether you go with or without your family. Covers everything from grub to gear, bugs to backpacking.

Wise Highs

MORE NATURE HIGHS

- If nature is a high and sports are a rush, imagine what happens when you combine the two. See Chapter 4: Sports, Exercise, and X-treme Highs for inspiration and resources.
- Skinny-dip in a cool mountain lake.
- Have a picnic.
- Watch a calf being born. Or, for that matter, watch any animal being born. It's an awe-inspiring, if slightly yicchy experience.
- Rescue earthworms after a rain. You may get a medal for valor.

A Garden of Earthly Delights

Gardening is a great way to feel at one with nature. You can experience deep tranquillity as you run your fingers through the cool, moist earth and keep your eyes peeled for snakes. Whether your garden consists of an acre of eggplants or a boxful of geraniums, there's nothing quite like the pleasure that comes from tilling soil, planting seeds, and nurturing life.

GROW YOUR OWN

If you're a city dweller and don't have any land handy, you can still experience the joys of floral parenthood by playing mommy or daddy to 12 little cacti on the windowsill. Or make a container garden. Set the pots on a porch or roof or fire escape (as long as they won't impede people in pajamas trying to get out of the building in a hurry).

"Earth laughs in flowers."
RALPH WALDO EMERSON

Tip: Talk to your plants. Many horticulturists believe this helps them to thrive. And if it doesn't, the worst that can happen is your plants will think you're crazy. But who cares what plants think?

There are literally hundreds of books on gardening (probably more), and they cover all types of gardens—from shade to rock, Japanese to water, container to rooftop, cottage to herb, prairie to small-space. You'll find books on irises and plant viruses. Cacti, bonsai, and Versailles. There's probably even a book on Italian roof-top herb waterfall gardens for shady, humid climates. Visit a library or bookstore and browse the gardening section. Or search an online bookstore for the type of garden you're thinking of (e.g., Japanese gardens, roses, container gardens).

Nature Highs

"If you have a garden and a library, you have everything you need."
MARCUS TULLIUS CICERO

Tree Highs

Would you believe there's an organization for people who like to climb trees? It's called Tree Climbers International. It was founded by an arborist and tree landscaper named Peter Jenkins. One day back in 1983, Jenkins was sitting in a tree during a blizzard when he got the idea of starting a club so others could experience the freedom and joy he found in swinging from limb to limb and getting to know trees on a first-name basis. When a bolt of lightning struck a nearby tree, he took this as a sign that he should pursue his idea. (And get out of that tree, pronto.)

One thing led to another, and before you could say wasp's nest, Tree Climbers Interna-tional was launched. There are now, er, branches in 20 countries. They sponsor weekend camps to teach people the ropes of tree climbing. Some-times club members spend the night in trees on spe-cially made hammocks *(Rock-a-bye baby, in the tree top...)*. All in all, it's a tree-mendous way to get a good physical workout, commune with nature, and make friends with squirrels.

Tip: A tree's bark is always worse than its bite.

COCO-NUTS

Each year, a Coconut Tree Climbing Competition is held at Sukana Park on Fiji. The record for climbing the 29-foot, 6-inch tree (4.88 seconds) is held by Fuatai Solo of Samoa. When he won the competition for the third time, Fuatai put the $100 prize money in his mouth and scampered back up the tree.

Wise Highs

"If you would know
strength and patience,
welcome the company
of trees."
HAL BORLAND

"Of all the wonders
of nature, a tree in
summer is perhaps the
most remarkable; with
the possible exception
of a moose singing
'Embraceable You'
in spats."
WOODY ALLEN

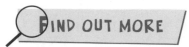

FIND OUT MORE

Tree Climbing.com
www.treeclimbing.com
The Tree Climbers International Web site bills itself as "Everything in the World About Tree Climbing," and it's true. Drop in to learn about recreational tree climbing, tree care, tree gear, and *much* more. Link to tons of related sites, visit the live chat room, and look at pictures of people climbing trees. There's even a section on rescuing cats from trees. Go there to find answers to those questions that have been keeping you up at night, such as *Why do cats climb trees, and why don't they come down?*

BUILD A TREE HOUSE

Now that you're in a tree-climbing mood, why not build a tree house? This can range from a couple of strategically nailed boards to an actual house complete with running water, electricity, and a connection for your modem. Of course, unless your parents own 10,000 acres of forest land, you may need to get building permits, as most towns don't take too kindly to people placing homes in trees without permission.

The best way to get started is to check out some of the books that have been written on amazing tree houses. You'll learn everything you need to know to find your own safe arbor.

FIND OUT MORE

Life in the Treetops: Adventures of a Woman in Field Biology by Margaret D. Lowman (New Haven: Yale University Press, 2000). Margaret Lowman never intended to climb trees as a career. But as a biologist interested in tree canopies and other ecosystems, she soon found herself up a tree. Many trees, in fact. And once she got married and became a working mother, she'd bring her small children with her to work...as in 75 feet above ground level. A fascinating and funny memoir of an unusual woman and her life.

Tree Houses You Can Actually Build by David and Jeanie Stiles (Boston: Houghton Mifflin, 1998). The basics and fun stuff, from secret escape hatches to rope bridges and swings.

Treehouses: The Art and Craft of Living Out on a Limb by Peter Nelson (New York: Houghton Mifflin Co., 1994). A brief history of tree houses from Ancient Rome to Victorian England, plus stories and gorgeous color photos of tree houses (including the author's own 200-square-foot octagonal tree house in Canada). Nelson has also written *Home Tree Home: Principles of Tree House Construction and Other Tall Tales.*

Get Wet

Nature Highs

We humans feel a powerful, primal connection to water. This may be because the earliest forms of life originated in the sea. Or because we begin our own lives floating in the womb.

Water is a metaphor for life. We speak of the river of time. Streams of consciousness. Going with the flow. When we are ex-hausted, we feel *drained*. When we are *drowning* in sorrow, we *dissolve* into tears.

Water provokes powerful emotions, images, and associations in ways that, say, a can of tuna fish doesn't. For example, picture a lake or a pond at dawn. The surface is like glass. Can anything be more still? More peaceful and serene?

Now picture sunlight dancing on the ocean. Or a vast jungle waterfall under a misty rainbow. Or the dark, hidden depths of the sea. What do you feel? Joy? Longing? Eternity? Mystery?

COOL IT

If it weren't for the cooling effect of the water present in human tissues, a person's exertion during one day could raise body temperature by as much as 300°F.

WATER WAYS

TRY THIS!

For a great natural high, get thee to water. Once you're there....

Sit by a pond. Can you be as still as the water?

Meditate on a waterfall. It doesn't have to be Niagara or Angel Falls in Venezuela (the world's tallest, by the way). A small cataract in a local stream will do nicely. Sit comfortably and stare at the flowing, sparkling, rushing water.

Relax by a river. Or stream, brook, creek, or canal. The water you're watching probably meets up with another river, stream, etc. a bit further on. Then that flow meets up with another. And another. Follow it in your mind.

Watch the ocean. Let the waves soothe you. The one that just broke on the beach; where do you think it came from? Watching the ocean is like watching eternity.

Play in the waves. Dive into breakers. When you're really tired, go lie on the beach. The world will spin.

DID YOU KNOW?

60 percent of our body weight is water. Research shows correlations between human moods and behaviors and the full moon. Perhaps the moon influences our internal "tides."

Wise Highs

Home Variations

1. If you don't happen to have a body of water nearby, consider getting a little indoor fountain. Just plug 'er in, fill 'er up, and listen to the gentle gurgle of cascading water. It's both a visual and aural treat. Great for falling asleep to, too.

2. Advanced water aficionados might want to set up an aquarium. Few things are more calming than watching brilliantly colored fish swim in circles. No wonder so many dentists have aquaria in their offices for patients to look at. If an aquarium can take your mind off of the fact that someone is about to stick a 6" needle into your gums, imagine what it can do for those little everyday stresses.

3. If an aquarium is too expensive or labor-intensive, you might get a lava lamp. There's nothing quite like the sight of colorful floating globules. And, unlike fish, you don't have to feed them. Next time you're feeling edgy and out of balance, turn off the light in your room, focus on the glowing lava, and meditate on your globs.

RIDE THE WAVES

This visualization will help you relax by letting the power and rhythm of the sea purge you of all anxiety.*

Find a quiet, comfortable room. Lie down. Close your eyes. Raise your arms and shake them until they feel like light, loose strands of spaghetti. Let them flop down to your sides. You already feel more peaceful and calm...

> You are lying on a deserted beach...the sand is warm...you hear the breaking of waves on the shore...
>
> As the tide comes in, an occasional wave gently laps your ankles and feet...slowly the waves reach further onto the beach...the warm water moves up your legs until you are surrounded by it...you feel yourself lifted off the sand as the water continues to rise...you begin to float...
>
> The sea draws you into its rhythmic embrace...you are weightless, rising and falling with the swelling of the waves...

* For more visualizations, see pages 41–47.

In your mind, turn over and stretch out your hands in front of you…ride the waves, surging with the crests…

Let the waves carry you back to shore…a long wave deposits you on the warm sand, high on the beach…

You lie there, filled with gentle waves of peace and joy.

Nature Highs

TAKE A BATH

TRY THIS!

Not that I'm saying you need one. But according to our survey of 2,000 teens, showers and baths are among the Top Ten ways they reduce stress and escape from reality. So the next time you're wired or just want to play with your rubber ducky, head for the tub, rub-a-dub-dub.

Tips: Try to find a time when you won't be disturbed. Lock the bathroom door to guard against intrusions by pesky siblings (not to mention parents). And never take a bath during a thunderstorm.

Variation: Psychedelic Bath

Turn your bathroom into a fantastic sound-and-light show. Set up a strobe or a mirrored ball with a spot shining on it. Or bring a lamp with a red bulb into the bathroom. (Always be sure that electrical devices and their cords cannot touch or fall into any water.) Or light a dozen candles. Play a tape or CD of your favorite music, or put on some weird electronic music or chanting. Add bubble bath to the running water. (See if you can find some that's luminescent and/or glows in the dark.) Now get into a nice, hot tub and zone out.

Fire Highs

Fire, like water, has a profoundly spiritual effect on humans. This is because we associate it with basic human needs such as warmth, security, and marshmallows.

Thousands of years ago, families didn't have televisions to sit around. So teens used to go over to each other's caves to watch fire. Good caveparents used to tell their children "Don't sit too close to the fire; you'll ruin your eyes."

"There is no need to go to India or anywhere else to find peace. You will find that deep place of silence right in your room, your garden, or even your bathtub."
ELISABETH KÜBLER-ROSS

Wise Highs

For a rousingly good, meditative time, build a fire. (Do this in a fireplace or woodstove, since most parents don't take kindly to towering infernos on the living room rug.) Then turn off all the lights. Stare at the fire. Lose yourself in it.

CAUTION!!! Even though I know you'd never, ever play with fire, get permission before building a fire of any kind, and be sure you know what you're doing.

 BUILD A BONFIRE

If you're camping, at the beach, or have a big backyard, you can build a bonfire. Invite your friends. Once the fire's ablaze, dance around it. Yell and sing. Pretend you're the kids in *Lord of the Flies*—after they've been through a conflict resolution workshop.

Important: Many parks, campgrounds, and counties have strict laws governing when and where you can build open fires. This is so you don't burn the state down. *Be sure to check local regulations and build your fire safely.* Nothing spoils the high of a fire more than the sound of fire engines.

Follow these tips to build a fire that's fun for everyone:

- Find a space that's sheltered from the wind and more-or-less flat. Otherwise, your fire will roll downhill and you'll have to keep moving to sit next to it. The area should be free of overhanging branches, awnings, and roofs.

- Clear the site of leaves, branches, trash, and other flammable materials. The best site is one on which the fire will not spread, such as sand, bare rock, or a riverbed. Never build a fire directly on a river, as it will tend to float away.

- If you use stones to build a ring around the fire, be sure they are absolutely dry. Wet or recently wet stones can explode when the moisture in them turns to steam and expands. Shards of flying rock embedding themselves in your brain will ruin the fun for everyone.

- Keep in mind that fires built on grass or lawns will burn off the ground cover. Therefore, never build a fire on your neighbor's lawn.

"Man is the only creature that dares to light a fire and live with it. The reason? Because he alone has learned how to put it out."
HENRY JACKSON VANDYKE JR.

158

The basic idea with fire-building is that little things ignite somewhat bigger things, which ignite still bigger things, and so on and so forth. So you'll want to start with tinder, which is material that will instantly light with a match or spark. Tinder includes dry grass, leaves, pine needles, and shredded bark.

Nature Highs

Once you light the tinder, build a little teepee over it out of kindling (dry twigs or split wood that will catch fire easily). Construct the teepee so air can flow through it. Once the kindling is ablaze, build a new teepee on top of the old one. Proceed in this fashion, adding larger logs or pieces of wood to the fire until it's a size you like.

TRUE HIGHS
Along Came a Spider

Once I was staying in a centuries-old farmhouse. In the living room was a huge fireplace with gigantic andirons and black kettles. I looked at the hearth and could feel 200 years of history. I pictured a colonial mom wearing a colonial bonnet cooking a colonial dinner. I pictured little colonial kids doing their colonial homework by the fire. I don't know where colonial Dad was. Probably at the tavern with Paul Revere.

The hearth was calling to me. ("Fire, Fire.") I gathered logs and kindling and newspapers. I checked that the flue was open. And before you could say Boy Scouts of America, I had a roaring conflagration.

As I was about to sit down in a Barcalounger, for some reason—call it fate—I happened to look at the steaming log. On it, to my horror, was a spider. It raced from one end of the log to the other, fire licking at its little spider heels. My heart pounded. This was all my fault! Was I to have a crispy spider on my conscience for eternity? I had to do something!

Heedless of the danger I faced, I grabbed the fire poker and placed the tip on the log. "Come on, Mr. Spider," I said. "Hop on board. This is your ticket to freedom." And in a rare moment of spider-human communion, that crazed and dazed little arachnid crawled onto the end of the poker, hanging on for dear life with all eight hands. I gently carried him away from the log, which was now completely engulfed in flames, set him down on the hearth, and squashed that little sucker dead. (Just kidding!)

Actually, I brought him outdoors and set him back in the woodpile. The high I experienced from saving a life was something I will never forget.

Thunder and Lightning

Big, dark thunderclouds roll in. Blinding flashes of light streak across the sky. Thunder roars and crashes. Wind howls, rain falls in sheets, and hail pounds expensive dents in your parents' car. What could be more exciting than a rip-roaring storm?

Not much, in my opinion. And since a storm isn't something you can go looking for (at least, not usually), know what to do when one comes looking for you.

STORM SAFETY

Storms are more fun when you're safe. Then you can sit back and enjoy the show.

You can *safely* watch a storm from inside a car, bus, or truck (with windows rolled up), inside a house, or inside a large, enclosed structure. It's *unsafe* to watch a storm from under an isolated tree, in an open field, on a golf course, near a flagpole or light pole, on a roof, on bleachers, in a gazebo or picnic shelter, or on or in water (lake, pool, ocean).

LIGHTNING FAST FACTS

- An average 8.6 million bolts of lightning strike the earth per day.
- In any moment of the day there's an average of 2,000 thunderstorms raging.
- Florida is the Lightning Capital of the U.S.
- There's enough electricity in the average flash of lightning to power a 100-watt light bulb for 3 months.

Source: National Weather Service Forecast Office— Melbourne, FL
www.srh.noaa.gov/mlb/tgcenter/lgt_facts.html

Remember that lightning normally *(but not always)* goes after the tallest object. If you're standing in the middle of a field, that's you. It's also dangerous to stand under a tree because trees are poor conductors of electricity. The current doesn't stay within the tree trunk but may leap out the sides and zap nearby objects (e.g., you).

If you're caught outdoors in a storm, immediately look for a safer location. Try not to stand right next to a tree. If you must, choose a tree that's shorter than the ones surrounding it. Assume a crouching position to keep your head and shoulders as low as possible. Keep your feet right next to each other and wrap your arms around your legs. If you're with other people, stand at least 20–25 feet from one another. This way, if one of you is zapped, chances are there will be someone left who can administer CPR.

Nature Highs

Tip: Sound travels about ⅕ mile per second. You can calculate (roughly) the distance of lightning by 1) counting the number of seconds between the flash and the bang, then 2) dividing by five. For example, if you count 6 seconds, the lightning is about 1⅕ miles away. If you count 0 seconds, your sneakers are on fire. ***Note:*** This ranging method isn't foolproof. Especially when there's a lot of lightning and thunder, you can't be sure you're matching the right flash to the right bang.

If you're indoors when a storm strikes, don't shower, bathe, wash your hands, do the dishes, use the telephone, or touch metal doors or window frames. Avoid contact with electrical wiring and plumbing.

FIND OUT MORE

Storm Chaser: In Pursuit of Untamed Skies by Warren Faidley (Chicago: Independent Publishers Group, 1996). Faidley is an award-winning photographer and storm chaser who makes his living by getting as close to tornadoes and lightning as he can. The book describes the meteorological phenomena Faidley encounters, as well as how he became a storm chaser, and what his life is like. *Eye of the Storm: Chasing Storms with Warren Faidley* (New York: Putnam, 1997) contains spectacular photographs of lightning, tornadoes, and hurricanes wreaking havoc.

Sky Diary
www.skydiary.com
Chris Kidler is a space reporter and storm chaser. His site covers lightning, tornadoes, hurricanes, and of course, storm chasing. Also check out www.weatherwizkids.com for tons of info on all weather phenomena.

> "We can never have enough of nature. We must be refreshed by the sight of inexhaustible vigor, vast and titanic features, the sea-coast with its wrecks, the wilderness with its living and its decaying trees, the thunder-cloud, and the rain...."
>
> HENRY DAVID THOREAU

Armchair Adventures

There are many famous books about nature and living in the wild. If you can't take a safari, you can read about one. And you won't risk getting eaten by a lion.

Your librarian (school or public) will be happy to point you toward great reading. Here are a few starter suggestions:*

The Endurance: Shackleton's Legendary Antarctic Expedition by Caroline Alexander (New York: Knopf, 1998). Just as World War I was erupting in Europe, Sir Ernest Shackleton set off to become the first person to sail across the Antarctic. His ship, *The Endurance,* was trapped by ice and eventually broke apart, stranding Shackleton and more than two dozen crewmen on floes. Enhanced with diary

---

* See page 178 for more recommended reading, this time by travel writers.

Wise Highs

entries from crew members and photos taken during the ordeal, this book chronicles one of the greatest, most arduous survival epics in the history of exploration.

The Hungry Ocean: A Swordboat Captain's Journey by Linda Greenlaw (Boston: Little, Brown & Company, 2000). Greenlaw is a swordfish boat captain—possibly the only female captain in the world. This gritty, exciting book describes her love of the sea and the grueling, harrowing, dangerous life she and her fellow fishermen lead.

Into Thin Air: A Personal Account of the Mount Everest Disaster by Jon Krakauer (New York: Anchor Books, 1999). When Krakauer joined an expedition up Mt. Everest, he expected to write about the commercialism of the mountain for *Outside* magazine. Instead, he wrote a harrowing account about a tragedy that claimed many lives.

The Perfect Storm: A True Story of Men Against the Sea by Sebastian Junger (New York: Harper, 1999). In October 1991, a massive storm hit North America's eastern seaboard. Meteorologists dubbed it a "perfect storm" because of the rare combination of factors that created it. Junger's meticulously researched best-seller tells the true story of six doomed fishermen caught in its 100-foot waves.

The Silent Spring by Rachel Carson (Boston: Houghton Mifflin, 2002). Written over the years 1958–1962, this book (now considered a classic) was one of the first to cry out against the degradation and destruction of our environment. Many people feel that it launched the environmental movement in the U.S.

Walden by Henry David Thoreau (a literary classic available in many editions). In March 1845, Thoreau built a cabin on the shores of Walden Pond. He stayed there for two years, "living deliberately" and waxing philosophical. Read all about it.

Altered States
Out-of-the-Ordinary Highs

Do you ever feel like you're in a rut? Every day, the same old thing. Get up. Shower. Eat breakfast. Brush teeth. Grab backpack. Go to school. Same bus or carpool. Same route. Same classes. Same teachers. Same friends. Same obnoxious jerks. Back home, same room, music, homework, parents, chores, TV, Web surfing, snacks, bed. Get up and start all over. Same, same, same.

Everybody has habits and routines. Some are self-imposed, based on our own interests and choices. Others are forced upon us by people, places, and things beyond our control.

Habits can be enjoyable and comforting. They can structure our day and provide a sense of security. They can give us something to look forward to. But habits can also trap us. They can keep us from new experiences. The more something becomes a habit, the more mindlessly we do it. We fall into a rut. We fail to notice all the rich stimuli around us. We become stagnant. When that happens, it's time to...

> "To escape from reality, I give my friend a dream. A fantasy I know she will enjoy. Then she does the same for me. We never want to come back."
>
> DREAMY KID

Change Your Habits

This is easy for nuns to do. They just go to the closet. For teenagers, it's a bit harder.

Start by examining your habits and routines. First, make a detailed list of things you do every day (e.g., wake up, take shower, make bed, eat breakfast, check email, go to school, meet friends, go to history class, etc.). Next, write down things you do on a weekly basis (e.g., music lessons, worship, Sunday dinner at Grandma's). Finally, list the things that occur regularly but less frequently (e.g., summer camp, summer job, your family's August vacation, soccer league every fall).

Now analyze your list. Using any symbols you like, flag the things you *love* to do. (These are activities that lift your spirits, fill you with joy, teach you new things, and help you to grow.) Next, identify things that you *have* to do. (These items may be required by parental units, the law, societal expectations, your "future," or the desire to avoid having the person sitting next to you on the bus say "Eee-yoooo, what's that smell?") Among these activities, identify the ones you enjoy, as well as the ones you dislike.

Continue to "handle" your list. As you scrutinize it, ask yourself these questions:

- Do I do something new every day?
- Which parts of my day make me want to scream or die from boredom?
- How much of my day happens by default, laziness, or indifference?
- How much of my day do *I* choose?
- What things do I do simply because my friends do them?
- What would I love to do that I'm not doing?

You'll begin to see patterns in your daily, weekly, and yearly calendar. You'll discover that almost every habit is made up of two parts: *behavior* and *content*. For example, you eat breakfast every day. That's the behavior. What you eat, where you eat, and what else you do while you eat (e.g., cereal, in the kitchen, watch TV)—that's the content. You wouldn't want to change the basic behavior, since eating breakfast is a good habit to have. But you could turn having breakfast into a fresh experience by changing the content. Eat something different. Meet a friend for breakfast. Put your meal on a tray and take it outdoors.

Here's another example. Let's say one of your routines is reading in bed every night before falling asleep. That's the behavior. You

> "Habits are safer than rules; you don't have to watch them. And you don't have to keep them, either. They keep you."
>
> FRANK CRANE

> "Habit is a cable; we weave a thread each day, and at last we cannot break it."
>
> HORACE MANN

could change the behavior by listening to music instead. Or taking a bath. Or writing in a journal. Or getting a massage from a sibling or roommate. Or you could change the content. You could read a *different* type of book from your usual choice. Either way, you bring something new into your life. You perk up your senses.

Look for ways to alter your routines. The most obvious places to start are activities and patterns that you do not enjoy. But don't overlook the habits that give you pleasure. You may find that changes here will bring you *more* pleasure, or renew your appreciation of the original activity should you choose to return to it.

Here are a few more examples of ways you can change your habits:

- Get up 20 minutes earlier. Use this newfound time to jog, exercise, meditate,* plan your day, sip a cup of tea, sit outside and listen to birds, etc.
- Choose a different destination for your family vacation.
- Take a different route to school.
- Sit next to a kid on the bus you *don't* know.
- Take a class you never dreamed of taking: drawing, fencing, acting, singing, painting, pottery-making, poetry-writing, cooking.

JUST FOR ONE DAY... TRY THIS!

Smile and say hello to every person you see...Walk backwards...Use your left hand if you're right-handed...Use your right hand if you're left-handed...Use your toes if you're ambidextrous...Keep your eyes closed whenever you're being driven somewhere...Change your name...Change your hairstyle...Change your underwear.

JUST FOR ONE WEEK... TRY THIS!

Don't go online...Don't watch TV...Don't listen to any music... Dress in a fashion completely opposite than usual...Meditate every morning...Have a conversation a day with your parents in which you ask them about their work, life, childhood, adolescence, first loves, dreams, regrets, beliefs, etc.

Out-of-the-Ordinary Highs

"Habit and routine have an unbelievable power to waste and destroy."
HENRI DE LUBAC

"The easier it is to do, the harder it is to change."
ENG'S PRINCIPLE

---

* See Chapter 3: Meditation Highs.

Wise Highs

"When I want to escape reality, I go swimming. I take a deep breath and go under the water and look up. It makes me feel like everything bad in the world is outside and I'm in my own world under the water, just looking from a safe distance."

SOGGY KID

"From naive simplicity we arrive at more profound simplicity."

ALBERT SCHWEITZER

THE SURVEY SAYS...

We asked teenagers "How do you escape reality without alcohol or other drugs?" Here are some of the things they do:*

act
go into the woods
daydream
look at old photo albums
go to the mall, sit on a bench, and play the people game, where you
   pick a person and make up a life story about that person
watch artsy movies and dream I live in the 18th century
fantasize about the future when we're successful and famous
visualize movie plots or novel plots in my mind
sit in the dark with candles lit
be alone in nature
run around with my friends and pretend
   to be kids again
dance alone
stand on top of a mountain
make up a dream world and imagine what it would be like

One teen responded "I don't want to escape from reality. I *like* reality."
Another wrote "I'm never involved with reality."

Deprivation Highs

Depriving yourself of the everyday patterns and perceptions of your life alters your reality. It forces you to find new balances. Things you consider "essential" may, in fact, be distractions.

Distractions from what? From serenity. Creativity. Inner growth and tranquillity. From the beauty around us. From noticing what people close to us are needing and saying. From knowing what's really important. From feelings of unity and oneness with all consciousness. When you deprive yourself of something, you don't end up with less. You end up with more. Hey, less *is* more! Here are some ways to bring more into your life by doing with less.**

---

* From a survey of 2,000 students ages 11–18.
** For more about sensory deprivation, see page 132.

Out-of-the-
Ordinary Highs

For a wet and salty high, floatation tanks are the way to go. A floatation tank is a box a little larger than a twin bed. It is filled with about 10 inches of water into which 800 pounds of Epsom salt have been dissolved. You get into the tank and float on your back.

Because the water is so salty, you float effortlessly and weightlessly—like a cork. The air and water in the tank are both heated to skin temperature (94 degrees Fahrenheit) so you don't feel any difference in temperature between those parts of your body that are submerged and those that are exposed to air. The tank has a lid you can shut, which allows you to float in near total silence and darkness. The idea is that you eliminate virtually all visual, audio, and tactile stimuli. That leaves just you, yourself, and you. Floating consciousness.

At first, your mind will probably prattle and chatter. All the trivia of the day will buzz around in your head like static: gripes, grievances, worries, plans, hopes, wishes, dreams, reminders, resentments, ideas, events, people, homework, tests, things to do.... Babble, babble, babble on. Let it—but don't focus on it. Ignore it. Think of it as background noise. Better yet, don't think about it at all. Just let it be. Soon—maybe not on your first float, but eventually—you won't notice it anymore. Deprived of sight, sound, and touch, your consciousness will take you to places and states you never even knew existed.

Scientists call this approach to relaxation and internal exploration REST, which stands for Restricted Environmental Stimulus Therapy. Many studies show that an hour of REST can decrease muscle tension, heart rate, blood pressure, and anxiety while promoting deep feelings of relaxation and well-being.

Bigger towns and cities usually have tank emporia where you can float by the hour (kind of like going to a tanning salon). If you should turn into a total tankophile, you can buy a fully-assembled tank, a kit to put together, or plans for making your own tank.

Tankless Variation

You don't need a tank to get some REST. Try floating in a warm swimming pool. Put on a life vest or other floatation device (unless the pool happens to be filled with salt water). Lie on your back with your arms and legs slightly outstretched. Your feet may sink, but that's okay. Close your eyes and relax. Let your mind go. Combine

> "There are places and moments in which one is so completely alone that one sees the world entire."
>
> JULES RENARD

Wise Highs

"Learn to get in touch with silence within yourself and know that everything in life has a purpose."
ELISABETH KÜBLER-ROSS

your float with some smooth, easy, deep breathing.* Do this for 15–30 minutes and you'll emerge a new (if somewhat soggy) person.

GO INTO THE CLOSET

You can create a mild sensory deprivation chamber for yourself out of a closet or a huge box (the sort a refrigerator, washing machine, or large piece of furniture might come in). Fill it with pillows so you can sit or lie comfortably. BE SURE AIR CAN FLOW IN AND OUT OF YOUR SPACE! If it isn't totally dark inside, put on a blindfold. Find something to place over your ears to muffle sound (e.g., headphones or ear muffs).

Once you're settled in, try not to move around. The more you cut off external sensory stimuli, the more you become aware of internal stimuli.

Don't stay in your deprivation "booth" for too long; 15–30 minutes is ample for your first time. If you increase the time on subsequent "visits," you will usually experience profound alterations of consciousness within a couple of hours.

WARNING!!! Sensory deprivation is serious stuff. (It is sometimes used to torture or brainwash people.) If you're in a "bad place" emotionally, sensory deprivation could lead to an unpleasant or upsetting experience.

Never enter a state or space of sensory deprivation without making sure there is someone nearby who can be summoned with a holler.

Fasting

Eating is a primal activity. Our survival depends on it—but eating also structures our day and creates rituals that are the basis for many social interactions. We chow down when we're emotionally upset or bored; we use food to impress people, initiate romance, convey sympathy, and show hospitality.

---

* See Chapter 2: Breathing Highs.

Depriving yourself of food is a simple way to alter your world. People have been fasting for centuries—sometimes for religious purposes, purification, or political protest, other times to achieve the altered consciousness many people report experiencing.

When you give up eating for a period of time, you feel liberated. Your body is no longer regulated by the rhythms of digestion. Your mind is no longer focused on what, when, or with whom you are going to eat. Without food as a physical, mental, and social anchor, you approach life from a brand new perspective.

People who fast report that they usually lose the sensation of hunger after three days. After four days, some people experience visual illusions and hallucinations, and enhanced color and depth perception. Some people actually "taste" foods and spices during their fast, even though they aren't eating them.

Out-of-the-Ordinary Highs

WARNING!!! Since eating disorders are a problem for many teenagers, you should *never* undertake a fast if:

- you see it as a way to lose weight
- you have ever been diagnosed with an eating disorder
- you have ever engaged in yo-yo dieting, binge eating, and/or intentional vomiting (purging)

Be sure to talk with your doctor before beginning a fast. I mean it!!! No exceptions!!!

Generally speaking, you shouldn't fast fast. Ease into it. S-l-o-w-l-y reduce your consumption of food over a day or two. Drink plenty of liquids during the fast. Your doctor may want you to take nutritional supplements and/or something to stave off infections which can grow during a fast. When you resume eating, do so in a moderate, healthful manner.

FIND OUT MORE

HealthWorld Online
www.healthy.net
Visit this site for articles on the pros and cons of fasting, the possible side effects of short- and long-term fasting, conditions under which people should *not* fast, the effects of fasting on the body and aging, and more. *Surfing this site is not a substitute for talking with your doctor.*

Being Alone

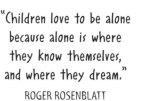

Wise Highs

Some of the greatest joys in life come from friends. In fact, most teenagers would rather hang out with their friends than do just about anything else. But it's possible to get addicted to people. You can reach a point where you become dependent on social stimulation. If you're not gabbing, gossiping, or gathering, you feel anxious, bored, and lonely.

When you're with people, you tend to focus on them. The social "environment" you carry with you provides its own stimulation and entertainment. This can cut you off from certain experiences. When you're by yourself, you tend to take greater notice of your surroundings. And you're more available to meet interesting new people along the way. Being alone can be wonderfully freeing—as this solo traveler discovered:

> *"I went to Seattle last week…my first trip by myself! I stayed at a hotel downtown, rented a car, got a book on Seattle gardens, and just had such a wonderful time popping from garden to garden. I was never bored or lonely—in fact, I evaded my friends the first night there so I could go to the fancy restaurant in the hotel by myself for dinner. Another first! And it was fine, it was better than fine, it was fun and delicious and just perfect! I am beginning to find out that I am my own best companion!"*
> **WOMAN ON HER OWN**

> *"In solitude the mind gains strength and learns to lean upon itself."*
> LAURENCE STERNE

> *"Children love to be alone because alone is where they know themselves, and where they dream."*
> ROGER ROSENBLATT

TRY THIS!

GO OUT WITH YOURSELF

Take yourself out on a date. Treat yourself to a fine dinner in a nice restaurant. (If the maitre d' is rude enough to say *"Just one?"* smile and say "One is all I need.") Go to a movie or concert by yourself. Or a museum. Go for a stroll. Take a day trip by train or bus to someplace interesting.

You might want to bring any or all of the following with you when you set off on your perambulations:

- 35mm camera (for those Kodak moments)
- videocam (for your first feature film)
- portable personal stereo (I find reggae excellent for city sauntering)
- journal (for writing your novel)
- sketchbook (people will amble over to see what you're drawing)

- book (great for café or park sitting)
- cell phone (so Mom and Dad won't worry)
- water, sunscreen, snacks (survival gear)

The amazing thing is that the more you enjoy being alone, the more attractive you'll be to others. Why? Because people will see you as a deep and fascinating individual. A person of mystery and inner resources. They'll sense your confidence and courage. And the more at one you are with yourself, the more pleasure *you'll* find in others.

Out-of-the-Ordinary Highs

Quiet Highs

Have you ever noticed how much talk there is in the world? Yak, yak, yak. And how meaningless, unnecessary, or even destructive so much of it is? Blah, blah, blah. We live surrounded by noise, virtually all of it made by humans. Except for people who are unable to hear or speak, language is the filter through which we experience much, if not most, of our lives. Even when we're alone, our minds chatter away.

> "Silence is the great teacher, and to learn its lessons you must pay attention to it. There is no substitute for the creative inspiration, knowledge, and stability that come from knowing how to contact your core of inner silence."
> DEEPAK CHOPRA

SHHHHHHHH

TRY THIS!

Take a vow of silence for a day. You'll be amazed at how difficult—and powerful—an experience this can be.

You'll need to set it up carefully. Shutting your pie-hole just before the debate finals is not a choice I would recommend. A weekend is probably your best bet. Tell your family and friends that you do not intend to speak that day. Your vow should include *all* forms of linguistic communication. There's little point in not speaking if you spend the day writing notes or email.

You may find that people won't take you seriously. They'll think you're doing it as a joke, or to be rebellious or weird. Some people may even get annoyed, as if you're clamming up just to make life difficult for *them*. This goes to show what a powerful force you've tapped into. Maybe your parents and/or siblings will join in for the day. (Frankly, I can't imagine parents who wouldn't be thrilled if their children took a vow of silence for a Sunday.)

Wise Highs

Good rules for a day of silence would be:

1. You're still responsible for being polite when interacting with others. If people ask you questions or do something for you, it's okay to smile, hug, wave, or nod your head in response.

2. You must break your silence in the event of an emergency. *Thinking* "FIRE!!!!" won't do.

3. No "mouthing" words.

4. You must abandon your vow if it causes genuine anguish. For example, an infant or toddler who is used to your voice and contact may become upset and inconsolable if you suddenly can't speak. He or she wouldn't understand your vow. Or a friend or loved one may really, really need to talk with you about something very important to him or her. Use good judgment; you can always be silent another day.

Tip: If you're going to be out and about, you may want to have a little card prepared explaining that you cannot speak. Or you can usually indicate as much through body language.

When you renounce speech, you relinquish your primary means of expressing your needs and opinions; of exerting your will; of controlling or influencing others. Your ego shrinks. You will find a peace in silence. Life slows down. Your other senses heighten. You'll feel calm.

Variation for Quiet Types

If circumstances allow, consider not speaking for a week. Spend a weekend with a friend during which you both remain silent. You'll be amazed at how it affects your relationship and how you experience each other.

School Variation

Maybe your school or one of your teachers would be interested in having a silent day. Classes shouldn't just be study halls, or periods during which you write an essay or read a book. Is it possible to have a class during which people learn without speaking?

TRUE HIGHS
A Silent Man

It was a Saturday night several years ago, and James Otis, a documentary filmmaker, was at a Hollywood party. He was attracted to the host, movie producer Lisa Henson, and asked her out on a date for the next day, Sunday.

"I mentioned that there was one small problem...I don't speak on Sundays," says Otis. "Before she said yes, she stopped and literally looked me over for five or six seconds.... But we spent the most lovely few hours hiking through the mountains. She talked just enough, and I got in a couple of nods maybe."

Like his hero Mahatma Gandhi, who retreated into silence on Sundays, Otis has maintained a similar vow of silence for over three years. He says that he has come to need the silence; that it slows him down and heightens his senses. "Generally my silence is much more awkward for other people than it is for me," he notes. Otis carries a card explaining that he doesn't speak on Sundays. He receives varied reactions. Airline reservationists have handed over upgrades; movie houses have let him in for free; and some people, who look on his silence as a handicap and feel sorry for him, offer extra assistance.

Clearly his silence didn't bother Lisa Henson, for she and Otis now live together and have celebrated the birth of their first child, Julian. Fortunately, he wasn't born on a Sunday, for Otis would have had to break his silence to offer encouragement in the delivery room. Otis does say that he is willing to talk on a Sunday in the event of an emergency or if it is causing someone genuine anguish.

Out-of-the-Ordinary Highs

"In the attitude of silence the soul finds the path in a clearer light, and what is elusive and deceptive resolves itself into crystal clearness."

GANDHI

SEEK SILENCE — TRY THIS!

Noise pollution is everywhere. Nitwits blast car radios and boomboxes. Nincompoops shout into cell phones. You can't go anyplace without having your eardrums assaulted by cars, trucks, airplanes, and heavy machinery. Beeping, blaring, banging, clanging; screeching, screaming, vrooming, booming. AAAAGGGGHHHH!!!!

Silence is one of life's greatest and most endangered luxuries. Silence isn't simply the absence of sound. It's the space *between* sound. Silence is a deep well of tranquillity. Balm for the spirit. Salve for the soul.

For a restorative pause in the din of life:

- Find a spot of natural beauty where all you hear is the breath of the wind or the burble of a stream. Go there and just be.
- Sit outside in your backyard and listen to the birds sing the day awake.

"In stillness there is fullness, in fullness there is nothingness, in nothingness there are all things."

QUAKER SAYING

Wise Highs

- Lie back in the tub and slip your ears under the water.
- Crawl under the covers in your room and enjoy the peace and quiet.

Seek silence whenever and wherever you can. Absolute silence is virtually impossible to experience in today's world, but some places are quieter than others. Find a few that work for you.

TURN OFF THE MUSIC

Are you a musicolic? Do you wake up to music? Ride the bus to music? Go through school to music? Do homework to music? Talk to friends to music? Go to bed to music? Would your parents recognize you if they saw you without headphones?

"Silence is more musical than any song."
CHRISTINA ROSSETTI

Music is fabulous*—but to appreciate it even more, leave home without it from time to time. Absent music to distract or entertain you, you'll turn inward and become more aware of your own thoughts and feelings.

Next time you're out driving or walking, turn off the tunes. You'll find yourself in a calm, meditative frame of mind. You'll notice more things in your surroundings. You'll enter a zone of altered consciousness.

No News Is Good News

"Nothing travels faster than light, with the possible exception of bad news."
DOUGLAS ADAMS

Of course you want to be a well-informed person who can speak knowledgeably about current events, politics, popular culture, the arts, and the state of the world. And that means getting the news— whether from a newspaper, the Internet, CNN, or local or national television news broadcasts.

The problem is, the purveyors of news tend to focus on the morbid, the negative, and the sensational. "Ten Thousand Planes Land Safely Today" is not news. "Plane Crashes, 42 Dead" is. There's an old saying in newsrooms: If it bleeds, it leads. In other words, for the best ratings, go with the gore. News media present a skewed picture of the world which makes life seem darker and gloomier than it really is.

In one fascinating study, researchers in England edited news broadcasts so they were upbeat, neutral, or negative in content. They then divided people into three groups. The people who viewed

---

* See pages 203–205.

the negative programs became sadder and more anxious than the people who watched the upbeat or neutral shows. They were also significantly more likely to exaggerate and worry about their personal problems.

The majority of news stories are about "victims"—of fate, injustice, illness, accident, crime, violence, or "acts of God." If you watch a lot of news, it's easy to become sad or depressed. You may even feel helpless and vulnerable.

Out-of-the-Ordinary Highs

TAKE A NEWS BREAK

TRY THIS!

When bad news gets you down, go on a news fast. Avoid all news for at least a day. If you're not that much of a news junkie anyway, do it for a week. Notice how you feel, what you miss, and what you do with the extra time you suddenly seem to have.

Then, when you bring news back into your life, take the following steps to keep it in perspective and limit the negative impact:

- **Place the news in context.** Remember, as you hear about a plane crash, that air travel is the safest mode of transportation there is. Remember, as you hear about a murder, that the homicide rate in America has been steadily declining—even though network coverage of murders has been increasing.
- **Don't read disturbing stories.** If you know that certain stories upset you, simply don't read them.
- **Take action.** It can be very upsetting to learn about a war or natural disaster that has affected thousands of innocent victims. You may feel a lot better if you make a donation or volunteer to help in some way.
- **Write a letter.** Some of the most disturbing news stories are about hypocritical politicians. Don't stew. Send a letter or email. Give them a piece of your mind.
- **Avoid pictures.** Seeing the aftermath of a massacre or earthquake can be much more upsetting than reading about it. Get your news from print media (e.g., newspapers, news magazines). You'll keep up with what's happening, but without the blood and guts.

INFORMATION OVERLOAD

Email, voicemail, faxes, pagers, cell phones, the Web. Newspapers, news magazines, electronic newsletters, newsgroups, books, around-the-clock cable TV news. Too much information! Researchers are linking information overload with specific symptoms including elevated blood pressure, increased cardiovascular stress, confusion, frustration, and feelings of helplessness and anger. What can you do? Try decreasing the quantity and increasing the quality of the news you consume.

"People everywhere confuse what they read in newspapers with news."
A.J. LIEBLING

175

Wise Highs

Variation: Flick the Switch

If you're willing to try a day without news, why not go further? Take a day off from electricity, or maybe just an evening after you get home from school. Make your room an electricity-free zone, or get your whole family to play along. Without TVs, radios, computers, and electric lights to distract you, you'll be in tune with the natural rhythms of the day, and you may rediscover the joys of simple things like reading, games, or conversation—it's what your great-great-grandparents did for fun.

Travel

Travel has always captured the human imagination. Think of all the explorers who set off to discover distant, exotic lands and brought back T-shirts. It's all so romantic: gondolas, pyramids, waterfalls, bazaars, sunsets, diarrhea. Just saying the words fills your soul with wanderlust: Timbuktu, rainforests, the Great Pyramids, Venice, Rio, London, Paris, Shanghai, Bangkok, Buffalo. When you travel, things look different. Sound different. Taste differ-

ent. Smell different...the outdoor food markets, the sweet smell of fresh-baked buttery croissants, the diesel exhaust of European cities.

Travel alters your consciousness by showing you new worlds. If you live in a modern city, imagine what it would be like to visit a town where the streets and houses are 500 years old, or to take a safari or explore a vast wilderness. If you live in the country, imagine what it would be like to travel to a bustling city of 10 million people. Visit a king's castle and you'll see unimaginable treasures; visit a third-world village and you'll see poverty you never dreamed of (for many families, their annual income is less than your weekly allowance). Visit a foreign land and you won't understand a word anyone's saying.

Travel expands your horizons. It gives you a perspective on life, history, culture, joy, and suffering that you just don't get shuttling between home and school. Travel gives you dreams, helps you to appreciate what you have, and reminds you that where you live is not the center of the universe. And travel lets you be whoever you want. Not that you're going to lie to people or pretend to be someone you're not, but travel gives you a clean slate. People you meet won't know your embarrassing nicknames. They won't know your past, your mistakes, your triumphs, whether you're popular, bullied, teased, or ignored. They will only know what you tell them and what you show them.

"I feel especially ecstatic at the thought of tropical or warm weather. When I go to Florida, I feel great. I feel at home with the sun, beach, and palm trees."

SUNNY KID

CORRECT TERMINOLOGY

Travel puts a fresh spin on everything. Ordinary experiences are transformed. For example, if you can't find your way around your home town, it's called "getting lost." If you can't find your way while traveling, it's called "exploring." Here are other ways everyday terminology changes when you're on the road:

At home	*When traveling*
Needing a bath	Roughing it
Toilet	Hole in the ground
Trespassing	Being a tourist
An embarrassing moment	A good story to tell when you get back home
Hanging out and doing nothing	Soaking up the atmosphere
Talking to strangers	Meeting the locals
Eating unrecognizable food	Sampling the cuisine
Making hilarious and unintelligible noises	Trying to speak a foreign language
Staying up past your bedtime	Being too excited to sleep
Belching loudly	Expressing your appreciation for the food*

LOW-COST TRAVEL

TRY THIS!

Travel doesn't have to be expensive. Start in your own backyard. It's amazing how many people live in the suburb of an exciting city and never venture forth to see its sights. What sights, you ask? Check with your local convention and visitors bureau. They'll steer you toward museums, galleries, theaters, attractions, parks, recreation, etc. you never knew existed.

You can also save money by visiting places where you have friends or relatives who can put you up for free. Often it's the hotel expense, not the plane fare, that breaks your budget.

Other ways to cut costs are backpacking, taking buses or trains, camping, and staying in youth hostels and dormitories. While these low-cost options can be inconvenient and uncomfortable, when

* Depending on what country you're in.

Wise Highs

we're on vacation we don't call this a "pain"; we call it an "adventure." And, by a happy coincidence of design, nature has seen to it that teenagers are most adaptable, intrepid, and energetic at the very time that their travel budget demands it.

No-Cost Variations

When you were learning to read—or when you were spending 100 percent of your time watching television and your parents were begging you to read—you probably heard this phrase (or something like it): "Reading is your passport to anywhere; you can travel the world in books." Well, guess what: IT'S TRUE. Curious about Paris? Read about it. London? Ditto. Siberia? Brazil? New Zealand? Amsterdam? Kenya? Indonesia? Santa's workshop at the North Pole? Open a book and *go there.*

Public libraries are free to anyone with a library card. Travel sections tend to be well-stocked. Ask your librarian for recommendations, or check out booksellers' Web sites (borders.com, barnesandnoble.com, amazon.com) to learn about popular travel books. Don't just read guidebooks; read travelogues, essays, and memoirs, too—first-person accounts by people who have been there/done that. Page through photography books. Curl up in a comfy chair and let your imagination wander.

> "I travel not to go anywhere, but to go. I travel for travel's sake. The great affair is to move."
>
> ROBERT LOUIS STEVENSON

A few suggestions for books to look for:

- Any travel book by James Chatwin *(In Patagonia, Songlines, What Am I Doing Here?)*, Jan Morris *(Destinations, Hong Kong, The World of Venice)*, Redmond O'Hanlon *(In Trouble Again, No Mercy, Into the Heart of Borneo)*, or Paul Theroux *(The Great Railway Bazaar, The Kingdom by the Sea, Riding the Iron Rooster)*.

- Any volume in the "Traveler's Tales" series, an award-winning, ever-growing collection of anthologies that gather great writing by today's best travel writers. A partial list of their tantalizing titles:

  Australia: True Stories of Life Down Under
  Danger! True Stories of Trouble and Survival
  Testosterone Planet: True Stories from a Man's World
  There's No Toilet Paper on the Road Less Traveled: The Best of Travel Humor and Misadventure
  Women in the Wild: True Stories of Adventure and Connection

Here's another way to travel for free: Watch your local newspaper for announcements of travel slide shows, video shows, or lectures.

Often these are held at public libraries, community centers, or places of worship. People who have recently returned from interesting places show pictures, videos, etc. and talk about their travels. It's not a bad way to spend an afternoon or an evening.

And one more: the Web is full of travel information, photos, first-person stories, itineraries, descriptions, etc. Visit any Web portal (yahoo.com, excite.com, about.com) and see where it takes you.

Out-of-the-Ordinary Highs

10 TIPS FOR TRAVELING WITH PARENTS

Taking your parents along when you travel is a great idea. Why? Because it's cheaper. They'll pick up all the bills. No, actually, it's a wonderful way to spend some quality time with the 'rents.

I know that to many kids, "fun" and "parents" sound like two things that can't happen simultaneously. But if you plan carefully and stay flexible, you'll discover what enjoyable companions your parents can be.

Here are some tips for harmonious traveling:

1. Go where nobody knows you. This way you don't have to cringe every time your mother tries out her Spanish or your father wears that ridiculous hat.

2. Get your parents involved in the planning. Let them choose some activities. But don't be critical when they say silly things like "We'll never be able to do the Louvre in just six days!"

3. If you're staying in a hotel, try to get your parents their own room. If this is impossible and you must share, make a point every few days of going for a long walk. Say something like "I'll just leave you guys alone for a while. I'll be gone at *least* an hour." It's amazing how this nap time seems to cheer them up.

4. Never use the expression "I'm bored." Instead, say "Wow, this place is great! Can we go now?"

5. Recognize that parents are going to act like adults from time to time. This means they'll do things like say they don't want any dessert and then eat half of yours. Or take a billion pictures. Or hang up their clothes. Parents also have peculiar priorities like wanting to unpack first and go to the pool second. Be patient. It's just a stage they're going through.

6. On occasion, while trying to find the Washington Monument or some other obscure landmark, you may notice that your father has just passed the same intersection for the fourth time. Do not ask him if he is lost. Fathers don't get lost.

"My favorite thing is to go where I have never gone."
DIANE ARBUS

"Half the fun of travel is the aesthetic of lostness."
RAY BRADBURY

Wise Highs

7. When driving along the interstate, parents get upset if you hold up signs in the car's back window that say "Help! I've been kidnapped!"

8. Parents do not understand that poking, pinching, tickling, and hitting are signs of affection between you and your brothers and sisters. This is why your mother will eventually say "If you don't stop that, somebody's going to get hurt." And because somebody always *does* get hurt, your mom will appear to have been right. To avoid this scenario, stick to silent face-making and rude gestures. Of course, now your mother will say "What's going on back there? It's too quiet."

9. Never ask "Are we *there* yet?" This exasperates parents no end. A better question, which you can ask in the same whiny voice, is "Are we *here* yet?" Since the answer to this is always yes, it keeps the mood positive.

10. Your parents, being on vacation, may get mushy and hold hands or even kiss in public. If this happens, all you can do is sigh and, if anyone is watching, put on an expression like "Who, them? They're not with me. I don't know why they're sitting at this table."

TRUE HIGHS
Getting High
by Going Down Under

by Kimberly Shearer Palmer, 19

I get my natural highs by taking risks that help me grow as a person. I recently discovered my personal favorite. I went to a place where I couldn't depend on food or housing—to Australia, where I didn't know anybody and nobody knew me. Every day, I woke up with two pressing goals: finding food and housing. I lived off of pineapple, watermelon, and sugarcane, and I slept in youth hostels for $10 a night.

I was living the life of a beat poet, with all my belongings on my back and everything that was really important in my head. I can't say that I never indulged in carnal pleasures—my friend and I spent all the money we had left by the last night on a luxurious dinner—but I can say that I always felt independent, which made me feel alive. I would even call the feeling of arriving at a youth hostel, realizing how dirty it is, and having the owner put me in a room with four shirtless, snoring guys, some kind of natural high.

Of course, traveling can be somewhat of an expensive way of finding thrills. But it doesn't have to be. The highlight of my trip came when I worked as a day laborer on a tropical organic farm, weeding jicama. I didn't even notice the blister on my finger until it had peeled off completely—I was concentrating too hard on distinguishing the "weeds" (which looked to me like miniature palm trees) from the jicama plants. Here I was, thousands of miles from home, sweating with a farmer who takes risks with experimental crops so he sometimes has to depend on unemployment benefits.

Who would choose to take mind-numbing drugs over discovering a new thrilling lifestyle?

Out-of-the-Ordinary Highs

Fodor's Great American Learning Vacations: Hundreds of Workshops, Camps, and Tours That Will Satisfy Your Curiosity and Enrich Your Life (New York: Fodor's Travel Publications, 1997). Vacations with a purpose, from archaeological digs to cultural tours, whale-watching cruises to foreign language immersion programs.

Volunteer Vacations: Short-Term Adventures That Will Benefit You and Others by Bill McMillon (Chicago: Chicago Review Press, updated often). Profiles hundreds of charitable organizations and projects worldwide that need volunteers.

Rough Guides to Travel
travel.roughguides.com
Explore more than 14,000 destinations, from the Al-Wad Road to Zaragoza and everywhere in between. Check out the *Rough Guide to...* books in your local bookstore or library. They're designed for independent travel and all budgets, from shoestring to expense account.

Roleplaying Games

You might have heard horror stories about roleplaying games, especially one called "Dungeons and Dragons." Supposedly these games promote violence among teenagers, lure kids into the occult, even cause teen suicides.

They don't.* In fact, if you've ever played any kind of let's pretend game (dressing up as a character on Halloween, playing a favorite character in a storybook, playing "house"), then you've

---

* For more on this topic, check out the Religious Tolerance Web site *(www.religioustolerance.org)* and do a search for role-playing.

Wise Highs

had personal experience with roleplaying. And you might enjoy roleplaying games. Millions of people do, and they're not all geeks, nerds, freaks, wackos, and weirdos. (Okay, some probably are, but most aren't.)

There are many different types of roleplaying games—fantasy ("Dungeons and Dragons"), horror ("Call of Cthulhu"), science fiction ("Traveller," "Fading Suns," "Alternity"), cyperpunk ("Cyperpunk 2020"), comic book ("Champions"), historical ("Boot Hill"), games based on movies and television series (*Star Wars,* James Bond, *Babylon 5*), and more. LOTS more. They all have their rules, characters, books, dice, figurines, art, etc. Some are fairly simple, others are incredibly complex. All require healthy doses of creativity and imagination.

If you're interested, ask around at your school, youth group, or community center to see who plays D&D and other roleplaying games. Or visit any Web portal (yahoo.com, excite.com, about.com) and search for roleplaying (or role-playing).

---

12 REASONS TO ROLEPLAY

With thousands of TV stations, movies, videos, computer games, card games, board games, books, magazines, Web sites, parks, sports, and other activities to choose from, why roleplay? Roleplaying doesn't provide aerobic exercise or flood your body with antioxidants, it isn't going to build up your résumé or get you into graduate school. So—why bother?

1. Because roleplaying is fun. Have you read those psychological studies about the importance of play to human health and mental well-being? First and foremost, roleplaying is about playing—it's "Let's Pretend" at its most refined. Playing isn't just for kids anymore.

2. Because roleplaying is educational. Roleplayers actively seek out new knowledge to enhance their gaming experience; they learn about mythology, history, weaponry, tactics, science, philosophy, codes, currencies, and even basic astrophysics; they learn phrases in different languages and traditions in different cultures. And here's a hint for students—more than one roleplayer has learned to make a dull class interesting by thinking "How could I apply [macroeconomics, military history, the history of the novel] to my game?"

3. Because roleplaying is social. Roleplaying requires players to interact with each other, whether face-to-face or through some form of computer-mediated communication. Roleplaying games (RPGs) are much more social than sitting in front of a television or computer game all day. And for some people—for example, those whose responsibilities or physical challenges keep them at home all day—roleplaying by computer can became a significant form of social interaction that would otherwise be closed to them.

4. Because roleplaying encourages teamwork. Roleplayers who only look out for No. 1 aren't going to be invited back to games very often. RPGs usually pose players with a problem to solve, and every player's participation is essential to achieving a successful solution. Players learn that their characters must work together to succeed—a good lesson to carry over into real life!

5. Because roleplaying is about more than winning and losing. Roleplaying games encompass far more than the win/lose scenario prevalent in most sports and board or card games. RPGs can include self-sacrifice (see how far that'll get you in a computer game!), romance, negotiation, and other scenarios that most other types of games simply can't handle.

6. Because roleplaying teaches conflict management. A good gamemaster (GM) encourages different methods of problem-solving within the game—sometimes problems are solved by combat, but other times they must be resolved by peaceful means. Players get a chance to explore different methods of conflict management within the safety of a fictional setting and can later apply those methods to the real world.

7. Because roleplaying encourages creativity. Many roleplayers enjoy painting miniatures, sketching characters, carving terrain and models, writing game-related poems or short stories, composing game-related songs, and even, especially in the case of live-action role players, sewing costumes or cooking "in-character" meals. Even those who just play the game exhibit creativity by developing their characters and interacting with the fictional world in which the game takes place.

8. Because roleplaying is relatively inexpensive. RPGs don't need memory upgrades, expensive equipment, or high-priced tickets. After the rulebooks and dice have been purchased, roleplaying can be as expensive or inexpensive as the players care to make it. RPGs can be run with nothing more than paper and pencil, or they can be run with detailed terrain and handpainted metal miniatures.

9. Because roleplaying doesn't discriminate. Roleplayers can be of any age, gender, religion, ethnicity, sexual orientation, shape, size, or level of fitness. A skilled GM can tailor a game to accommodate all sorts of special needs or considerations.

10. Because roleplaying improves speaking skills. Roleplaying is a verbal game (textual, if you play over email or in chat), and through practice, players

Out-of-the-Ordinary Highs

"Roleplaying games (RPGs) are a great way to escape the day-to-day grind. You can be anyone you want—a medieval knight, a warrior, captain of a spaceship, a secret agent, a spy, a king, a queen, Sherlock Holmes or Indiana Jones. RPGs prove that the best highs happen in your imagination— no drugs needed."

TEEN ON A ROLE

Wise Highs

improve their verbal (or writing) skills as they play. It's also a form of acting, and players learn to convincingly present themselves to others while they play.

11. Because roleplaying is extremely portable. At the minimum, most RPGs require dice and character sheets…and maybe a rulebook, although if the players know the rules, they can often get by without one in a pinch. RPGs can be played just about anywhere, unlike many physical sports, and they don't require batteries or a nearby electrical outlet, unlike many computer games.

12. Because roleplaying is wish-fulfillment. The daily grind gets everyone down sooner or later, so it's a relief to become a devil-may-care space pilot, a fearless warrior princess, a gorgeous rock star, or a brilliant computer pro-grammer for a while. Players can step out of their own lives by roleplaying characters of different genders, ethnicities, social classes, physical or mental abilities. Roleplaying allows everyone to become someone else for a while… and most of us need that break in our lives.

So, why roleplay? Why not? Not only is roleplaying fun, but it's been used by educators and counselors for decades to improve skills and encourage learn-ing. So, if you don't roleplay, consider finding a group and trying it out. And if you do roleplay, remember these reasons the next time somebody asks you what the hobby is all about. Roleplaying is about a lot more than books and dice and funny metal figures!

Alter Your Altitude

> "It is not the mountain
> we conquer but ourselves."
> EDMUND HILLARY

Human beings are made to walk (run, crawl, dance) on the earth. Unless you make a frequent habit of soaring overhead during out-of-body experiences* or climbing mountains**, and unless you live at a high altitude, chances are your everyday view of things is anchored on terra firma.

It's a high to get high—literally. Whether you scale a local prom-ontory and stare out over the landscape, climb up on your roof and look down on your backyard, take a plane ride and gaze out the window, learn to walk a high wire, or visit the observation deck of a skyscraper, you'll get an exhilarating new view of the world.

---

* See page 57.
** See page 85.

HIGH HIGHS

Out-of-the-
Ordinary Highs

Go to the top of a skyscraper. On a clear day you may not see forever, but you will see for 50–60 miles! Amazing. Look down at the people and cars scurrying about like tiny ants. Press your nose against the glass and wonder what would happen if the window suddenly popped out...and so did you.

If you live in New York City, you can go up the Empire State Building. If you live in Chicago, there's the Sears Tower, which, while not the tallest building in the world, has the highest occupied floor. And all of you who live in Kuala Lumpur, Malaysia, can marvel at the Petronas Towers. At 1,483 feet, these are currently the tallest inhabited structures in the world. (And they're the scene of an exciting chase in the movie *Entrapment* starring Sean Connery.)

If you live in Prairie Flats, Kansas, you may be out of luck when it comes to finding an observation deck on the 60th floor. But you can look forward to visiting a big city and getting your first skyscraper high. Or maybe you can climb a mountain. There's nothing quite like the feeling you get when you're standing on top of the world. The air is thin. The sun burns bright. Everything is so quiet. And you feel as if you're the first person to set foot on Earth. There's something about being high that just . . . gets you high.

Great Buildings Online
www.greatbuildings.com
This beautifully designed site documents over 750 of the world's greatest buildings from ancient times to modern day. You can search by architect, building name (e.g., Monticello, Chrysler Building, Parthenon), and location. Entries contain photographs, 3-D models you can "walk" through, facts and descriptions, and references to other sites and materials.

Wise Highs

Space Out

Environment and mood are related. The type of space in which you live, sleep, do homework, daydream, listen to music, and entertain your friends can affect the way you feel. It can affect your concentration, organization, and peace of mind.

Different people like different environments. Some people like a serene, minimal look. Others like a cozy, busy decor. Find the style that complements your mood. For example, I live in a loft in what used to be a pillow factory. It's a huge space with tons of windows. Because my mind is so cluttered and anxiety-prone, I keep my loft spare and serene. It's a quiet, meditative space that calms me. When the light pours in, I feel as if I'm on vacation. I use the design, just as one might use music, to shape my moods.

Use your space to alter your consciousness. Depending on what works best, this might cause some conflict with your parents. Many parents, for example, don't realize that clothes on the floor can have a calming effect. Or that three-day-old sandwiches are excellent objects for meditation. I've even heard of parents who balk at the idea of their child painting a bedroom black! So you may need to negotiate. (If you share a room, you'll have to negotiate with your roommate.)

In general, I believe that a child's room is his or her castle, and as long as the room doesn't pose a hazard to life or limb, the child should be able to keep it any way he or she likes. (Isn't this why doors were invented?) In return, the child must respect the standards of orderliness and cleanliness established by his or her parents for the rest of the house.

The most immediate way to alter a room is by painting it a different color.* If this is too drippy, smelly, or labor-intensive, you can change the look with fabrics, posters, wallpaper, art, rugs, etc. Move the furniture around. You may be able to create cozy corners or hidden hideouts. Lighting can transform a room, especially at night.

Since clutter and disorganization create stress for most people, you may want to run a "mess check" on your space. Can you quickly lay your hands on a homework paper or book or CD? How much of your time do you spend looking for things? Do you have enough space to store your belongings? Are surfaces inches-deep with papers, magazines, clothes, books and supplies? Does your room look like a hurricane blew through it?

> "We make the world we live in and shape our own environment."
> ORISON SWETT MARDEN

---

* See pages 117–118.

If your space is out of control and causing distress, you can either throw your sibling out on the lawn or create better storage and organization systems. Consider getting more bookshelves, or a filing cabinet, or one of those modular storage systems they make for closets.

FIND OUT MORE

Redoing your room on little or no money? These books are full of fun ideas.

Flea Market Style: Decorating with a Creative Edge by Emelie Tolley and Ali Hanan (New York: Clarkson Potter, 2005). Keys to successful secondhand buying at flea markets, consignment shops, rummage sales, garage sales, and tag sales.

Junk Style by Melanie Molesworth (New York: Stewart Tabori & Chang, 2002). How to find treasures at garage sales, flea markets, auctions, thrift stores, attics, and more, plus irreverent "rules" for decorating ("If you frame it, it's art").

Any book by Rachel Ashwell with *Shabby Chic* in the title.

Messing with Your Mind

Creative and Intellectual Highs

Chapter 10

If you've ever...

read an amazing book
built a model
talked into the wee hours
surfed the Internet
shot a film
pursued a hobby

composed a song
cooked a fabulous meal
worked on a sculpture
written a story
developed photos in a darkroom
acted in a play

> "When we are writing, or painting, or composing, we are, during the time of creating, freed from normal restrictions, and are opened to a wider world, where colors are brighter, sounds clearer, and people more wondrously complex than we normally realize."
>
> MADELEINE L'ENGLE

...then you know the hours fly by like minutes when you're absorbed in a creative or intellectual passion. You enter another world. It may be a world of fantasy; of characters coming alive. It may be a world of your mind, where ideas ricochet and multiply and lead you down paths of intrigue and discovery. It may be a world of friends and kindred spirits joined in joyful pursuit of a common goal.

One thing that sets human beings apart from most other species is our ability to be aware of, and take pleasure in, our own thought processes and creative activity. Maybe cats hold lengthy debates as to the proper construction of hairballs, and maybe lizards have sleepovers during which they ponder the origin of life, but I doubt it. Until a geranium wins an Oscar or a fish writes a bestseller, I'm going to keep believing that creative and intellectual highs are one of the privileges of being human.

Virtually anything can be a creative or intellectual high. If you paint battle scenes on the heads of thumbtacks (and, in so doing, enter a zone of impenetrable concentration), that's a high. If you talk late into the night with a friend about time travel and suddenly realize it's dawn, that's a high. If you pick up a guitar and compose a love song so sad your eyes well up with tears, that's a high.

You'll discover your own intellectual adventures and creative cruises. In the meantime, here are some tried-and-true mind highs.

Creative and Intellectual Highs

Writing

Writing isn't just a high. It's actually good for your health. Studies show that putting your thoughts and feelings down on paper improves immune function, lessens anxiety and depression, and reduces the likelihood that you'll come down with colds or flu. In one study, people with arthritis and asthma actually got better after writing about painful and stressful events in their lives. In another study, college students who wrote about traumatic events cut way back on their visits to the campus health clinic. Researchers have also found that writing about emotionally charged or stressful life situations can raise your grades, help you get a job, and make you feel more cheerful and positive.

Benefits come from writing as little as 20 minutes a day for three or four days in a row. Just venting or complaining doesn't help. You need to explore what's most on your mind or in your heart to reap the rewards.

Why is writing so therapeutic? Scientists aren't exactly sure. When they measure changes in the body that occur immediately after writing, they find that blood pressure and heart rate decrease. This suggests a state of relaxation. Writing also helps you to think, process ideas, and discover things about yourself, which can lead to creative problem-solving. Plus it's a positive way to deal with emotions such as grief, sadness, longing, disappointment, even joy.

Whether you're interested in better health or a career as a novelist, do the write thing. It's free, it's easy, and you can do it anytime, anywhere.

> "I write down what I'm thinking. This can be so relieving. Sometimes, when I look back on it, I think 'This isn't so bad.'"
> WRITING HIGH STUDENT

GENDER DIFFERENCES?

While the benefits of writing cut across all ages, races, and levels of intelligence, they seem to be slightly greater for men than for women. This may be because men tend to *talk* less about their feelings than women do, which makes *writing* about their feelings even more powerful and effective.

> "Writing down my thoughts makes me happy, especially when I reread them and they sound good."
> HAPPY HIGH SCHOOL STUDENT

Wise Highs

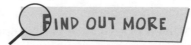

FIND OUT MORE

Writing Down the Days: 365 Creative Journaling Ideas for Young People by Lorraine M. Dahlstrom (Minneapolis: Free Spirit Publishing, 2000). A fact, person, or event for each day of the year prompt you to think, reflect, and write.

KEEP A JOURNAL

Only you can write the book of your life. Get a blank book. Find one that "feels" good, for it's about to become one of your closest friends. (If a computer feels most "friendly," there's nothing wrong with writing your journal on a word processor. You can still include pictures and photos. You can even print out a hard copy to put in a special binder.)

> "How can I know what I think unless I see what I write?"
>
> ERICA JONG

Take 20 minutes a day and write about anything that pops into your mind: the view out your window; your dog; the color of hope; someone you love; something you're upset about; your fondest wish, biggest regret, or most secret fantasy. Remember that writing about your deepest worries and feelings can reduce stress and improve your health.

Tip: If you get stuck on the first sentence, start with the second.

> "I write to clear my own mind, to find out what I think and feel."
>
> V.S. PRITCHETT

FIND OUT MORE

Spiritual Journaling: Writing Your Way to Independence by Julie Tallard Johnson (Rochester, VT: Bindu Books, 2006). This book guides readers through exercises to unlock individuality and independent thinking through exploring the power of creative journaling and self-expression.

WRITE POETRY

TRY THIS!

Writing poetry (or, as an English teacher of mine always pronounced it, "poy-tree") is a great way to get lost in your thoughts and feelings. Unfortunately, many teenagers turn off to poetry in school. This is because teachers assign dense, boring, unreadable poems. You spend hours trying to figure one out, and then, when the teacher finally explains it, you think *If that's what the poet wanted to say, why didn't he just come out and say it?!?* Poems follow my "whole artichoke" theory of learning: If getting to the edible part isn't worth the effort, people will pass on the dish.

Actually, poy-tree can be neat. Some types of poems, like sonnets and haiku, follow strict rules which dictate the rhythms, rhymes, line lengths, number of syllables in a line, number of stanzas, etc. The more you know about the poem's structure, the more you'll appreciate its beauty. Other poems are totally free-form. They make and break any rules they like about punctuation, capitalization, rhyme, rhythm, and reason. These types of poems are especially fun to write because you don't have to worry about grammar and such things.

Try writing some poems. You may discover it's just the high for you. To get you started, here's a poem that a student wrote especially for this book.

alternative high

by Annie Wengenroth, 17

I don't want to drink like them
I would rather sink creative teeth into my art
and devour it ravenously
until the colors blend like the passion of lovers
and the music thrills my brain
I don't want to get high
no, I don't want to be the attraction of the part
I can let the words writhe
across the page like exotic dancers
and entice my dreams through a camera lens
the feel of a paintbrush in my hand
the sound of pencil scratching words on paper
the songs I play for an eternity
these are my drugs
this is my high

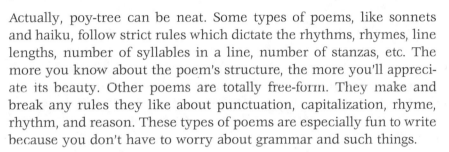

Creative and
Intellectual Highs

"Any time is the time
to make a poem."
GERTRUDE STEIN

"Breathe-in experience,
breathe-out poetry."
MURIEL RUKEYSER

"Poetry is life distilled."
GWENDOLYN BROOKS

Wise Highs

Poem-Making by Myra Cohn Livingston (New York: HarperCollins, 1991). Covers many types of poems, poetic forms, and figures of speech. Also includes writing exercises.

"Writing is a way of cutting away at the surface of things, of exploring, of understanding."
ROBERT DUNCAN

"Becoming a writer is about becoming conscious."
ANNE LAMOTT

12 REASONS TO WRITE

1. Writing helps you discover who you are. When you put pen to paper and pour out your thoughts, you begin to discover what you know about yourself and the world. You can explore what you love or hate, what hurts you, what you need, what you can give, and what you want out of life. This helps you better understand yourself and your place in the world.

2. Writing can help you believe in yourself and raise your self-esteem. The very act of making something out of nothing produces a feeling of pride and a sense of accomplishment. Knowing that you're able to fill up a journal with your thoughts, write a story, or put together a research paper helps you believe in your own abilities, talents, and perseverance. Your increased self-confidence can inspire you to take more risks in your writing and in other creative activities.

3. When you write, you hear your own unique voice. Poet William Stafford once said that a writer is not someone who has something to say as much as someone who has *found a way to say it*. Writing allows you to communicate in your own words and voice, without the filters and blocks you might use when talking to people you want to please, avoid, connect with, impress, or run from. Writing also gives you an opportunity to listen to your own distinctive voice, recognize it, and know it better.

4. Writing shows what you can give the world. As you write, you can explore your particular talents, interests, and passions. What are you good at? What do you feel compelled to throw energy into? What do you want to improve? Writing allows you to delve deeper into yourself and put into words what it is you want to be and do. It helps you find your calling.

5. As you write, you seek answers to questions and find new questions to ask. Because writing forces you to sit and think, it can be a way of finding answers to questions in your life. Writing is introspective by nature; it gives you the opportunity to carefully review choices and decisions about everything from what to study, to who to hang out with, to how to tell someone what's on your mind. In the process of writing about your issues and examining your questions, you may find answers that are right for you.

6. Writing enhances your creativity. Creating anything means asking questions, dwelling in doubt and confusion, and finally reaching a breakthrough.

When you write, you immerse yourself in the creative process. The more practice you get, the more easily you can transfer these skills to other areas of your life (school, activities, a job) that require creative solutions.

7. You can share yourself with others through writing. Many people believe that the written word allows for more freedom of expression than the spoken word. Writing lets you reveal aspects of yourself that don't always come across in face-to-face communication, phone conversations, or class discussions. Your writing self, in contrast to your talking self, has more time to reflect on what you believe, what you want to say, and why you think or feel a certain way.

8. Writing gives you a place to release anger, fear, sadness, and other painful feelings. Feelings are intense. They can hurt you to the core. (According to writer Oscar Wilde, their main charm is that they don't last!) When you're feeling angry, scared, upset, or depressed, it helps to get these emotions on paper rather than bottle them up. Writing is a safe way to release your feelings, explore them, and begin to cope.

9. You can help heal yourself through writing. It's no secret that many writers derive at least some healing benefits from writing. Whether it's their career, passion, hobby, or all three, writing offers writers a way to examine their wounds and, if they want, share them with the world. You, too, can take what has hurt you and turn it into something that helps you. The very act of creating can be a way to heal.

10. Writing can bring you joy and a way to express it. It's fun to put into words what's important and meaningful to you, then read what you've written. But the *process* of writing can be fun, too. It's exciting to put words onto paper and fill up pages with your ideas and opinions, not knowing exactly what you're going to say or what will come next. When you allow yourself to relax and see what happens on the page, you experience the thrill of creative expression.

11. Writing can make you feel more alive. The words, the images, the delight or grief that surfaces, the discoveries, the answers or questions that come to you as you write—all of this helps you feel more alive. Writing, like any art, is a way to connect with yourself, other people, and the world. In doing so, you may feel more involved, engaged, and interested in life. You may even be compelled to embrace it wholeheartedly.

12. You can discover your dreams through writing. Through the quiet and solitary act of writing, you can discover your greatest dreams (not what other people *think* they should be, but what *really* calls to you). You can think about these dreams, what it would take for them to become real, and what you can do to start making things happen. Then you can write your way there.

Creative and
Intellectual Highs

"When you're writing, you're operating out of some different part of the brain. When it's happening, you're not aware of it, you don't know where what you write is coming from. And when you read it later, you think, Wow. I did that? It's like a surprise."
JUDY BLUME

"I've learned a lot I could not have learned if I were not a writer."
WILLIAM TREVOR

Wise Highs

Many writers write about writing. So there are many books available for you and other writers to read. Here are a few suggestions to start with; almost any book about writing will include lots more.

The Artist's Way: A Spiritual Path to Higher Creativity by Julia Cameron (Los Angeles: J.P. Tarcher, 2002). This famous book takes you through a self-directed 12-week writing program designed to dissolve blocks and recover creativity. It's especially useful for writers who feel they have lost some of their ability to create and want help getting it back.

Writing Down the Bones: Freeing the Writer Within by Natalie Goldberg (Boston: Shambhala, 1998). This fun, very readable book is based on Goldberg's Zen master's premise that "if you go deep enough in writing, it will take you every-place." Includes dozens of tested ideas, suggestions, and exercises to help new writers get started and experienced writers keep going.

TRY THIS! DIFFERENT STROKES FOR DIFFERENT FOLKS

Do you know what *arms, ears, tails, links, stems, spines, counters, strokes*, and *beaked serifs* have in common? They are all terms used to describe parts of letter forms. By using word processing software, you've probably discovered that there are hundreds of different fonts, or typeface designs. Each has a distinct character and set of associations.

A CAREER IN CALLIGRAPHY?

Don't laugh. A man named Donald Jackson, known as the "Queen's Calligrapher" (he has a part-time job writing official decrees for the British government), is busy with a big new project. In 1999, St. John's University in Collegeville, Minnesota, commissioned him to write the complete Bible by hand, and he's doing it the way medieval monks and scribes did: with goose quill pens on vellum ("paper" made of fine calfskin leather). Jackson designed a new style of lettering especially for the St. John's Bible; he's also ornamenting the pages with gold leaf, elaborate letters, and illustrations. The project is expected to take six years and cost three million dollars.

Calligraphy is the art of lettering by hand. The earliest books were all handwritten; you've probably seen examples of ancient illuminated manuscripts that made you gasp and say "How could anyone do that without spilling ink all over it?"

If you take up calligraphy, you'll enjoy it just as people enjoy drawing or painting. With practice, you'll be able to reproduce gorgeous alphabets and even design your own. In addition, calligraphy is a practical skill you can use to create beautiful hand-penned invitations, announcements, signs, cards, and books (hmmm, you could go into the lettering business and charge your friends for custom work). Plus calligraphy has an added benefit: the meditative high you get from losing yourself in the discipline of practicing your strokes.

FIND OUT MORE

Teach Yourself Calligraphy by Patricia Lovett (Lincolnwood, IL: NTC Publishing Group, 2004). The title says it all.

Creative and Intellectual Highs

Storytelling

Do you treasure memories of your parents telling you bedtime stories? Have you ever curled up in a sleeping bag around a campfire while a counselor turned your blood cold with a scary tale? If so, you know the power of oral storytelling.

The tradition goes back thousands of years. Stories have been told for many purposes, including:

- entertainment
- explaining physical and natural phenomena
- communicating emotion and experience
- preserving history
- passing on tradition and ancestral legacies
- teaching religious doctrine
- getting children to go to bed

STORIES IN THE BOARDROOM

Stories are a great way to share knowledge, and some companies are starting to use stories and storytellers to share business information and improve their image. For example, CapitolOne (a financial organization) has hired a professional storyteller to talk about the company. Other companies have staff people who use stories to explain difficult concepts.

Kids today are so used to getting their stories from books and movies that many never experience the pleasures of listening to a live human being. Luckily, you can do something about that.

ONCE UPON A TIME...

TRY THIS!

For a profound high, learn the art and craft of storytelling and tell stories to children. There are books with hundreds of wonderful stories. You may know stories that were passed on to you, or you can make up your own stories. If you have younger brothers or sisters, you've already got an audience. Or volunteer to tell stories at schools, libraries, and pediatric hospitals. The spell you weave will enthrall your young listeners—and their attention and adoration will put you on cloud nine.

> "The story...is one of the basic tools invented by the human mind, for the purpose of gaining understanding. There have been great societies that did not use the wheel, but there have been no societies that did not tell stories."
>
> URSULA K. LE GUIN

Wise Highs

FIND OUT MORE

Storytelling Encyclopedia: Historic, Cultural, and Multiethnic Approaches to Oral Traditions Around the World, edited by David Adams Leeming and Marion Sader (Phoenix, AZ: Oryx Press, 1997). This award-winning 560-page tome will tell you everything there is to know about the art of storytelling. See if your local public library has a copy.

Collecting

The urge to collect probably stems from our hunter-gatherer past. Long ago, our ancestors ventured forth from the cave to bring home food and other necessities of survival, such as sticks for making fire, gourds for holding water, and videos for keeping the children entertained. At some point, pottery replaced gourds, lighters made sticks obsolete, and DVDs followed videos. But by this time, the urge to collect was ingrained in our species. Gourds looked *pretty* so people  continued to gather them as well as many other items such as rocks, spears, eggs, leaves, and arrowheads. Many famous historical figures were known for their collections. For example, Norman the Conqueror collected countries. Henry the Eighth collected heads. And to this day, most humans continue to enjoy collecting.

The joy of collecting doesn't stop with the gathering of objects. True collectors love to look at, use, and/or handle their collections. My father, for example, has a collection of several hundred canes and walking sticks. Some of them have swords inside; others have removable handles that conceal flasks, compasses, and daggers. The handles themselves are made of pearl, ivory, wood, or brass; many are hand-carved in the shape of birds, dogs, and snakes. At least once a year, my father examines, cleans, and polishes all his canes—which is as much a part of the pleasure as acquiring them.

MAY THE FORCE BE WITH HIM

Stephen Sansweet, 53, is one of the world's most avid collectors of Star Wars items. He has more than 30,000 pieces linked to the first three movies alone (including movie tickets in Japanese, an authentic Darth Vader costume, and Chewbacca barrettes). His collection is so huge that it won't fit in his house; he stores most of it in a building he hopes to turn into a Star Wars museum someday.

Creative and Intellectual Highs

If you haven't already, find something to collect. It could be anything: books, bugs, baseball cards; postcards, posters, photos; coins, cars, candy wrappers. Maybe you're into watches or globes or model rockets. Be the first on your block to collect 18th-century thimbles or "Inspected By" labels.

While you may want to collect boulders or washing machines, keep in mind that it's easier to collect things that can be readily carried. And, if it's something that can be found anywhere in the world, you can look for additions to your collection anytime you travel.

FIND OUT MORE

> "One cannot collect all the beautiful shells on the beach. One can collect only a few, and they are more beautiful if they are few."
>
> ANNE MORROW LINDBERGH

Kovels' Yellow Pages by Ralph and Terry Kovel (New York: Three Rivers Press, 2003). With over 3,000 references to books, Web sites, clubs, auctions, services, and suppliers, this is the ultimate directory for collectors. Whether you want to refinish a table, sell a toy, buy a carousel, repair a broken doll, or find out if that lamp in the attic is worth $45,000, this up-to-date guide will steer you in the right direction. The authors (who have written over 70 books) also put out an annual publication called *Kovels' Antiques & Collectibles Price List: The Best-Selling Price Guide in America.*

Explore the Arts

Imagine a world without paintings, drawings, songs, symphonies, dances, plays, musicals, operas, ballets, sculptures, films, photographs, concerts, poetry slams, jewelry, tattoos, and T-shirts with designs on them. A world without theaters, amphitheaters, concert halls, jazz clubs, galleries, cultural centers, museums, and Shakespeare in the park. Without posters, prints, music videos, cartoons, comic books, and lots of other things you probably take for granted every day but would really, really miss if they suddenly disappeared.

Imagine a world without the arts. Dull. Boring. Scary!

Do your part to consume the arts. And make some of your own.

LOVE ART, LIVE LONGER

Researchers in Sweden surveyed 15,000 people to find out how often they went to plays, concerts, museums, and ballet performances. Ten years later, the researchers found that of the people who regularly attended these events, only 67 had died, compared to 399 of those who rarely or never went.

Wise Highs

"Art is the only way
to run away without
leaving home."

TWYLA THARP

THE SURVEY SAYS...

We asked teenagers "How do you relieve stress, have fun, escape reality, and/or get high without alcohol or other drugs?" Many enjoy the arts. Here are some of the things they like to do:*

• •

write

write poetry

act

make art/look at art

draw

paint

make a comic book

take pictures

make music/listen to music

sing

play a musical instrument

listen to music and sing along at the
        top of my lungs

listen to a tape I made of all my
        favorite love songs

go to a concert

One student responded "Walking through a museum is a hallucinogen for me." Another wrote "For me, acting and being on stage is a high. I love the feeling you get when you take on a different character." Another said "I love to play the guitar—particularly the blues."

TRY
THIS!

DRAW AND/OR PAINT

"I enjoy drawing. It
helps me calm down."

TRANQUIL MIDDLE SCHOOL
STUDENT

There are many reasons to take up drawing and painting besides nude models. Creating art is one of the most spiritual, exhilarating, rewarding experiences a person can have. Why else would Michelangelo have spent all those years on his back painting the Sistine Chapel ceiling?**

Of course, the creative process can also be painful and torturous. It can take a thousand sketches before you end up with one you like. It can take years of study and practice before your hands and eyes are skilled enough to create the vision in your head. But nothing beats art as a means of expressing the joys, riddles, and torments of human emotion and experience.

---

* From a survey of 2,000 students ages 11–18.
** Okay, the real reason: Pope Julius II made him do it.

Take a drawing or painting class. Check local museums, galleries, art schools, and community centers; many offer classes to the public. Whether you use watercolors, ink, gouache, charcoal, pastels, or oils; whether you dab, drip, roll, spray, or brush; whether you create on canvas, cardboard, vellum, or newspaper; whether you prefer landscapes, portraits, still lifes, or abstractions—creative passion will give you one of the best highs there is.

TRUE HIGHS
A Passion for Art

by Annie Wengenroth, 17

When I was four years old, I used to sit up in my dad's studio and draw or paint. I would write stories and draw illustrations for them.

When I was in third grade, I started taking piano lessons. Unlike most kids, I liked to play and would sit for hours playing or writing songs. This ignited a new passion for music, which became one of my outlets, along with other forms of art.

My interest in visual arts comes as no surprise to my family, because both of my parents attended art school and many of my dad's relatives are artists. However, I don't see it as simply an inevitable interest for me. I also see my art—whether it be writing, painting, music or photography—as what I like to call an alternative high.

"Art...is as much a source of happiness for the beginner as for the master. One forgets everything in one's work."
MARIE BASHKIRTSEFF

VISIT A MUSEUM OR GALLERY   TRY THIS!

Like poetry, museum-going can be ruined for kids if they are "forced" into it. There's nothing like being dragged by your parents along miles of corridors lined with portraits of dead people in starchy collars to create a lifelong distaste for art.

If you've gotten turned off to museums and galleries, give them another chance. And if you've already discovered the incredible riches of these places, you know how consciousness-altering and transforming museum-going can be.

When no one is lecturing you on what to appreciate, art is just so amazing! Stand close to an Impressionist painting. (Not *that* close or you'll set off the alarm.) Look at the brushwork. You'll see little dabs of color. They won't "represent" anything. Each is simply a brush

"Art is not a luxury, but a necessity."
REBECCA WEST

Wise Highs

stroke, a place where the artist applied some paint. Now stand five to ten feet away. Those thousands of dabs of colors become a shimmering landscape, a church facade, a field of hay. Unbelievable! You can't help but be filled with awe. And every one of those artists was once a teenager just like you—playing video games, checking for email, cruising malls.

Where but an art museum or gallery can you take a stroll and see epic battle scenes; somebody's thousand-year-old mummy; sinners cast into hell; sculptures so sensual you'd swear they're alive; a man wearing nothing but a helmet; or a nude woman reclining on a couch?

Most cities and universities have museums and galleries. Explore the ones near you. Many galleries are free (or free to students). Some have admission fees but are free at certain times. A lot of museums have comfy chairs, courtyards, and cafés that are great for getting away from

it all. If your home is like Grand Central Station, spend a few hours at a gallery after school. Besides being a great place for learning about and enjoying art, galleries are wonderful for doing homework, meditating, daydreaming, and meeting girls or guys.

FIND OUT MORE

Many of the world's great art museums are online. Visiting Web sites isn't the same as standing in front of a Rembrandt (or a Picasso, Monet, Magritte, or Warhol), but it's exciting to tour the Louvre or the Museum of Modern Art even if only virtually. Plus Web museums never close.

A great place to start exploring art on the Web is the **WebMuseum, Paris.** This ever-expanding network has mirror sites all over the world; in the U.S., go to www.ibiblio.org/wm or search for WebMuseum on any Web portal (examples: yahoo.com, excite.com, about.com).

Other sites to visit:

The Art Institute of Chicago
www.artic.edu

Le Louvre
www.louvre.fr

J. Paul Getty Museum
www.getty.edu/museum

The Metropolitan Museum of Art
www.metmuseum.org

Guggenheim Museum Bilbao
www.guggenheim-bilbao.es

Museum of Fine Arts Boston
www.mfa.org

Museum of Modern Art www.moma.org	**State Russian Museum** www.rusmuseum.ru	
National Gallery of Art www.nga.gov	**Stedelijk Museum of Modern Art** www.stedelijk.nl	
Smithsonian Institution www.si.edu	**Uffizi Gallery** www.uffizi.firenze.it	

You can also visit any Web portal, do a search for museums, and find lots more possibilities to explore.

Dance

When movement meets music, you've got dance. Dance is probably the oldest, most widely practiced, and most accessible of all the arts. We don't know exactly when dance started or what prehistoric dances were like, since no one bothered to save the tapes of Cro-Magnon *Soul Train*. But we do know that virtually anybody can dance. All you need is a body, a rhythmic accompaniment, and something to stand on.

Over the centuries, dance has been a means of recreation, communication, and religious expression. It is used to commemorate such milestones as births, deaths, marriages, and rites of passage. Primitive cultures use dance to invoke the powers of the gods, acknowledge the passing of the seasons, and celebrate fertility. Dancing is a mating ritual in many societies. Teenagers, for example, use dance as a means of expressing romantic interest, shocking their elders, and stepping on the toes of their classmates.

Dancing is so universal, it seems as if the urge to move and shake is wired into our genes. Just think of all the different types of dance: waltzes, polkas, minuets, and rhumbas. The twist, tango, shimmy, and bunny hop. The jerk, monkey, hora, and frug. Tap dancing, break dancing, clog dancing, square dancing; folk dancing, step dancing, line dancing, dirty dancing. Not to mention the fandango. And disco. And swing.

Some dances are very formal and stately; others are loose and wild. Some are comprised of specific steps; others let you make up your own. In Eastern dances, every gesture and movement has a specific meaning. In Western dances, you don't even have to know what you're doing to dance.

> "There are short-cuts to happiness, and dancing is one of them."
> VICKI BAUM

OLYMPIC DREAMS

Modern ballroom dancing, dubbed DanceSport, demonstrates the fusion of entertainment and sport. It has been given full recognition by the International Olympic Committee and may become an event at the 2008 summer Olympic Games.

Wise Highs

And then, of course, you have ballet, one of the most artistic forms of dance. Ballet, which developed in the late Middle Ages, was originally performed by amateur dancers at festive balls. (The Italian word *balletti* means "ballrooms.") Over time, ballet turned into dramatic works performed in theaters by highly trained dancers.

Fortunately, you don't have to put on tights or balance on your toes to experience the highs of dance. All you need to do is—DO IT!

TRUE HIGHS
Fun, Food, and Friends

by Hunter Strong, 15

There are so many ways to get high without taking drugs. This is my favorite.

My best friends and I make a night of it. We normally get together at one friend's house because she has a balcony that overlooks the ocean. We make sure there is plenty of food to get hyper from. After stuffing our faces with sugar, we carry the stereo out on the balcony, make sure there is a disco CD in the player, and *dance.* We have so much fun! We dance until we are sore! We hop around laughing and giggling at each other the entire time. The people passing by all laugh at us, but we are having so much fun that we don't mind. We call this "discotheque on Annie's roof!"

All you need to have fun as we do is plenty of ice cream, soda and/or coffee, a place to dance, a stereo, and of course, the most important thing, YOUR FRIENDS!

Big Dance List
www.bigdancelist.com
THE place for links to funny animated dances on the Web. And to think it all started with a hamster.

Music

Nobody has to tell you that music is one of the most powerful and immediate ways to alter consciousness.* But just in case you don't already know this, here's what other teens have to say:

"When I listen to music and I am about to fall asleep, I am in total bliss."

"When I am stressed, the best thing I can possibly do to ease my tension is to find some soothing music like Nirvana Unplugged in New York *and turn the volume up really loud and lie flat on my back and just concentrate on Kurt Cobain's voice. The clarity of the music eases all the stress in the world."*

"To get 'high,' I usually turn to music. I don't know what it is; there's something in me that I was born with that just spins around and lights up when I'm playing my own music, or I'm listening to someone I like. It's a great feeling to go over to the piano or pick up the guitar, close your eyes, and just pour out sweet music."

"I carry a tape with me wherever I go. I listen to it wherever I go. I have a mix tape and there is a song to put me in every kind of mood imaginable. I listen to that while I take a 3 1/2 mile walk each day to clear the mind and take stress off, or to pump me up."

> "Whenever I play, I throw myself away. It doesn't matter where I am. I close my eyes and leave this earth."
> MARY LOU WILLIAMS, JAZZ PIANIST

You know what music does to you:

- You're driving along, a song comes on the radio, and you're instantly happy. You can't help it, your body just wants to get up and dance!
- Or you hear another song and it transports you to a place of such melancholy that you feel like crying.
- Or you're watching a movie, the soundtrack turns ominous, you get goosebumps, your blood runs cold, and you *know* that you're about to be scared out of your skin.

> "I was born with music inside me.... Music was one of my parts. Like my ribs, my liver, my kidneys, my heart. Like my blood."
> RAY CHARLES, SOUL SINGER

Use music as a mood-altering substance. Learn which types of music make you feel happy, silly, and joyful. Which types help you to relax or concentrate. Which help you to have a good cry. Orchestrate your life.

> "You don't need any brains to listen to music."
> LUCIANO PAVAROTTI, TENOR

---

* See also "Visual Music," pages 125–126.

Wise Highs

HEALING MUSIC

Music has been used for healing since ancient times. Around 3,500 b.c., Egyptian physicians were prescribing chants to treat their patients. Music was used as medicine in ancient China (and still is today); the Chinese character for "medicine" is very similar to the character for "music." Plato and Aristotle believed that music could heal.

Today music therapists work in psychiatric clinics, rehab facilities, hospitals, nursing homes, schools, and hospices. They use composing, listening, and performing to induce relaxation and assist in the treatment of post-operative pain, migraines, brain injuries, psychiatric and emotional disorders, Alzheimer's disease, and many other injuries and illnesses. There are now 69 approved college programs in music therapy in the United States alone.

There is even a type of music called "healing music." Composers, scientists, musicians, researchers, and therapists are joining forces and making music specifically designed to ease stress, promote well-being, enhance relaxation, boost creativity, deepen concentration, and more. Some healing music matches the natural rhythm of the resting heart (about 70 beats per minute); some uses sound pulses to influence brainwave frequencies. It's a fascinating field and one worth exploring, if you're interested.

Visit your library or music store and look for recordings by Steven Halpern (*In the Key of Healing*), Dr. Jeffrey Thompson (*Alpha Relaxation System, Brainwave Suite*), Anna Wise (*High Performance Mind*), Dr. Andrew Weil (*Sound Body, Sound Mind*), Bruce BecVar (*The Magic of Healing Music*), Randy Crafton (*Inner Rhythms*), and other artists. You might start by checking the New Age section.

If you want to know more about music therapy and healing music, here are three Web sites you can explore:

Canadian Association for Music Therapy
www.musictherapy.ca

Institute for Music Research
imr.utsa.edu

Steven Halpern's Inner Peace Music
www.stevenhalpern.com

Doo-dee-doo-doo-doo-doo-doo. It's hard to whistle and *not* feel cheerful. For a nice little mini-high, whistle a soundtrack for your life.

There are two primary techniques for whistling. One involves the insertion of fingers into your mouth, the other doesn't. What if you're pucker-impaired? That's all right. You can probably learn to whistle. And if, after extensive practice, you still can't make anything come out of your mouth except your tongue, there's always the kazoo.

FIND OUT MORE

ehow.com
www.ehow.com
This fun site offers instructions on everything from fixing a running toilet to cleaning miniblinds and carving a turkey. But we were talking about whistling. Search for "how to whistle" for step-by-step instructions.

Highbrow Highs

Why do people seek advanced degrees? Why do they spend hours, weeks, months, and years doing library research? Or surfing the Web for answers, information, and facts? Or reading mountains of books? Or solving math problems that would give any normal person a headache? Or going to lectures? Or learning foreign languages…for fun? When shopping malls are open seven days a week, why would anyone spend time learning and studying if he or she didn't have to?

I'll admit it's nice to have a few extra letters after your name. And it's not the worst thing in the world to be seen as a bright, intelligent person. But the main reason is this: Exploring and playing with ideas is one of the greatest highs there is.

Besides, if humans weren't meant to think, we'd all have pineapples for heads. Following are a few not-just-for-brainiacs highs you can try.

> "You are led through your lifetime by the inner learning creature, the playful spiritual being that *is* your real self."
> RICHARD BACH

Wise Highs

Zen koans are profound philosophical riddles that Zen teachers use to guide their students. Here's an example:*

Kyogen Mounts the Tree

Kyogen said: "Zen is like a man hanging in a tree by his teeth over a precipice. His hands grasp no branch, his feet rest on no limb, and under the tree another person asks him: 'Why did Bodhidharma come to China from India?'

"If the man in the tree does not answer, he fails; and if he does answer, he falls and loses his life. Now what shall he do?"

Zen koans can't be solved by the use of logic, science, math, or online encyclopedias. They can only be solved by moving outside of and beyond ordinary consciousness.

You reflect on a koan morning, noon, and night. It becomes the mantra of your existence. You get more and more frustrated because you can't come up with "the answer." This is because there are many right answers...and no right answers. Eventually your mind can't stand it anymore and goes to an "extra-cerebral" dimension where it finds the solution. The giddy high of enlightenment you experience comes from recognizing that the "answer" applies not just to the riddle, but to many other aspects of life.

Even though Zen koans are designed to be contemplated by one person, there's no law that says you can't ponder them with others. Pose a riddle to a group of friends and see where the discussion goes.

> "I dreamt that I was a butterfly, flitting around in the sky; then I awoke. Now I wonder: Am I a man who dreamt of being a butterfly, or am I a butterfly dreaming that I am a man?"
>
> CHUANG TSU

FIND OUT MORE

Zen Flesh, Zen Bones: A Collection of Zen and Pre-Zen Writings compiled by Paul Reps and Nyogen Senzaki (Tokyo: Charles E. Tuttle Co., 1998). First published in 1957, this book introduced a generation of Americans to Zen. Consider it a sort of "Zen 101." Includes ancient writings (in translation) and koans to ponder.

---

* This comes from a classic Zen text called *The Gateless Gate* which was written by the Chinese master Ekai, called Mu-mon, who lived from 1183–1260. (Text transcribed by Nyogen Senzaki and Paul Reps.)

The idea that you can get high off of math may seem a bit far-fetched when you're cramming for a test on the square roots of sine curves of negative quadratic equilateral logarithms.* Schools tend to teach math for its practical uses: balancing a checkbook, converting currency, computing fuel consumption, and, of course, the application we all use most often upon graduating from high school: figuring out story problems.

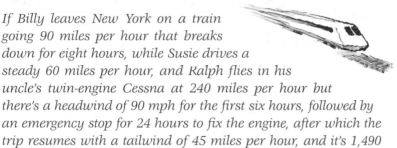

If Billy leaves New York on a train going 90 miles per hour that breaks down for eight hours, while Susie drives a steady 60 miles per hour, and Ralph flies in his uncle's twin-engine Cessna at 240 miles per hour but there's a headwind of 90 mph for the first six hours, followed by an emergency stop for 24 hours to fix the engine, after which the trip resumes with a tailwind of 45 miles per hour, and it's 1,490 miles from New York to Kansas, who will get to Kansas first?

The answer, of course, is WHOOOOOO CAAAAAARES?

When the purpose of learning math is so you'll know the answers on the test, it tends to obscure the fact that mathematics is a thing of beauty and elegance. There is a perfection to math that creates its own reality. The most chaotic and unfathomable aspects of the universe may all one day be explained by mathematical equations. Perhaps so-called "random" events aren't random at all.

Dive into mathematics. What you learn may alter your consciousness forever. For starters, here are five neat things about math.

Magic Squares

In magic squares, the sums of each full row, column, and diagonal add up to the same number. In the following magic square, the constant sum is 15.

$$2 \ 7 \ 6$$
$$9 \ 5 \ 1$$
$$4 \ 3 \ 8$$

Try making a magic square of your own. Need help? Go to:

Grog's Magic Squares
www.grogono.com/magic

---

* You can tell that I was very good at math.

"I see a certain order in the universe and math is one way of making it visible."
MAY SARTON

"People who don't know what math is don't know what math isn't."
SHEILA TOBIAS

Wise Highs

Music and Math

Musical harmony can be expressed by mathematical formulas. Don't believe it? Read:

Math and Music: Harmonious Connections by Trudi Hammel Garland (White Plains, NY: Dale Seymour Publications, 1995). This fascinating book explores the connections between music and math—and there are plenty.

Nifty Nines

All multiples of 9 have 9 as the sum of their digits. *Examples:* 2 x 9 = 18; 1 + 8 = 9. 6 x 9 = 54; 5 + 4 = 9.

Yes, it works with bigger numbers, too. *Example:* 45,932 x 9 = 413,388; 4 + 1 + 3 + 3 + 8 + 8 = 27; 2 + 7 = 9.

Now you'll always have something to do while waiting for a bus or a dentist's appointment.

Number Meanings

Throughout history, different numbers have been assigned different attributes, symbolic meanings, or "powers." Some numbers are considered lucky (7) or unlucky (13). In Greece, odd numbers were masculine and even numbers were feminine; in China, odd numbers were yang and even numbers were yin. In Central America, 20 was a sacred number, associated with the sun god; in Hebrew tradition, 21 meant wisdom.

Curious to know more? Visit your local library and wander through books on symbols and numerology.

Fabulous Fibonaccis

Leonardo Fibonacci (no relation to Leonardo DiCaprio) was a famous mathematician who lived around the 12th century. One day he was bored (probably after having watched *Titanic* for the 157th time), so he wondered how many rabbits would be produced if a pair had two babies each month, and those two (after two months) produced two more rabbits of their own each month thereafter who, two months later, produced two more who also began to produce offspring at the rate of two a month and...well, you get the picture. After a lot of mental hopping around, Fibonacci ended up with a sequence of numbers that is now called the Fibonacci Series. It looks like this:

Month	1	2	3	4	5	6	7	8	9	10	11	12...
Couples	1	1	2	3	5	8	13	21	34	55	89	144...

There are two amazing things about this series of numbers. The first is that each number of rabbits produced in this series (1, 1, 2, 3, 5, 8, 13, 21, 34…) is the sum of the two preceding numbers (1 + 1 = 2, 1 + 2 = 3, 3 + 5 = 8, etc.). The second is that this sequence can be found in many of nature's designs (e.g., pinecones, shells, flower petals).

Has this brief introduction tickled your inquisitive mind? If so, check out:

Fascinating Fibonaccis: Mystery and Magic in Numbers by Trudi Hammel Garland (White Plains, NY: Dale Seymour Publications, 1987). Explores Fibonaccis in nature and math.

Fibonacci Fun: Fascinating Activities with Intriguing Numbers by Trudi Hammel Garland (White Plains, NY: Dale Seymour Publications, 1998). Sounds like just the ticket for a rainy afternoon.

Fibonacci Numbers, the Golden Section, and the Golden String
www.mcs.surrey.ac.uk/Personal/R.Knott/Fibonacci
Facts about Fibonacci, the Fibonacci numbers, and where they appear in nature, plus puzzles where the answers all seem to involve Fibonacci numbers. This award-winning site is hosted by the Department of Computing of Surrey University in the United Kingdom.

Want to know more neat stuff about math? Of course you do! Just carrying these books around will make you look and feel smarter. Reading them is challenging but worth it.

- *e: The Story of a Number* by Eli Maor (Princeton, NJ: Princeton University Press, 1998).
- *Fermat's Enigma: The Epic Quest to Solve the World's Greatest Mathematical Problem* by Simon Singh (New York: Bantam Books, 1998).
- *Gödel, Escher, Bach: An Eternal Golden Braid* by Douglas R. Hofstadter (New York: Basic Books, 1999).
- *A History of Pi* by Petr Beckmann (New York: St. Martin's Press, 1976).
- *The Mystery of Numbers* by Annemarie Schimmel (New York: Oxford University Press, 1994).
- *The Nothing That Is: A Natural History of Zero* by Robert Kaplan (New York: Oxford University Press, 2000).

When you're on the Web and hungry for some tasty math, go to:

Eric Weisstein's World of Mathematics
mathworld.wolfram.com
From abacus to Zsigmondy theorem, this massive site has it all. Online nirvana for math freaks.

Creative and Intellectual Highs

"The more I learn, the clearer my view of the world becomes."
SONIA SANCHEZ

"I can't understand why people are frightened of new ideas. I'm frightened of the old ones."
JOHN CAGE

Science is the systematic study used to prove how things work…until someone comes along later to prove that what was proved earlier was wrong. For example, people used to think that the Earth was flat. Now, thanks to science, we know that it is sausage-shaped.

Science is all about matter and energy, quantum physics and quarks, atoms and crystals, time and speed, mating praying mantises and, and, and—EVERYTHING!!!! People sometimes think that science just deals with "material" things like chemical compounds and pistils and stamens. But science can be used to explore the deepest mysteries of life. For example, scientific methods are increasingly being used to study spiritual matters. Studies show that people who are prayed for recuperate from illness or surgery faster than people for whom no prayers are said.*

If you want to think about things you've never thought about before; if you want a whole new perspective on life and reality and God and the universe, get into science.

"The true definition of science is this: the study of the beauty of the world."

SIMONE WEIL

FIND OUT MORE

Want to know more neat stuff about science? Sure you do! Like the math books listed on page 209, these titles aren't easy reading. Roll up your mental sleeves and give them a try anyway.

- *A Brief History of Time* by Stephen Hawking (New York: Bantam Doubleday Dell, 1998).
- *The Elegant Universe: Superstrings, Hidden Dimensions, and the Quest for the Ultimate Theory* by Brian Greene (New York: W.W. Norton & Co., 2000).
- *Six Easy Pieces* by Richard P. Feynman (Reading, MA: Perseus Press, 1996).
- *The Tao of Physics: An Exploration of the Parallels Between Modern Physics and Eastern Mysticism* by Fritjof Capra (Boston: Shambhala Publications, 2000).

Other more readable recommendations: Pretty much anything by scientist/physician Lewis Thomas *(The Lives of a Cell, The Medusa and the Snail)*, amateur astronomer/former journalism professor Timothy Ferris *(Coming of Age in the Milky Way, The Whole Shebang)*, and zoologist/geologist/paleontologist/biologist Stephen J. Gould *(The Panda's Thumb, Questioning the Millennium)*.

In the mood for some anti-science? Visit this Web site:

Ask Dr. Science
www.ducksbreath.com
"America's foremost authoritarian on the world around us," used to be heard daily on the radio. Now you can listen to the archived shows on this site.

---

* For more on prayer, see pages 238–239.

MATH AND SCIENCE UNDER THE BIG TOP

When you go to the circus, you expect to see jugglers and acrobats (and lions and tigers and bears). Along with death-defying tricks, you're also seeing scientific laws in action. For example, juggling is a form of math—both math and juggling are based on patterns that can be changed. Changing the pattern brings a different answer…or a gasp of surprise from the audience. Acrobats use the same techniques to perform basic patterns, then complicate them in exciting ways. For example, a full-body somersault demonstrates the conservation of angular momentum. That's the long way of saying that the smaller and more compact the acrobats can make their bodies, the faster and easier they move through space.

PHILOSOPHY

TRY THIS!

People who major in philosophy in college are very brave, because I can guarantee you'll never see a classified ad reading "Philosopher Wanted." There can be only one reason why somebody would study philosophy: the sheer love of ideas.

You probably won't learn it in school—at least, not until you get to college, and even there philosophy won't be required (unless you're one of those fearless souls who major in it). You won't learn it on tele-vision. There aren't many movies about philosophy. You won't hear about it on the radio or read about it in the newspaper or the latest issue of *Seventeen* or *People*. Bottom line: If you want to study philosophy, you'll have to get started on your own.

> "Philosophy is a kind of journey, ever learning yet never arriving at the ideal perfection of truth."
>
> ALBERT PIKE

FIND OUT MORE

Philosophy for Dummies by Tom Morris (Foster City, CA: IDG Books Worldwide, 1999). How to think about life's big questions, apply the insights of great philosophers, develop your own personal philosophy, and more. The author is no dummy; he taught philosophy at Notre Dame for 15 years.

Internet Encyclopedia of Philosophy
www.iep.utm.edu
Timelines, texts, biographies, and more, from Aenesidemus the Skeptic to Zeno the Eleatic.

Performing Highs

Many teens dream of performing—but it doesn't have to be a dream. You can do it and enjoy the same highs these teens feel:

"My joyous times are when I'm on stage, either dancing or acting, and knowing that everyone's eyes are on me. I've been performing for 11 years, and every time I set foot on stage during a performance, I get this huge adrenaline rush and feeling of power that makes me forget what's going on in my life at that time, or the stress that goes along with being a teenager. Acting allows me to take on an entirely new character, so I can forget about myself and become a new person." **NIKKI ROUTHIER, 17**

"I remember my first violin recital with my current teacher. I was extremely nervous. I got up on stage and took a deep breath. I felt that I played beautifully with only a few minor mistakes. The confidence was in my veins. I felt great. When I completed the piece, everybody clapped and congratulated me. That performance really turned me on to music, and I have loved putting on shows ever since." **RACHEL COVERT, 14**

"When I get off any stage, anywhere, for anything, I always, always feel good inside!" **EVELYNN SAWYER, 12**

"When I perform, I get lost in the music because it's all I can think about. I usually forget the audience is there, and the only thing that makes me realize they're there is when they applaud me at the end. Even though I've been playing for quite a while, I've never tired of playing and performing and probably never will. Because both make me feel great." **ELLEN SAWYER, 14**

Look into your school's drama program or clubs. Contact community theaters and ask about auditions and casting calls. Or start your own theater. (Why not? That's how lots of established theaters began.) Stage a variety show with people in your neighborhood—little kids, other teens, seniors. Join your school choir or glee club. If your parents want you to play piano for your grandparents when they visit, don't moan and groan and hide in your room. Play a tune or two and bask in the applause.

Some people may have more natural talent than others, but even the stars take classes and lessons. The more you learn and practice, the more confident you'll feel.

PERFORMING STUDENTS MAKE THE GRADE

In a Department of Education study, researchers found that students who were deeply involved with any kind of instrumental music scored higher on math tests than those who weren't. Students involved in drama had better reading skills—and were less likely to tolerate racism, perhaps because actors learn empathy.

Creative and Intellectual Highs

How wonderful it is that humans are endowed with a built-in musical instrument. I'm not talking about the popping sounds we can make by placing an index finger in our cheek. I'm talking about the *la-la-la* human voice. About the *do-ron-ron-ron-da-do-ron-ron* ability to sing.

So *do-re-mi-fa-so-la-ti-do* and let yourself go. Whatever singing means to you—belting out a sultry blues song, screaming at the top of your lungs, harmonizing with a hundred voices in a choir, scatting with Ella or rapping with Snoop—it's a great way to express the music in your soul.

"But I can't sing!" you say. No matter. The ability to sing doesn't seem to be a requirement for becoming a fabulously successful singer. Actually, anyone can learn to sing. Part of the process involves finding your own style and learning what kinds of music your voice is most suited for: opera, choral, jazz, rap, barbershop, or being the person who goes *bop-bop-a-bop-bop* in the background.

> "When we want to get high, we listen to music and sing at the top of our lungs."
> SINGING HIGH SCHOOL STUDENTS

Follow Your Muse:
Four Steps to Success

1. Write down something creative you've always dreamed of doing (e.g., paint a mural, write a screenplay, play guitar).

2. List all the reasons you haven't yet pursued your dream. Be as detailed and complete as you can.

3. Examine your list. How many of the obstacles are *practical* (e.g., lack of money or time, no place to work) and how many are *motivational* (e.g., afraid to try, haven't looked for a teacher)? Identify each type.

You'll probably find that *you* are standing in the way of your own dream. Even factors seemingly "outside" of you, such as a lack of money or equipment, are surmountable.

For example, you want to take piano lessons, but you can't afford it. Well, if it's really your dream, you can make it happen. How? Here are some starter ideas:

- Find a student at your school who already plays piano and ask him if he'll teach you. His rates will be a fraction of those of a professional teacher.

> "When inspiration does not come, I go for a walk, go to the movie, talk to a friend, let go…. The muse is bound to return again, especially if I turn my back!"
> JUDY COLLINS

Wise Highs

- Contact music schools in your area. See if they offer scholarships.
- Talk to people until you get the names of accomplished amateurs who play piano for enjoyment. They may teach you for free.
- Make a list of all the piano teachers in your area. (You can get names by calling music schools, asking musicians you know, and/or talking to your own school's orchestra, band, or choir leader.) Call every teacher on the list. Explain your situation and offer to barter for lessons. You could care for their lawn, shovel snow, wash cars, baby-sit, or do carpentry, housecleaning, shopping, or laundry.

Adults are impressed by teenagers who are motivated and eager to learn. If you're persistent, you *will* find someone who wants to help.

4. Go over your own list of obstacles and brainstorm ways to overcome them. If you *really* want to do something, you can. It's just a question of how much you want it.

Friends, Family, and Heavy Petting
Connecting Highs

What matters most in life to you? What makes you feel most alive? What fills you with the most joy?

Chances are you'll say "family," "friends," "my pet Schnauzer, Wolfgang," "playing in a band," "going dancing," "helping others," "watching a sunset," "skiing through the woods," "creating something." Whatever you say, I bet it involves making a *connection* of some sort or another.

In his book *Connect*, Dr. Edward Hallowell says that connectedness is "a feeling of being part of something larger than yourself," and that connecting is essential to health and happiness.

Connecting to what? To family and friends, tradition and history, art and music, ideas and fantasies; to the natural and spiritual worlds; to physical exuberance and sensuous delight; to people we need and people in need; to memories and dreams. According to Dr. Hallowell, connections open your heart, lengthen your life, and deepen your soul. According to me, an open heart, a long life, and a deep soul add up to quite a high.

Another way to measure the importance of connections is to think about life *without* them. When are you most miserable and unhappy? Is it when you feel lonely and isolated? That nobody understands or cares? That nothing matters? That you can't trust

"Intimate relationships cannot substitute for a life plan. But to have any meaning or viability at all, a life plan must include intimate relationships."
HARRIET LERNER

215

Wise Highs

anybody? That you're bored and there's nothing to do? That you'll never fall in love? That you're no good at anything? If so, you can see how every one of those feelings represents a *disconnection*—from your friends and parents; from humanity; from hope and creative passion; from faith in your own abilities and future.

What rescues you from these feelings of loneliness and despair? Reconnecting! Talking to a friend. Holding a baby in your arms. Having a heart-to-heart with your parents. Being appreciated. Listening to a fabulous song. Creating something that pleases you. Seeing a rainbow. Falling in love.

Life today is increasingly disconnected. So many people are busy and stressed. Families find it hard to sit down together for a meal. Young professionals pick up and move every few years. Neighbors don't know the people living next door. We walk down the street in a cocoon of suspicion and on-guardedness. If we smile at someone, they don't think we're being friendly; they think we're nuts!

Ironically, as computers and the Internet *connect* the world, the "net" effect is *disconnection.* Things we used to do person-to-person we now do electronically: banking, buying a book, filling a prescription, answering the phone. Have you tried to reach a live human being in a business lately? Impossible! How many shopkeepers or bank tellers do you know personally?

One of the best things you can do to feel happy and stay healthy is connect to as many people, places, and things as you can. This chapter explores some of the different types of connections Dr. Hallowell describes—and ways you can maintain and strengthen those ties.

CONNECT OR DIE!

Dr. Lisa Berkman conducted a study of some 7,000 people over a period of nine years. She measured their "connectedness" by examining whether they lived alone or with someone; how much they interacted with relatives and friends; whether they were members of a church or other religious community; and whether they did volunteer work and/or belonged to any groups. The results were amazing. The people with the fewest connections were *three times* more likely to die over the nine-year period of the study than the people with strong social ties. In other words, the more isolated you were, the more likely you were to die! Over a dozen subsequent studies have confirmed this link between connection and mortality.

Connect with Your Family

Connecting Highs

Our family relationships—with parents, siblings, children, spouses, partners, aunts, uncles, grandparents, cousins—are tremendous sources of warmth, joy, and security.

And heartache. Where there's love and caring, there's also hurt.

An investment in family connections is one of the best you'll ever make. But, because family is always "there," it's easy to take for granted the people we care about most.

If you think about it, every one of us was *literally* connected at birth. Once the umbilical cord was cut, growing up became a steady process of increasing *separation* and *individuation* (to use a couple of "shrink" terms). The happiest families are those that allow each family member to grow; that find appropriate balances between dependence and independence, between family identity and personal identity.

Here are some ways to build, sustain, and strengthen your family connections.

"Call it a clan, call it a network, call it a tribe, call it a family. Whatever you call it, whoever you are, you need one."
JANE HOWARD

TALK TO YOUR PARENTS

TRY THIS!

Find out what makes them tick. Ask them about…

…their childhood, adolescence, and schooling
…their relationships with their own parents
…their friends, first loves and dates
…their years in college or when they first started working
…their jobs, dreams, and regrets

If your relationship allows, ask them about…

…their experiences with (and attitudes towards) sex and drugs when they were your age

Ask them what they *think* about things going on in the world. Ask them how they *feel* about things going on in the world—or in your city, town, or neighborhood. Let them know that you believe their thoughts and feelings are important. Who knows, they might turn around and ask about *your* thoughts and feelings. That's the start of an ongoing dialogue.

Tip: Connecting doesn't always have to mean talking. A parent and child throwing a ball back and forth are connecting. Two people watching the sunset are connecting. A family sitting in the living room— one person reading, another knitting, another doing homework, two

"The best inheritance a parent can give his children is a few minutes of his time each day."
ORLANDO A. BATTISTA

Wise Highs

playing a game—are connecting. The unspoken sharing of a moment or experience is connecting.

 TRY THIS!

HAVE FAMILY MEETINGS

Get together at least every two to three weeks (more often, if possible) to make plans, coordinate schedules, and discuss family goals. If there's family conflict afoot, use the meeting to identify and solve the problem.

Tip: It's never conflict *per se* that damages a relationship. It's *unresolved* conflict or *unfairly resolved* conflict.*

Here's how to make family meetings work:

1. Establish a regular time to meet. If someone can't come because of an unavoidable conflict, try to reschedule. If one or more family members just decide not to show up, don't reschedule. It's their loss, and they have to abide by decisions made without their input.

2. Post an agenda in a conspicuous place. Encourage your parents and siblings to write down items they'd like to discuss. While late-breaking issues can always be brought up, the agenda lets people do some thinking ahead of time.

3. Appoint a "chair" for each meeting. This is the person who brings the agenda and runs the meeting. The position should be rotated among all family members so no one person dominates.

4. Don't meet for too long. When people get restless, tempers flare and thinking gets sloppy. Better to schedule another meeting than to run overtime.

5. Take notes. Appoint a scribe for each meeting. The scribe's job is to write down ideas, decisions, plans, etc. He or she can also remind people between meetings of actions they need to take.

6. If you have a family problem, work together to solve it. Virtually any conflict can be resolved if you:

"The support of family and friends to do well gives me the greatest 'high.' Every time someone says they're proud of me or care about me, a huge smile runs across my face and I know I'm safe. Once one has that, one can do anything."
NIKKI ROUTHIER, 17

---

* I could write a book about resolving family conflicts and solving family problems. Come to think of it, I *did* write a book. It's called *Bringing Up Parents: The Teenager's Handbook,* and it's published by the same folks who brought you *this* book.

- Define it in terms that don't accuse people of wrongdoing (*example:* "I can't study with music on," NOT "Your music is driving me crazy!").
- Brainstorm solutions together.
- Discuss the options available to you.
- Pick the best one and make a plan of action.
- Monitor and adjust the solution as needed.

Connecting Highs

7. Keep the mood positive. While family meetings are the place to bring problems and complaints, they shouldn't degenerate into gripe sessions. This can be avoided if you all agree to stick to the following rules:

- Listen when others speak.
- Think constructively. Focus on solving the problem rather than finding blame.
- Don't label people's ideas as lame, clueless, or silly.
- Don't accuse. Say how you feel.
- Make sure there's a fun item on every agenda (for example, taking a trip, getting a dog, deciding what to do for Grandma's birthday).
- End each meeting on an upbeat note. Rent a video, make ice cream sundaes, play a game. Try not to end a meeting when people are angry or upset.

MAINTAIN AND INVENT FAMILY TRADITIONS

TRY THIS!

Children who grow up in families that maintain rituals are less likely to have behavioral or emotional problems, and less likely to get into trouble with alcohol and other drugs, than are children who grow up in families without rituals.

What's a ritual? Eating meals together. Celebrating birthdays and holidays. Parents reading to their children before bedtime. Family swim night every Thursday. Taking a vacation together once a year. Ordering a pizza once a week.

Don't feel bound by the rituals of others. If your family chooses to celebrate Thanksgiving by going bowling and eating take-out Chinese food, that's fine. It's also fine to change rituals, to let them evolve. For example, if you're 16 years old, you may no longer want your father to pretend he's a spider and tickle your back every night before bed. But you might like to take an after-dinner walk together a few nights a week.

"Ritual is one of the ways in which humans put their lives in perspective."
CLARISSA PINKOLA ESTÉS

Wise Highs

EAT DINNER TOGETHER

Of all possible family rituals, eating together at least once a day is probably the most symbolic of "being a family." Studies document the importance of shared mealtimes in maintaining healthy families.

Of course, it only works if you use the time to have interesting discussions and find out what's going on in people's lives. It *doesn't* work if people nag, criticize, tease, or belittle one another.

If your family dinners often decay into sniping sessions or free-for-alls, you'll need to work on family problem solving and communication strategies. See "Have Family Meetings" on pages 218–219.

DO SERVICE WORK TOGETHER

This is multiple connectedness. Not only will you enjoy your family's company, you'll also feel good about doing good.*

You don't have to commit to a huge, time-consuming project. Service can mean shoveling a neighbor's sidewalk, picking up litter in a park, visiting someone who's homebound, or watching a single mom's kids for a couple of hours while she runs errands or goes to a movie.

If and when you're ready for a bigger commitment, try these suggestions from Susan J. Ellis, president of Energize Inc., an international training, consulting, and publishing firm specializing in volunteerism:

1. Have a family meeting to consider this whole idea. Make sure everyone, no matter how young, participates in the discussion.

2. Make a list of all the volunteering each member of the family is doing now. Would the others like to help with any of these activities?

3. What causes interest you? Allow everyone to suggest a community problem of concern to him or her. If some of the ideas intrigue the whole family, start exploring what organizations in your community are already working on these. Use the Yellow Pages, go to the library, visit the Volunteer Center, or search the Internet.

"My parents and I spend every Christmas day at a shelter serving dinners to homeless people. The first year, I didn't want to do it; I wanted to stay home opening presents and lazing around as usual. But now I really look forward to it. It feels great to be helping people."
SERVING STUDENT

* See also "Connect by Giving" on pages 229–233.

4. Consider what types of work everyone wants to do. Make two lists: one for Things We Know How to Do and one for Things We Would Like to Learn How to Do. Make sure something is listed for each member of the family. (This is a great opportunity to acknowledge each other's talents. The lists will also prove helpful when you interview with an agency.)

5. Call several organizations for appointments and screen your options. See whether the agency representatives are comfortable talking to children and teens as well as to adults. Ask if the agency has something meaningful for you to do as a group.

6. You may want to begin with a one-time activity. This will test the water to see how everyone likes volunteering together.

7. Once you commit to a volunteer project, take it seriously. Talk about it during the week and plan ahead to do it, even when things get hectic.

8. Enjoy the many benefits of volunteering as a family: spending quality time together, getting to know each other in new ways, demonstrating skills and learning new ones (which builds mutual respect), working together toward the same goals—and having something to talk about all week!

Connecting Highs

"Service to others is the rent you pay for your room here on earth."
MUHAMMAD ALI

STAY IN TOUCH WITH RELATIVES — TRY THIS!

Call, email, or write to your grandparents at least once a month. Keep in touch with uncles, aunts, cousins, and siblings who are away at school or have moved out of the house. Plan visits or family get-togethers so you see close relatives at least once a year.

As families become more geographically scattered, family reunions are becoming more popular. If you're the take-charge, super-organized leader type, you might offer to plan a family reunion. Or find out if anyone else in the family is interested and offer to help.

You might also start a family newsletter, with new "editions" once a year—or once a month, depending on how much news your family has and wants to share. Call, visit, write, or email relatives asking for the latest news. Then whip something up on your computer at home, at school, or at your local public library. Print out copies to send by snail mail, or send them by email to relatives who have computers of their own.

"Family is just accident.... They don't mean to get on your nerves. They don't even mean to be your family, they just are."
MARSHA NORMAN

Wise Highs

FIND OUT MORE

Creating Family Newsletters: 123 Ideas for Sharing Memorable Moments with Family and Friends by Elaine Floyd (St. Louis, MO: Newsletter Resources, 1998). Shows and explains several different newsletter formats and styles, from text only to Web sites. Includes worksheets.

The Family Reunion Sourcebook by Edith Wagner (Los Angeles: Lowell House, 1999). Practical guidelines, advice, and anecdotes from the founder and editor-in-chief of *Reunions* magazine.

Connect with Friends

Nobody has to tell you how important friends are. Friends are your partners in life. Here's what teens told us about their friendships:

"Friends are the family
we choose for ourselves."
EDNA BUCHANAN

"A single rose can be my
garden...a single friend,
my world."
LEO BUSCAGLIA

"In my opinion, the main way to get high without actually using drugs is to spend time with friends. We share so many common interests and it never gets boring. We can always think of things to do regardless of the situation. We have so much fun, whether just listening to music or going to a concert. This is one of the best ways I can think of to feel happy and confident. Being with my friends definitely gives me a natural high." **ANNIE BELL, 15**

"My friends and I have giant bonding sessions where we all spend the night together and do goofy stuff we would never do around anyone else." **GOOFY STUDENT**

"I sit with my friends and talk about my hopes and dreams in life. It helps me escape from reality, especially when my friends encourage me, because I begin to believe it will happen". **DREAMY STUDENT**

"My friends and I will just sit down and talk. We might explain our anger, yell, cry, laugh, and many more emotions spill out when we do this. It is very rare to find someone you can do this with, but you know when you find them." **EMOTING STUDENT**

The quality of your connections with friends is probably a pretty good barometer of how you're feeling at any given time. When you want to nurture and strengthen those connections, try these ideas.

SEE YOUR FRIENDS REGULARLY

TRY THIS!

Connecting Highs

Many friends you see automatically; you live next door to each other, you're in the same class, you play on the same team. But how about friends you don't automatically see? Someone you met at camp. Someone you really liked from a community play you were in a year ago. Don't let these friendships slip out of your life. Keep them alive.

Make plans to see each other regularly. Meet once every week or so at a café or ice-cream shop; play a sport together; see a movie; go to each other's houses. If the friend lives out of town, stay in touch by email. And try to see each other once a year.

BROADEN YOUR FRIENDSHIPS

TRY THIS!

Some of the best friendships you'll ever have may be with people you wouldn't normally think of. Humans have all sorts of needs which peer friendships don't always satisfy.

Make friends with older people. And I don't mean only people over 30; I mean people over 60, too. You know—those in upper middle age. You may find their experience valuable. And there won't be that edge of competition that sometimes surfaces between friends.

Make friends with neighbors, crosswalk guards, bus drivers, salespeople, gas station attendants, restaurant owners. You may not choose to share your love life with these people or put them in your will, but it *is* nice to have warm, human contact wherever you go.

Make friends with little kids. Notice them, smile at them, learn their names. Say hi to them when you see them on the street, at the park, at the mall. Act glad to see them. Talk with them. Include them in conversations. Remember their birthdays. Let them know they're important in your life, because you'll certainly be important in theirs. Little kids look up to big kids like you.

Become friends with teachers you like. *Tip:* Sometimes friendships with teachers sort of simmer while you're still their student, then start to percolate when you move on from their class. Teachers don't have to grade you anymore, you don't have to explain why your homework was late anymore, and you can actually get to know each other as human beings.

> "There is nowhere you can go and only be with people who are like you. Give it up."
> BERNICE JOHNSON REAGON

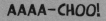
AAAA-CHOO!

Researchers at Carnegie Mellon University asked 276 healthy men and women for the lowdown on their professional, social, and love lives. Then they squirted cold viruses up their noses. The *more* active and diverse a person's social life, the *less* likely he or she was to feel sluggish or come down with a cold.

223

Wise Highs

The Internet is changing the way people communicate. Who would have thought ten years ago that teenagers could sit in their bedrooms and carry on real-time conversations with their peers on the other side of the globe? Or that a group of 20 people who share similar interests could have a live chat? It's beyond amazing, and ten years from now we'll probably be doing things on the Internet that we can't even imagine.

Used wisely, the Internet is a fabulous resource for connecting. Find chat rooms you like. You'll inevitably make online friends. If you hear of an author or expert who will be a guest in a chat room, pay a visit. You'll have a front-row seat without needing to find a parking spot.

The Internet has some pitfalls, though. People aren't always who or what they represent themselves to be. To help you stay on the safe side, here are four simple tips:

1. Watch out for cyber-pals who seem overly friendly. The Internet is no different than real life. There are tons of wonderful, trustworthy people out there—and a few creeps. Beware of people who seem overly intimate, who want to know what you look like, where you live, what your sexual fantasies and experience are. Follow your instincts. If something or someone feels weird, it probably is. And if it feels okay, it probably is. But because you can't be 100 percent positive either way...

2. Never go alone to meet someone in person you've met online. Just in case the self-described 17-year-old stamp collector turns out to be a 47-year-old human eyeball collector, always bring several friends, preferably several BIG friends. Good people won't be offended by your caution. Imposters will, and won't you be glad you came prepared?

This doesn't mean you have to approach everyone as if he or she is a serial murderer. You may meet someone online, and it will be so clear from his or her knowledge of your school or classmates, or of the tournament it turns out you both played in last year, that you'll know it's safe to meet him or her without NATO troops watching your back.

> "The antidote for fifty enemies is one friend."
>
> ARISTOTLE

> "If I don't have friends, then I ain't nothing."
>
> BILLIE HOLIDAY

3. Don't give out personal information. Never reveal your full name, phone, address, credit card numbers, or passwords. NO legitimate Internet service provider, telephone company, or business will EVER ask you for your password. Many sites will ask you for a lot of personal information. Beware that if you provide it, you may be spammed with 400 useless emails every day for the rest of your life.

4. Don't go overboard. If you race home from school to check your email and spend every evening and weekend in chat rooms; if you can't remember the last time you went to a movie or the mall with a friend or group of friends—you might have a problem. Cyber-relationships can be genuine and close, but you also need relationships outside your computer with people you can tickle, wrestle, and share a bag of popcorn with.

Connecting Highs

LOVE AND SEX

Love happens. And sometimes it doesn't. It pops up when you least expect it. And when you want it most, it's nowhere to be found.

Love isn't exactly something you can just go out and look for, like a post office or laundromat. But if you make new friends, stay connected, and keep your heart open, it'll come to you. And when it does...

> *You're on top of the world. Your stomach churns, your heart races, your mind wanders, your spirit soars. Your feet don't touch the ground. Everything matters. Nothing matters! You're silly. You're serious. Love will daze you and craze you. Hours go by like minutes. And minutes can take hours.*

Love will make you adore life. It might even make you be kind to your little brother and take out the trash.

Savor the "firsts" of love: holding hands, confiding, sharing, kissing, cuddling. Whispering secrets. Talking on the phone for hours. Sending mushy emails. Having your special table at the coffee shop. There's no greater high than romance.

When you're in love, you'll discover whole new parts of yourself. (And I don't just mean *those* parts.) In fact, nothing can spoil a good relationship more than sex—especially if you're not really, really ready and mature enough to handle it. Stay innocent and romantic for as long as you can. Save the high of making love for the right person at the right time.

"When a guy tells you he loves you for the first time, you get really high!"
LOVE-LY GIRL

"I feel high when a girl who hasn't liked me before gets interested and we start to go out and get close."
LOVE-LY BOY

Wise Highs

ᗾIND OUT MORE

The Teen Survival Guide to Dating & Relating: Real-World Advice on Guys, Girls, Growing Up, and Getting Along by Annie Fox, M.Ed. (Minneapolis: Free Spirit Publishing, 2005). How to have healthier, happier relationships with all the people in your life—including yourself. The author created Talk City's The InSite, an award-winning Web site for teens and young adults; her book is based on hundreds of emails she received and answered.

Teenwire
www.teenwire.com
Sexuality and relationship information, articles, advice, and more from Planned Parenthood Federation of America.

Connect with Your School

Studies show that the more you identify with your school and feel that it's a fair and respectful place, the more likely you are to stay in school, do well, and keep out of trouble.

Get to know as many teachers as you can. Join a school team. Play in the orchestra. Sing in the choir. Work on the yearbook or school paper. Run for student council.

Don't limit your social connections to one clique. Ignore the labels that so often create an exclusive "caste" system. Get to know as many classmates as you can. You'll connect with interesting people you would have otherwise missed.

CONNECTIONS COUNT

Researchers led by Michael Resnick of the University of Minnesota wanted to find out what factors put teenagers at risk, and what factors protect them from emotional and behavioral problems, suicide, violence, depression, promiscuity, and substance abuse. So they asked some 12,000 students in grades 7–12 about their feelings, thoughts, and behaviors.

They found that two factors above all others protected these adolescents from emotional distress, substance abuse, and violent or self-destructive behaviors: 1) feeling close to and loved by their parent(s) and family members, and 2) feeling close to and part of their school. In other words, feeling *connected* in the areas that matter most to teenagers: family, friends, and school.

Connect with Other Adults and Mentors

Connecting Highs

Search Institute in Minneapolis has surveyed children and teenagers since 1989 to learn what helps them succeed in life. According to their research, kids need at least three adults in their lives (besides their parents) they can go to for advice and support.

Do you know at least three adults you can talk to? Adults you admire, trust, and respect? An aunt or uncle? Grandparent? Teacher? Neighbor? Coach? Religious leader? Counselor? If you can't think of anyone, try broadening your friendships.* Or join a youth program—a team, club, organization, or group led by caring adults.

FIND A MENTOR
TRY THIS!

What exactly is a mentor? The dictionary definition is "a trusted counselor or guide." The Points of Light Foundation defines a mentor as "any caring adult who makes an active, positive contribution to the life of a child who is not his or her own. It's someone who has found ways to succeed in life—and cares enough to pass those lessons along."

What will your mentor be? That depends on what you want and need. A mentor can be someone who listens to you and gives you advice. It can be someone who takes an active role in your life and motivates you to succeed. It can be someone who helps you plan for your education, find a job, or learn a particular skill.

1. Start by asking yourself "What do I need from a mentor?" This will guide you in finding the right person.

2. Make a list of all the people you know who might make good mentors for you. For each person on your list, ask yourself:

- Is this someone I trust?
- Is this someone I would feel comfortable talking with and being around?
- Is this someone who cares about other people? Who cares about teenagers?
- Is this someone I can count on to be there for me?

"By far the best natural high is talking with adults who are my closest emotional friends in the universe. I have two such people in my life. I am lucky."
LUCKY STUDENT

* See page 223.

Wise Highs

3. Pick one person from your list and ask if he or she is willing to be your mentor. Explain what that means to you, what you need, and why you think that person would be a positive influence in your life.

4. If the answer is yes, set up a time for your first meeting. If the answer is no (maybe the person doesn't have time), ask if the person can suggest someone else who might be a mentor for you.

BE A MENTOR

You can make a big difference in the life of a younger person. There are so many kids out there who would love to have you as a friend—to have someone to play sports and go places with; someone to help them with their homework or problems; someone who will remember their birthday.

You don't have to have any special talents. Just a willingness to give and some time to spend. Your involvement with a younger child could become the most important thing in his or her life—and yours.

Need a few more reasons to be a mentor? Try these:

- Think of the many people who have helped you. Now it's your turn.
- Think of how great it will feel to be a hero in a child's life. That's what a mentor is.
- If you won't help, who will?

MENTORS MATTER

A lot of kids grow up in tough circumstances. They endure poverty, abuse, neglect, or loneliness. They may be shunted from one foster home to another. They may have a parent who's an alcoholic or drug addict. They may have trouble forming relationships, doing well in school, or feeling good about themselves.

But many of these kids make it anyway. They grow up to lead happy, successful, and rewarding lives. They become wonderful parents.

Researchers have studied these "resilient" kids to figure out why they thrive when other kids don't. One factor stands out above all others: Those kids had someone they could count on at crucial times in their lives. It might

have been a parent, older sibling, friend, or neighbor; an aunt, uncle, or grandparent; a tutor, teacher, coach, or mentor. Whoever it was, the person was there for them. Showed an interest in them. Treated them with love and respect. Gave them hope and encouragement.

A study done for Big Brothers Big Sisters of America found that kids who got together with their mentors an average of three times a month for a year or more were significantly less likely than kids without mentors to skip class, skip school, or start using alcohol or other drugs. In addition, the children with mentors got along better with their families and were more confident about their school performance.

FIND OUT MORE

The National Mentoring Partnership
1600 Duke Street • Suite 300 • Alexandria, VA 22314
(703) 224-2200 • www.mentoring.org
The National Mentoring Partnership is a resource for mentors and mentoring initiatives across the United States. Visit the Web site to learn more about mentorship and why it's so important, how to find a mentor, how to be a mentor, and how to start a mentoring program. The site also lists many local and national organizations that connect mentors with kids and kids with mentors.

Connect by Giving

In his book *Connect,* Dr. Edward Hallowell writes:

> "The minute you volunteer to be a part of something, you take on a responsibility.... Without responsibility, connection lacks power. If you are connected only as long as the connection pleases you, then this is not true connection. It is merely attendance. In this sense, connection is a burden. You have to be there in bad times as well as good."

Teens who lead connected lives understand that connection is a two-way street. Think of your closest friendships. They are among the strongest connections you have. They enrich your life immeasurably. But there are also times when friends can be a big pain in the butt. Like when they need something from you (your time, your help, your shoulder to cry on, your understanding, your forgiveness, your new sweater) and you don't particularly want to give it. But you

> "The best way to find yourself is to lose yourself in the service of others."
> GANDHI

229

Wise Highs

give it anyway, because you accept your responsibility for maintaining and nurturing that connection.

Operating at peak levels of trustworthiness and generosity produces a real high. Here are some ways to get it.

 ## MAKE THE SMALL GESTURE

Tiny, thoughtful gestures make people feel terrific. Surprise a friend with a little gift from your travels. Cut a neighbor's lawn. Send a thank-you note or congratulatory postcard. Bring a batch of chocolate chip cookies to school and share them at lunch. Offer to relieve your parents of certain obligations for a day. Send a card to a friend on his or her birthday.

These gestures don't have to cost a lot of money. Recently I gave someone a quart of my homemade chocolate mint iced coffee, and by her reaction you'd have thought I'd given her a new car. Not bad for a gift that costs $21,398 less than a new car.

 ## PRACTICE KINDNESS

Kindness is contagious. If someone does something kind for you, the goodness you feel will make you more likely to be kind to someone else. Unfortunately, the reverse is true, too. If someone cuts you off in traffic or commits a selfish act, you're more likely to think *Why should I be nice? Nobody else is!!!!*

Being kind is a gift you can give to others. It's also a gift you can give to yourself. Because being kind to others makes *you* feel good.

This brings us smack-dab to the philosophical question "If you benefit from giving, does it still count as giving? Or is it selfish because you know it'll make you feel good?" Clearly, the answer is "WHATEVER!!!"

If you give to someone else and that makes you feel good, the net sum of good feeling in the world has increased. And because kindness is contagious, the two of you are likely to continue giving, which, according to the Theory of Exponential Kindness Contagion, means that in less than 24 hours there will be...hmm, let's see, carry the 9, multiply by 285 squared...at least 1,357,998 people encompassed by your circle of giving. This is good.

It's a fact that teens who help others are less likely to join gangs, use drugs, or get pregnant. They also get better grades and stay in school longer. Why? Because they're connected. They're busy and motivated. And they have positive self-esteem. Self-esteem doesn't come from looking in a mirror and telling yourself how great you are. It comes from doing esteemable things—like giving.

Connecting Highs

FIND OUT MORE

Random Acts of Kindness, More Random Acts of Kindness, and *Kids' Random Acts of Kindness* by the editors of Conari Press (Emeryville, CA: Conari Press, 2002 and 1994). Inspiring true stories of people who have been the givers or recipients of caring and compassion.

TRUE HIGHS
Lawnmower Boy

In the summer of 1997, 12-year-old Ryan Tripp wanted to get his name in the *Guinness Book of World Records* as the person who traveled farthest by lawnmower. A few days before setting out on his trek, Ryan learned that a baby in his hometown needed a liver transplant. So he decided to dedicate his trip to raising money for the operation.

Ryan drove his lawnmower 3,366 miles from Salt Lake City to Washington, D.C. in 45 days, not only setting a record but also raising $15,000. The 25hp mower was outfitted with extra springs, special road tires, and a padded seat to minimize wear and tear on Ryan's butt.

Soon after completing his trip, Ryan appeared on *Late Night with David Letterman,* who dubbed him "Lawnmower Boy."

Two years later, Ryan embarked on another journey—this one to raise awareness about organ donation. His plan was to cut the grass of every state capitol in the nation. So if the lawn in front of your State House is looking extra spiffy, chances are good that Ryan came through town.

"The most important yardstick of your success will be how you treat other people—your family, friends, and coworkers, and even strangers you meet along the way."
BARBARA BUSH

"Each person has inside a basic decency and goodness. If he listens to it and acts on it, he is giving a great deal of what it is the world needs most."
PABLO CASALS

231

Wise Highs

TRY THIS! VOLUNTEER

Volunteering is a good example of connection at its most responsible level. The list of groups and organizations that welcome volunteers is practically endless. These can range from churches to clinics; soup kitchens to homeless shelters; social service agencies to schools. Many hospitals seek volunteers to entertain or tutor children, and even to hold and rock newborns. Now *there's* a high for you!

TRY THIS! CREATE A WEB SITE

Looking for alternative highs? If you live in Montgomery County, Maryland, log on to Things 2 Do *(www.things2do.org)*. This terrific site, created by 25 public and private high school students, provides information on events, places, people, and activities. You can learn about ballet auditions, movies, homework hotlines, cooking classes, theater performances, activity and special interest clubs, where to find a darkroom, and *much* more. It's the ultimate antidote to boredom.

SERVICE IS GOOD FOR YOU

Research shows that teens who participate in service programs do better in school, and are less likely to use drugs, get pregnant, or join gangs than are teens who don't volunteer or help others in a structured way.

What if you don't live in Montgomery County? Then your antidote to boredom is to start one of these Web sites in your community. It's a great way to exercise your mind, flex your creativity, perform a public service, and become a computer whiz so you can start an Internet company when you're 19 and sell it for 80 billion dollars when you're 20.

You'll need computer experts and Web designers; researchers, writers, and a Webmaster (to maintain the site); capital (a.k.a. money, moolah, dough); a computer or server space; and pizza for late-night brainstorming sessions. It shouldn't be too hard to raise the cash you need to get started. Your school may be willing to contribute, as might local foundations, businesses, and service organizations. You can also look into state and federal grants. Parents should certainly be solicited, since they tend to support activities that keep teens occupied, off the streets, drug-free, and doing good for others.

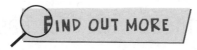

Connecting Highs

ServeNet
www.servenet.org
Enter your zip code in the box to find volunteer opportunities in your community.

Youth Service America
1101 15th Street, Suite 200 • Washington, DC 20005-5002
(202) 296-2992 • www.ysa.org
A resource center and alliance of more than 200 organizations, YSA promotes volunteering among young Americans at the local, national, and global levels. YSA is the organization behind National Youth Service Day (the third Tuesday of April), which mobilizes millions of kids each year to volunteer in their communities.

Connect with Animals

Cats and dogs are great stress relievers (especially Golden Relievers). They will shower you with love and affection. They will never say "Can't you do *anything* right?" If you're allergic to animal hairs or just don't appreciate four-legged mobile flea homes, get a goldfish. Goldfish will never drop a dead mouse at your feet.

> "Our perfect companions never have fewer than four feet."
> COLETTE

HEAVY PETTING

Studies show that caring for a pet can reduce anxiety, lower blood pressure, decrease feelings of loneliness, and provide opportunities for play, entertainment, and caretaking. It doesn't seem to matter whether you own a dog, bird, cat, or fish—although it may be hard to play "Go fetch" with a parakeet.

SOUNDS FISHY

Researchers found that dental patients who have an aquarium to look at while waiting exhibit significantly less stress during their visits than do "tankless" patients. Gazing at fish even worked better than hypnosis in allaying fears.

Connect with Your Past

We are all part of a multi-thousand-year chain of history. This concept is summed up in a phrase you may have heard: "No man is an island."* We are all connected. Even when we deny or don't feel those connections.

Many teens today aren't aware of the threads of history and tradition that have woven together so seamlessly over the centuries to stitch the fabric of their lives. Yes, the strands of culture and ancestry that embroider our families tell quite a yarn if we are willing to listen. Sew, let's look at some ways to connect with your past.

LEARN ABOUT YOUR FAMILY HISTORY

CLIMB YOUR FAMILY TREE

Tracing one's family history is a popular hobby in the U.S. today. There's even a name for it: geneaology. Millions of amateur geneaologists spend their free time looking for information about their ancestors in census data, church records, marriage certificates, armed service records, inscriptions on tombstones, etc. If you're interested, a quick search with an Internet search engine will turn up thousands of sites on geneaology. Or visit your local library.

There's an old joke about a five-year-old who asked his mother where he came from. After listening for 30 minutes to her detailed explanation of the birds and the bees, the startled little boy said, "No, I mean *where?* Tommy says he's from Boston. Where did I come from?"

Do you know where your family came from? Have you heard stories about your famous, infamous, or eccentric relatives? Talk to your parents and extended family members. Grandparents and great-grandparents are treasure troves of information—and they love to share it. Dig out old photos. Make a family tree. Discover your roots. See how the little twig of *your* life attaches to the ancestral branch.

LEARN ABOUT YOUR CULTURAL AND NATIONAL HISTORY

Many American teenagers know little about U.S. history beyond the fact that Martha Washington was Father of Our Country. Even teens who are aware that Paul Revere warned the colonies of a British invasion by placing lanterns in the Old North Church ("One if by land,

---

* Of course, today we would say "No *person* is an island."

two if by interstate") often don't know much about their own ethnic or cultural history.

Connecting Highs

If, like most Americans, you're the offshoot of immigrants, learn all you can about your country of origin. If your family can afford it, take a trip there. Or go alone to visit relatives who still may be in the "old country."

Dig into the history of your own county, town, or city. Wouldn't it be amazing to learn that your house sits on the very site where a famous massacre, deadly epidemic, or toxic dumping took place? This type of knowledge can be used to better understand your current life and feelings. For example, if your house was a make-shift morgue during the Civil War, those things going bump in the night may really *be* ghosts. Of course, you may discover that absolutely nothing of any consequence ever happened in your bland and boring suburb.

Still, it's worth the effort to investigate your past. The connectedness you'll feel will give you a great present.

"The history of one is the history of all."
GRACE KING

Connect with Groups and Other Organizations

These are some of the most rewarding connections we can make. The bonds that develop between people with similar passions, interests, and problems are an essential part of our connection collection.

JOIN TOGETHER

TRY THIS!

If you've ever worked with others towards a mutually shared goal, you know how rewarding that can be. It doesn't matter whether the goal is to win a pennant, clean up litter, put on a play, learn karate, or decorate a gym for a Halloween party. It's the *working together* that makes the experience special.

Find projects and groups you'd like to participate in. If you have an interest, take a class in it. If you have a hobby, find a group of like-minded enthusiasts.

Wise Highs

"Those whom we support
hold us up in life."
MARIE VON EBNER-ESCHENBACH

"Nothing is really work
unless you would rather be
doing something else."
JAMES MATTHEW BARRIE

Everyone needs a support structure. There may be times when you want or need help from sources other than parents, teachers, or friends.

For example, if one of your parents is a substance abuser, you might benefit from joining Alateen, where you'll find others in similar situations. Or you may have a chronic medical problem or physical disability. Find a support group of similar people. This type of bonding makes you feel less alone with a problem and better able to cope with it.

Connect at Work

Connections at work are among the most important and satisfying you can have. They involve the relationships you have with your coworkers as well as your relationship to the work itself.

Be as friendly and open as you can with your fellow denizens of the workplace. This doesn't mean slapping your boss on the back and calling him Billy Bob. You need to behave appropriately and respect the particular culture of the place in which you work. Clearly, different standards are afoot if you're a sales clerk at a shoe store as opposed to an intern at the White House.

Whatever the environment, think of yourself as an agent for positive human contact. Flash people your brilliant smile. (Check first for spinach in your teeth.) Express empathy if someone is tired or frustrated. Lend a helping hand if a coworker makes a mistake (like falling into the deep-fat fryer). Remember the details of people's lives. Ask about their vacation or how their child's recital went. Be the organizer of an office picnic or volleyball game. These human moments add immeasurably to everyone's enjoyment.

The other type of connectedness involves your feelings towards the *mission* of the place where you work. "Mission" is really just another word for the *purpose* of the establishment or service. For example, an environmental organization's mission might be to save whales or rescue the speckled cockroach from extinction. A restaurant's mission might be to create an ultimate dining experience at affordable prices in a setting of unparalleled beauty. A dry cleaner's mission might be to see how many new wrinkles they can add to your shirts.

For many teens, the mission of the workplace is secondary to their *personal* mission of stashing some cash. This is understandable. And, if you're only working a few hours a day, or during the summer months, the mission may not be as important as it would be if you were starting a career. But the more you believe in the work you're doing, the more pleasure you'll take from it, and the more you'll want to give to it.

Connecting Highs

Spiritual Connecting

For many people, the most important connection in life is to a "higher power." Some people call this higher power God. Others call it Allah. Or Buddha. Or Fred. Still others don't know what to call it.

This higher power is our connection to the universe, to all that is unknown and beyond fathoming. It is faith—that life has meaning; that there is a purpose and plan, even if we will never understand what it is. At least in this life.

For some people, this connection is built through religion. For others, it is built through music, art, literature, nature, meditating, reflecting, creating, caregiving. Whatever we call this connection, however we build it, it's unique to us. It is *our* spirituality.

I think of spirituality as the state of our soul. Our deepest sense of being and purpose. Our center, our self, our contact with that which lies beyond self. Spirituality is what fills our heart. It is our relationship to a higher power, to God *as we understand Him.* Or her. Or it. Or them.

If we think of spirituality as the essence of our connectedness to self, to others, to the universe, and to God, we can experience its thrill and comfort by working to improve each of these relationships. Many of the highs described elsewhere in this book—those found through nature, creativity, community, ideas—contribute to spiritual growth. Another way to deepen our connectedness to the "beyond" is through prayer.

> "Tell me what kind of God you believe in and I'll tell you what kind of person you are."
>
> T.S. ELIOT

DID YOU KNOW?

Research shows that young people who are involved in religious communities are less likely to engage in risky behaviors (like using alcohol or drugs) than teens who aren't. Religious communities also give young people opportunities to make strong connections with others, particularly adults they might not meet otherwise.

> "Good for the body is the work of the body, and good for the soul is the work of the soul, and good for either is the work of the other."
>
> HENRY DAVID THOREAU

237

Wise Highs

"I believe in prayer.
It's the best way we
have to draw strength
from heaven."
JOSEPHINE BAKER

"I believe in prayer.
It's the best way we
have to draw strength
from heaven."
JOSEPHINE BAKER

"Prayer...is the
most potent instrument
of action."
GANDHI

All teenagers are familiar with prayer.

Please, God, don't let me strike out.
Please, God, make this zit go away in time for the dance.
Please, God, don't let him call on me.

Almost two thousand years ago, a Greek historian by the name of Plutarch (not to be confused with Pluto) observed: "If we traverse the world, it is possible to find cities without walls, without letters, without wealth, without coin, without schools or theatres: but a city without a temple, or that practices not worship, prayers and the like, no one has ever seen."

It seems that no matter how far back in history you go, prayer and worship have always been around. And while the form may vary—words, silence, meditation, music, chanting, drumming, dancing—its purpose is always the same: to communicate with and/or seek help from powerful spirits, gods, or higher powers.

Why has prayer survived for so many millennia when, for example, dodo birds have not? Some scientists believe it's because prayer has evolutionary value. Evolutionary theory (as those of you who have been paying attention in biology class know) posits that behaviors and traits that promote the survival of a species are perpetuated, while those that don't are not. They die out.

So, what might the advantage of prayer be? There are several "scientific" explanations for the evolutionary value of prayer. Such as:

Prayer focuses the mind. It encourages us to *visualize* hope, help, courage, or success. If we believe that things will get better, or that we have the strength to endure, we're more likely to get off our butts and work to help ourselves. As the old saying goes: "God helps those who help themselves." People who visualize a way out of their problems may be more likely to "help themselves" and, thus, solve their problems.*

Prayer reduces stress. Dr. Herbert Benson of Harvard's Mind/Body Medical Institute found that people who pray or meditate for 10–20 minutes a day can lower their blood pressure and heart rate, reduce

---

* For more on visualization, see pages 41–47.

their need for oxygen, and decrease the number of breaths they take per minute. These physiological and metabolic responses are associated with reduced stress. Benson called this "the relaxation response" and wrote a pioneering book on the subject by the same name. People who can cope with stress and keep their lives in perspective are less likely to commit suicide, become depressed, or suffer from stress-related illnesses.*

Connecting Highs

Prayer brings people together. People often pray in groups. They come together for comfort, companionship, and baked goods. Research shows that people who have friends and social support networks live longer and enjoy better physical and psychological health than do people without such connections.

Prayer embraces ritual. Rituals and other traditions can provide a feeling of belonging and security. Studies show that children who grow up in families that maintain rituals (e.g., family dinners, celebrations, holiday traditions) are less likely to become substance abusers.

Throughout history, people prayed when they needed help. They prayed out of fear or desperation, or when they faced hunger, sickness, or death. They prayed for strength and hope, courage and enlightenment. They prayed to give thanks and blessings. According to evolutionary theory, if prayer had no value, if it made no difference, it would have died out as a human behavior.

You can see how the traits and behaviors associated with prayer— vision, motivation, strength, serenity, community—might advance the survival of the species. Our ancestors must have sensed the psychological and physical benefits of prayer, even if they didn't have the methods and tools to study them.

However you see prayer, you might want to give it a try.

"The life of prayer is so great and various there is something in it for everyone. It is like a garden which grows everything, from alpines to potatoes."
EVELYN UNDERHILL

FIND OUT MORE

The Power of Prayer, edited by Dale Salwak (Novato, CA: New World Library, 1999). Former president Jimmy Carter, Reverend Billy Graham, Sue Bender, Brooke Medicine Eagle, Mother Teresa, and other spiritual leaders, thinkers, and writers share their thoughts and reflections on prayer.

* For more on stress reduction, see Chapter 1: Serenity Highs.

More Readings and Resources

The Alternative Medicine Handbook by Barrie Cassileth (New York: W.W. Norton and Co. 1998). A comprehensive reference guide to the most commonly used complementary and alternative therapies—diet and herbs, bodywork, mind-body work, etc. The author discusses each approach, the beliefs on which it is based, relevant research findings, impact on the patient, and where to get it.

Buzzed: The Straight Facts about the Most Used and Abused Drugs from Alcohol to Ecstasy by Cynthia Kuhn, Scott Swartzelder, *et al.* (New York: W. W. Norton & Co., 1998). A comprehensive, objective book written by experts in the field and college students. *Buzzed* will tell you virtually everything you could ever want to know about legal and illegal drugs such as alcohol, caffeine, hallucinogens, inhalants, marijuana, steroids, etc. The book doesn't take "sides" for or against drug use; it simply presents the facts.

The Healing Power of Humor: Techniques for Getting Through Loss, Setbacks, Upsets, Disappointments, Difficulties, Trials, Tribulations, and All That by Allen Klein (Los Angeles: J.P. Tarcher, 1989). Ha, ha, ha, ho, ho, hee, hee, hee, hoo, haw. The title pretty much says it all. How to use humor and laughter to help you make your way through difficult and even tragic times.

Quick Fixes to Change Your Life: Making Healthy Choices by Judy Ann Walz, M.S.N., R.N. (Midland, GA: Creative Health Services, Inc. 1995). A good book for busy people on the go, with quick strategies for feeling energetic and maintaining a positive outlook on life. Covers everything from nutrition to stress reduction, spirituality to sexuality.

Timeless Healing: The Power and Biology of Belief by Herbert Benson, M.D. (New York: Fireside, 1987). If you're interested in the connection between faith, prayer, belief in a higher power, and physical and emotional well-being, this is the book for you. Benson believes that humans are genetically designed to believe in a higher power, and that meditation and prayer are just as important to your health as medicines, surgery, and visits to the doctor.

The Wellness Book: The Comprehensive Guide to Maintaining Health and Treating Stress-Related Illness by Herbert Benson, M.D. (New York: Fireside, 1993). A great guide to maintaining your health and staying stress-free through exercise, diet, and stress management techniques.

Freevibe
www.freevibe.com
This colorful, informative, teen-friendly site is filled with reliable facts about drugs and has a teen chat room where you can talk about drug-related issues.

Hazelden Foundation
PO Box 176 • Center City, MN 55012-0176
1-800-257-7810 • www.hazelden.org
Renowned as a treatment center for drug and other addictions, Hazelden is the world's leading publisher of materials on chemical and other dependencies, recovery, and healthy "abundant living." You can find books, pamphlets, and videos on just about any drug-related issue here.

Health World Online

www.healthy.net

This amazing site has tons of useful health-related information on just about every-thing, from acupuncture to nutrition, sports medicine, creative visualization, self-applied massage, breathing and relaxation exercises—even colon hydrotherapy!

National Institute on Drug Abuse

6001 Executive Boulevard, Room 5213 • Bethesda, MD 20892-9561

(301) 443-1124 • www.nida.nih.gov

NIDA is part of the National Institutes of Health (NIH), the principal biomedical and behavioral research agency of the U.S. Government. The Web site provides factual data and is a valuable resource for parents, teachers, and teenagers look-ing for information about alcohol and other drug use. Links to everywhere.

Natural Healers

www.naturalhealers.com

An educational resource for people interested in studying "the natural healing arts." You can search by location for references to hundreds and hundred of schools that teach massage therapy, acupuncture, aromatherapy, hypnotherapy, reflexology, Shiatsu, Trager, Reiki, Rubenfeld Synergy, Lomi Lomi, and other healing arts about which I don't have a clue.

Partnership for a Drug-Free America

405 Lexington Avenue • Suite 1601 • New York, NY 10174

(212) 922-1560 • www.drugfree.org

Private, nonprofit, and nonpartisan, PDFA combines advertising with the power of the media to reduce demand for illicit drugs in America. The Web site pro-vides current, accurate information about drugs, prevention, and intervention, an extensive reading list, and addresses for free publications.

Bibliography

Benson, Herbert, M.D. *The Relaxation Response*, revised edition. New York: Avon Books, 2000.

———— *Timeless Healing: The Power and Biology of Belief.* New York: Fireside, 1997.

Das, Lama Surya. *Awakening the Buddha Within: Tibetan Wisdom for the Western World.* New York, Broadway Books, 1997.

Feldman, David. *What Are Hyenas Laughing At, Anyway? An Imponderables Book.* New York: Berkley Publishing Group, 1996.

George, Mike. *Learn to Relax: A Practical Guide to Easing Tension and Conquering Stress.* San Francisco: Chronicle Books, 1998/

Gunaratana, Venerable Henepola. *Mindfulness in Plain English.* Somerville, MA: Wisdom Publications, 1993.

Hallowell, Edward M., M.D. *Connect: 12 Vital Ties That Open Your Heart, Lengthen Your Life, and Deepen Your Soul.* New York: Pantheon Books, 1999.

Hendricks, Gay. *Conscious Breathing: Breathwork for Health, Stress Release, and Personal Mastery.* New York: Bantam Books, 1995.

Kabat-Zinn, Jon. *Wherever You Go, There You Are: Mindfulness Meditation in Everyday Life.* New York: Hyperion, 1995.

Kirsta, Alix. *The Book of Stress Survival: Identifying and Reducing the Stress in Your Life.* New York: Fireside, 1987.

Rosenberg, Larry, David Duy, and Jon Kabat-Zinn. *Breath by Breath: The Liberating Practice of Insight Meditation.* Boston: Shambhala Publications, 1999.

Rosenfeld, Edward. *The Book of Highs: 250 Methods for Altering Your Consciousness Without Drugs.* New York: Quadrangle/The New York Times Book Co., 1973.

Rushkoff, Douglass, and Patrick Wells. *Free Rides: How to Get High Without Drugs.* New York: Delta, 1991.

Schwager, Tina, and Michele Schuerger. *Gutsy Girls: Young Women Who Dare.* Minneapolis: Free Spirit Publishing, 1999.

———— *The Right Moves: A Girl's Guide to Getting Fit and Feeling Good.* Minneapolis: Free Spirit Publishing, 1998.

Somer, Elizabeth. *Food & Mood: The Complete Guide to Eating Well and Feeling Your Best,* 2nd edition. New York: Owl Books, 1999.

Speads, Carola. *Ways to Better Breathing.* Rochester, VT: Inner Traditions International, Ltd., 1992.

Turkington, Carol, and David Barlow. *Stress Management for Busy People.* New York: McGraw-Hill, 1998.

Walz, Judy Ann, M.S.N., R.N. *Quick Fixes to Change Your Life: Making Healthy Choices.* Midland, GA: Creative Health Services, Inc. 1995.

Weil, Andrew, M.D. *The Natural Mind: An Investigation of Drugs and the Higher Consciousness,* revised edition. Boston: Houghton Mifflin, 1998.

Index

Wise Highs

Index

Wise Highs

Index

Wise Highs

Index

About the Author

When not in a state of serene bliss, Alex J. Packer, Ph.D., is president and CEO of FCD Educational Services, a nonprofit, Boston-based organization that provides alcohol, tobacco, and other drug education and prevention programs for schools throughout the United States and abroad. An educator and psychologist, he is the author of numerous books for parents and teenagers including *Parenting One Day at a Time, 365 Ways to Love Your Child*, and the award-winning bestsellers *Bringing Up Parents: The Teenager's Handbook; How Rude!® The Teenagers' Guide to Good Manners, Proper Behavior, and Not Grossing People Out;* and *The How Rude!® Handbooks for Teens.*

After attending Phillips Exeter Academy, Alex received undergraduate and master's degrees from Harvard University and a Ph.D. in educational and developmental psychology from Boston College. A specialist in substance abuse prevention, adolescence, and parent education, he was head of an alternative school for children ages 11–15 in Washington, D.C., for eight years, and has since served as Director of Education for the Capital Children's Museum.

Alex's favorite natural highs that can be mentioned in this book are eating, reading, writing screenplays, watching movies, renovating old buildings, flying ultralights, driving sports cars, and sitting in the Luxembourg Gardens in Paris on a sunny day with his feet up, listening to reggae music, and watching the world go by.

When asked to supply a photograph, Alex refused, saying "What?!?! And never be able to watch a sunset again without hordes of adoring teenagers whispering 'Look, the guy who wrote *Wise Highs* is getting high!'"

Other Great Books from Free Spirit

How Rude!®
The Teenagers' Guide to Good Manners, Proper Behavior, and Not Grossing People Out
by Alex J. Packer, Ph.D.
For ages 13 & up. *480 pp.; softcover; illust.; 7¼" x 9"*

Respect
A Girl's Guide to Getting Respect & Dealing When Your Line Is Crossed
by Courtney Macavinta and Andrea Vander Pluym
For ages 13 & up. *240 pp.; softcover; two-color; illust.; 7" x 9"*

Bringing Up Parents
The Teenager's Handbook
by Alex J. Packer, Ph.D.
For ages 13 & up. *272 pp.; softcover; illust.; 7¼" x 9¼"*

Life Lists for Teens
Tips, Steps, Hints, and How-Tos for Growing Up, Getting Along, Learning, and Having Fun
by Pamela Espeland
For ages 11 & up. *272 pp.; softcover; 6" x 9"*

What Teens Need to Succeed
Proven, Practical Ways to Shape Your Own Future
by Peter L. Benson, Ph.D., Judy Galbraith, M.A., and Pamela Espeland
For ages 11 & up. *368 pp.; softcover; illust.; 7¼" x 9¼"*

Be Confident in Who You Are
Middle School Confidential™ Series
by Annie Fox, M.Ed.
For ages 11–14. *96 pp.; softcover; full-color; illust.; 6" x 8"*

Too Stressed to Think?
A Teen Guide to Staying Sane When Life Makes You Crazy
by Annie Fox, M.Ed., and Ruth Kirschner
For ages 12 & up. *176 pp.; softcover; 6" x 9"*

Boy v. Girl?
How Gender Shapes Who We Are, What We Want, and How We Get Along
by George Abrahams, Ph.D., and Sheila Ahlbrand
For ages 10–15. *208 pp.; softcover; illust.; 7" x 9"*

Fighting Invisible Tigers
Stress Management for Teens
Revised and Updated Third Edition
by Earl Hipp
For ages 11 & up. *144 pp.; softcover; two-color; illust.; 6" x 9"*

The Teen Guide to Global Action
How to Connect with Others (Near & Far) to Create Social Change
by Barbara A. Lewis
For ages 12 & up. *144 pp.; softcover; two-color; illust.; 7" x 9"*

For pricing information, to place an order,
or to request a free catalog, contact:

Free Spirit Publishing Inc.
217 Fifth Avenue North • Suite 200 • Minneapolis, MN 55401-1299
toll-free 800.735.7323 • local 612.338.2068 • fax 612.337.5050
help4kids@freespirit.com • www.freespirit.com

Fast, Friendly, and Easy to Use
www.freespirit.com

Browse the catalog **Info & extras** **Many ways to search** **Quick check-out** **Stop in and see!**

Our Web site makes it easy to find the positive, reliable resources you need to empower teens and kids of all ages.

The Catalog.
Start browsing with just one click.

Beyond the Home Page.
Information and extras such as links and downloads.

The Search Box.
Find anything superfast.

Your Voice.
See testimonials from customers like you.

Request the Catalog.
Browse our catalog on paper, too!

The Nitty-Gritty.
Toll-free numbers, online ordering information, and more.

The 411.
News, reviews, awards, and special events.

 Our Web site is a secure commerce site. All of the personal information you enter at our site—including your name, address, and credit card number—is secure. So you can order with confidence when you order online from Free Spirit!

For a fast and easy way to receive our practical tips, helpful information, and special offers, send your email address to upbeatnews@freespirit.com. View a sample letter and our privacy policy at www.freespirit.com.

1.800.735.7323 • fax 612.337.5050 • help4kids@freespirit.com